To Debbie,

The Extraordinary
Tale of Kate Marsden

roki teller-Mum

The Extraordinary Tale of Kate Marsden

and

My Journey Across Siberia in Her Footsteps

by

JACKI HILL-MURPHY

Maps by Jon Harris
Cover design by Jim Starr

A catalogue record for this book is available from the British Library.

ISBN 978-0-9931054-1-8

Published by Adventuress Publishing For more copies of
this book, please email: info@adventuresses.com

Designed and Set by Hewer Text UK Ltd, Edinburgh
Printed in Great Britain

Although every precaution has been taken in the preparation of this book, the publisher
and author assume no responsibility for errors or omissions. Neither is any liability
assumed for damages resulting from the use of this information contained herein.

The people in the author's story are composites of the people met and travelled
with, and bear no precise resemblance to anyone you may know.

Picture credits:
Map on inside cover drawn by Jon Harris; p xvi, page 82, p123, p272, p302, p307,
1871 map on inside back cover, Royal Geographical Society; p6, p 14, Women's
Herald; p 12, p43, p44, p119, p126, p159, p164, p 178, p181, p186, p 204, p 205, p
211, p213, p215, p218, p221, p224, p264, p347, From 'On Sledge and Horseback to
Outcast Siberian Lepers' by Kate Marsden, artists unknown; p38 and p39 Tea Trakt
by Kosharov 1890, Tomsk Regional Museum of Local Lore (Tomskiy Kraevedcheskiy
Musey); p50, Grivita 1877 by Henry Dembitsky; p56 plectocycle, from the Online
Bicycle Museum free public database; p65, p75, p202, p288 and cover, The Girl's Own
Paper, courtesy of Lutterworth Press; p 67 Kate Marsden's medal, courtesy of RGS,
drawn by Jon Harris; p92 tarantass George Kennan (February 16, 1845 – 1924) public
domain; p104 Richard Blanshard; p151, The Ultimate Plum Pudding Company; p268,
from 'Travels of Miss Marsden to the Yakutsk Region'; p141, p267, p283, p306, p319,
p321, p323, Bexhill Museum Archive; p276 The Isabel F. Hapgood File, Manuscript
collection New York Public Library (thanks to Kate Renouf for this); p285 Wikipedia,
public domain; p294, p295, p296 donated by Telie - Ivanov Semen Victorovich; p311
Flora of the Canadian Arctic Archipelago; p313, p315, p316, p317, p318 public domain;
p345, Morgan Hill-Murphy; all the rest are taken by the author or travel companions.

Dedicated to the hospitable people of
Vilyuisk and Sosnovka
in Sakha Province, Siberia

Contents

Kate's life   2013 journey   *Jacki meeting Kate*

Preface

This is a story that defies all reason: a Victorian spinster and nurse, so obsessed with the fate of leprosy-sufferers worldwide that she was prepared to journey, in winter, nearly ten thousand miles across pre-revolutionary Russia, to one of the most inhospitable areas on earth. First to find a legendary plant that might be a cure, next to report to the world on living conditions of sufferers in the remote Siberian forests, and finally to prompt local community leaders to set up a properly regulated hospital. Here the sufferers, brought in from their wretched shacks in the snow-filled taiga, could lead a decent communal life, and receive treatment.

In the 1890s, Kate Marsden's courage achieved these primary ends. She would have done so much more, and equalled the renown of Florence Nightingale – who endorsed her mission – and Edith Cavell; and, in her public appearances and fund-raising. But, unfortunately there were sophisticated detractors who 'wished she'd never been born' namely Isobel Hapgood whose successful campaign against her, stopped Kate's career in its tracks.

Her personality was magnetic, if not endearing and having followed her footsteps – not of sledge, tarantass or horseback, but using public transport – to Yakutsk, I find that Miss Marsden still has many questions to answer: I have tried, in this account, to do just that. I conclude that if her aims were ridiculous her achievements were admirable, the Siberian leper colony, built in her name, brought relief to lepers for many years and she raised awareness of the disease worldwide.

Today, the remains of the leper colony in Vilyuisk, are subsumed into the psychiatric hospital bearing her name and is in the process of renovation, they are due to be conserved; alongside stands a statue to this 'local hero', and a Kate Marsden day is part of the Viyuisk calendar – all demonstrating the community's love for her.

By going back in time and visiting her I'm trying to do two things, introduce a Russian readership the world in England she lived in, and to show Kate the outcome of the new agenda she and her generation set for women. And I wanted to tell Kate, this sad lady who died alone and in poverty in a London mental asylum, that she is loved and appreciated today as a great explorer and enlightened nurse.

Foreword

Kindly contributed by the Minister of Social Development,
Republic of Sakha (Yakutia), Russia

Not everyone can be born under the sign of genius and not everyone can make the greatest discoveries but certain work and deeds
of concrete people leave memorable marks in the history of the
mankind. For Sakha people – the population living in Yakutia, the
coldest place in Siberia, one of such recognised figure is the intrepid
Sister of Mercy from far England Kate Marsden.

In Yakutia the name of Kate Marsden is associated with the
image of the Saviour, who showed heartfelt participation in
improving miserable lives of the Siberian lepers. A rumour about
daring and greatness of the spirit of the courageous English woman
is still alive in the memory of the Sakha people. The value of her
mission is supported by her concrete actions. She tried hard to ease
the leper's bad conditions and moreover she succeeded to arouse
the interest of local authorities and church to her mission. As a
result of her great efforts taken in finding financial aids, a colony
for lepers was built in Vilyuisk. Kate also insisted on building a
chapel which had become the place of relieving sufferings and the
last destination on the Earth for the most of sick people. That's
why many local people regarded her visit as God's mission and
called her the Angel sent by God.

People of Yakutia consider that the name of Kate Marsden is
worthy of an outstanding place in the history of the region as an
example of kindness, tolerance and selfless serving to people.

Sadly, for certain reasons Kate Marsden's considerable feat had
vanished into obscurity in her homeland. However due the truly

inspirational modern explorer Jacki Hill-Murphy who is recreating the gruelling journey of her Victorian predecessor to make others aware of it, the interest to Kate Marsden`s epic journey to Siberia is increasing. Inspired by the deepest gratitude of Sakha people towards Kate Marsden Jacki had visited Vilyuisk twice. In her book "The Extraordinary Tale of Kate Marsden" Jacki Hill-Murphy shares her experience of the visits and tries to find out what motivated Kate Marsden and what she had gone through.

I want to thank Jacki Hill-Murphy for her titanic work to preserve the good memory of Kate Marsden in the world. This book will help to keep the fire burning in Kate Marsden`s name and celebrate her noble mission for the benefit of mankind.

Alexander Druzhinin,

Translated for me, in Vilyuisk, by Ulyana Vasilieva.

Credits

I could not have written this book without the editorial help and encouragement of Jon Harris, who once more untangled my prose and drew the wonderful map.

For the journey to Siberia, my team mate Ellie, Belinda Kirk founder of Explorers Connect and The Ultimate Plum Pudding Company. In Tomsk; Anna Ishkova, Kirill, Elena Bondarenko, Yulia Mikhaleva, and Pavel Rachkovskiy, Maxim Miroshnikov who has answered many questions while writing the book, Father Victor and Vladimir. In Irkutsk; Alex. In Yakutsk, Sardarna and Irina for including us in the First Yakutsk International Film Festival and the Minister for Culture, Mr Andrei Boris and Nadia Noeva translator.

In Vilyuisk and Sosnovka, Dr Kleopatra Koryakina, Director of the Kate Marsden Hospital in Sosnovka, Ulyana Vasilieva and Zinaida Alekseeva, the translators who have worked tirelessly on my behalf, Margarita Sokolova, Sosnovka event organiser, Dr Margarita Alekseera, for treating my swollen face; Sergey Vinokourov, Matrena, Zakhar, Mikhail Tomsk. Principal of the Teacher Training College, Svetlana Egorovna Kirillina, Director of the Khomus Museum, Augustina Filippova and Nina Protopopova. The village of Chineke.

For access to the Yakutsk archive: Venera Tikhonova and Ulyana Vasilieva and Petr Ivanovich Koryakin, archive researcher and Ivanov Semen Victorovich, for the old photographs of the leprosarium, whose father Telie Victor Victorovich, worked there from 1910 to 1920.

For plant identification, Peter Rooney and F. Rumsey.

And special thanks to: Nimi Akinkugbe from Nigeria who sponsored the 2,500 postcards, Edward Surov in Moscow, the authority on Kate Marsden who publishes the Russian Kate Marsden Wikipedia site. Gwen and John Sankey and Michael Forbes Smith, (President) of the St Francis Leprosy Guild, Irene Allen at Lepra. Also, the staff at the Windsor Castle Archives, the British Library, the RGS Library, Cambridge University Library and Kate Renouf for the Hapgood files. John Betts and Julian Porter from Bexhill Museum. Also, Jim Starr, Jane Sparrow, Ken Hames, Helen Thornton, Becky Condron, Richard Creasey. Richard Blanshard, Victoria Hughes-Crosier, Alice Avis, Siffy and Tor Torkidson, Nicola Tagart and Morgan Hill-Murphy.

In a North London Victorian
cemetery, is an unmarked,
forgotten grave overlooked by
chipped stone angels with blackened
wings; obscured by once grand tombs
and lost to everyone's gaze
since a sad burial in 1931
that few witnessed . . .

Kate Marsden in her Jaeger travelling outfit in 1891

Chapter 1

The plane from Moscow landed gingerly at the town of Biysk, close to the Kazakhstan border, and through the steamy window an early morning white-out, like snow, welcomed my travelling companion Ellie and myself.

It was a blow: we were meant to be 200 miles away. In Tomsk, there were representatives from the region's department of culture waiting to meet us, fog was the cause of the diversion, a frequent hazard in September and now nobody was going anywhere. We people-watched the other passengers disembarking from the plane who hung about with travel-weary gazes, large Russian ladies in hand-knits clutching the hands of small children, young suited businessmen speaking urgently into their phones, the rest lolling on hard airport chairs staring into space.

If I ever felt weary of civilisation and my urban surroundings, and wanted to escape as far away as possible from them, Siberia was the right place to go to. Few regions come wilder; in few regions of the earth has mankind struggled so valiantly, and for so long.

As Westerners we don't know very much about it and I couldn't blame my friends for their concern – as they pestered me with questions such as "Have you packed special underwear for the arctic temperatures? Are there bears? Are there still gulags? Is there anything out there? Why Siberia for God's sake, Jacki?"

Crossing a region that at over 5 million square miles, makes up three-quarters of Russian territory, by any means of public transport I could muster – was going to bring me into contact with a huge diversity of Russians. This alone would be a unique and privileged experience and I couldn't wait. But there was a purpose to my journey, and I had company, a strange Victorian woman, by

1

turns deceitful and misunderstood, but undoubtably heroic, and it was my resolve to rescue her reputation, or at the very least establish the truth about her.

I had left an England in bloom and a Somerset countryside that had never been so beautiful. A last genial gathering in evening sunshine in my small garden, swathed in the sharp perfume of overgrown jasmine bushes, had ended with concerned farewells and musings on the remoteness of my trajectory. "Take good care of yourself", they said as they left.

"I will." I replied, and placated my mother in Sussex by telephone.

As Lady Florence Dixie wrote in her book 'Across Patagonia' of 1880: "On the eve of a long journey one cannot help thinking of the uncertainty of everything in the world".

One hundred and thirty three years later, it was curious how her words stand for my own sentiment so precisely.

I hate saying goodbye, and at the Heathrow departure gate a particularly fond farewell was to keep me smiling and warm inside for the many hours to come; and now, while I waited at this remote and unknown airport lounge, that parting lived on. I cursed its unfortunate timing: it left me hankering to return, when I should be eager to move on across Siberia and, there, embrace the opportunities that awaited me.

I would get used, in Siberia, to extraordinary experiences: I soon knew to expect them day by day. This was no ordinary journey that I was embarking on; later on I would discover that the glances we attracted from the passengers in that grey airport in Biysk, while we waited for the sky to clear, may have been the result of my imminent arrival being broadcast on All-Russia TV the night before. How could I have possibly known? I had been camped out under powerfully bright lights, on the hard and highly-polished marble floor, outside the executive offices of Moscow's Domodedovo Airport at the time.

By now into the fourth hour of inertia in Biysk departure lounge, I was beginning to feel awkward about the committee awaiting my arrival in Tomsk; fortunately the sun burnt off the fog, and we re-boarded.

Tomsk appeared below us as a brown smudge in a blanket of rich, vivid green stretching to the horizon. From Bogashevo Airport we were soon heading into town in the 'Tourism Department's auto' along the wide Bogashevsky Trakt on the city's south-east, which gave me my first glimpse of Siberian forest from the ground.

Only when my translator handed me an extensive itinerary for the next couple of days did it fully dawn upon me what my visit meant to these Russians. Through email and phone, via a contact in Edinburgh, to a friend's friend's sister-in-law in Tomsk, the message had filtered down to the local Head of the Tourism Board and, for the first time, they heard a name that created huge excitement, that of a woman who had visited their city long before the railway and the road had arrived, and whose book about her journey was cherished as a true record of the hardest known equestrian journey ever undertaken by a woman. She had travelled 11,000 miles across Russia by train, sledge, horseback and boat. So gruelling was the journey that when her book was published in England in 1895 its Victorian audience laughed it off as a piece of gothic-orientalist opportunistic fiction and for the rest of her life this hardy nurse, initially supported by Florence Nightingale and Queen Victoria, was hounded by a coven of detractors, from different parts of the world, hell bent on her unmasking and punishment. But not here in Siberia, which could attest to both the courage of her physical adventure and, (even after seventy years of Marxist-Leninism), the long-term benefits of the leper colony built in her name, in the years that Tsarism was beginning to unravel: here, Kate Marsden is a secular saint, and her name is revered everywhere.

She was born in 1859 and the epic journey to find the herb that might become a salve for leprosy, and to gather information about lepers that she had heard were cast out into the Siberian forest, was undertaken in 1890-91. In my personal quest to rescue the names of early women traveller's names from obscurity, Kate Marsden is up there with the pluckiest of them.

From my first reading of 'On Sledge and Horseback to Outcast Siberian Lepers', I loved the way her quirky nature revealed itself with that dramatic title that left the Victorian readers so confused! With its mixture of gung-ho-ness and piety, the title alone must have put the readers off the track. No wonder that a quarter century later she had to follow it with 'The Vindication', a heart-felt plea to her host of detractors to believe she really had under-taken the most foolhardy of all journeys. In 1921, it did little to quell their animosity towards her, and today it reads as an exten-sion of the heroic narrative of the first.

THE BOOK OF THE SEASON.

ON SLEDGE AND HORSEBACK
TO
OUTCAST SIBERIAN LEPERS.

(With Illustrations from Photographs and Drawings.)

BY

KATE MARSDEN,

Member (Special Badge) of the Royal British Nurses' Association, Member and Medallist of the Russian Imperial Red Cross Society, &c., &c.

Will be ready shortly, Crown 8vo., price Six Shillings.

(A Limited Edition of richly bound, large paper Copies, numbered, and signed by the Authoress, price One Guinea.)

This Book will be Published under the Auspices of the KATE MARSDEN LEPER FUND COMMITTEE, BY THE RECORD PRESS, LIMITED, 376, STRAND, LONDON, W.C., TO WHOM ALL COMMUNICATIONS SHOULD BE ADDRESSED.

From the security of an armchair, the critical hostility is under-standable; she makes limited attempts to describe her surroundings, she is a shameless name dropper, she goes out of her way to thank Almighty God for nearly everything she sees and does even if her real religious beliefs seem doubtful. Compared with the beautifully graphic narrative of Mary Kingsley and Isabella Bird, her prose makes little attempt to add detail or humour to the journey; but it is still a legendary tome.

My first experience of Russian hospitality greeted me at the Stary Zamok, the Old Castle. Under a glass atrium a large table was laid with a white tablecloth but the abrasion of many people waiting for all those hours was evident in the drunk angles of forks, knives and empty water glasses. But all changed when the beautiful Yuliya, the smiling boss of the Department of Culture and Tourism for the Tomsk region, stood up in her long flowery summer dress, introduced herself, and hugged me tightly.

A waterfall swirled and bubbled in its man-made watercourse through the restaurant before disappearing into the shadows of a small pond. There was an image of a fairytale castle with turrets and a winding stone path on the wall; at the top of a flight of real stone steps a lone balalaika player sang soulful Russian songs perched on a wooden chair. Now they all wanted to step forward and clasp my hand, first Elena, a specialist in the Culture Department, followed by Kirill, who I later discovered, was an expert on the old historical houses of the region and next came Paval, the head of the Cultural Legacy and Ethnocultural Policy Division, and last of all came the young and handsome Maxim, eager to translate for me the excited babble of chatter and questions.

I now understood: it was all down to this vibrant group of professionals that my arrival had been broadcast on Russian tv the night before; they had devoured the archives for information about Kate Marsden, who they realised had played a part in the history of their city. They turned what they could find into a short documentary to follow the evening news, to highlight the fact that an Englishwoman called Jacki Hill-Murphy, would be arriving the next day to replicate Kate's journey, not on horseback but by public transport.

With this new knowledge, I promised myself, I would live up to the exciting challenges awaiting me.

Chapter 2

MISS KATE MARSDEN
Amongst the Lepers in Siberia.

'The hardships which have been, and are still to be, undergone by this young and refined woman might well daunt the strongest and most active men.'

Helena B. Temple

The bright and appealing 'Woman's Herald', was launched in 1888 by Henrietta Muller who believed strongly in the cause of suffrage. The paper became a major breakthrough in the lives of women at the end of the Victorian era and no other publication before or since, has blown the trumpet so vigorously for women's rights. It instantly became the leading feminist paper of its time; with its fresh, lively and uncompromising style of journalism and bold illustrations, it proudly set the agenda for the new age by declaring itself 'The only paper conducted, written and published by women'. Despite endless difficulties, no doubt exacerbated by the lack of male support, it published over 200 editions before being absorbed by the 'Woman's Signal', and finally folding in 1899.

Henrietta Muller didn't hide the fact that she felt humiliated by the way that women's interests and opinions were left out from the World's Press. She was deeply upset that women's views were only represented by a little monthly leaflet, not worthy of the name of a newspaper, called the 'Women's Suffrage Journal'.

So she established her newspaper, realising that it was vitally important that women should have a newspaper of their own through which to voice their thoughts, and she did it because as no one else had come forward to do it she would try and do it herself. When asked why she had given herself a pen name she replied:

'My chief reason is in order that my own individuality won't give a colouring to the paper, but that it should be as far as possible, impersonally conducted and therefore open to reflect the opinions of women on any and all subjects.'

The paper was feminist and progressive, without any party allegiance; Henrietta made sure that the contents were refreshingly varied. The front page usually featured an interview which ran on inside; the range of interviewees included: Catherine Booth, A Modern Priestess; Mrs Brander, Inspector of Girls' Schools in Madras; Elizabeth Barrett Browning, The Priestess of Poetry; Lady Florence Dixie, Patagonian Explorer; George Eliot, Novelist; Elizabeth Fry, Prison Reformer; Mrs Pankhurst, suffragist; Mrs Beatrice (sic) Potter, author and amazingly, her Majesty the Queen.

On September 5th, 1891, Henrietta printed a long interview with Ada Field although the photograph accompanying it was of Kate Marsden, whose great story you are about to hear. Henrietta sent her editor at the time, Helena Temple, to conduct the interview.

Here is what Helena said about it:

I was pleased to secure the interview with Ada Field. Kate Marsden's name has been prominent recently; how marvellous it is that a woman is working so selflessly amongst the unfortunate lepers in Siberia and here was the woman who had travelled with her. 'Woman's Herald' loves to catch the early worm and to interview Miss Ada Field would make a great front page spread.

I caught the late train to Buxton, her home town, from Euston and stayed at The Railway Tavern before calling on her after breakfast the following morning.

Miss Field opened the door; she is a petite lady with a soft voice and she gripped my hand warmly and ushered me into a comfortable sitting room with chintz covered chairs and a splendid view of the surrounding hills. She announced at once that she would give me all the information she could and I immediately liked her and was assured that she was fully recovered from all the illness she had suffered travelling long distances in the sledge with Kate Marsden.

"This portrait," (above) said Ada, "is the only one of Miss Marsden which has not been published, and shows her in her nursing dress as a Red Cross sister."

Such was Miss Field's thoughtfulness towards other people she began by offering this picture and pointing out the great kindness and help which Kate and she had received from the Russian authorities. It was hard to find a way of getting Ada to talk about herself. "Ada can I begin by asking you what happened after you realised you were too ill to carry on with Kate across Siberia." Ada paused, seeming awkward.

"It wasn't an easy journey, I had to retrace my previous footsteps after a good long rest in Omsk . . . I had some ailments that took time for me to recover from . . . but the Lord assisted me and I was accompanied."

I suspected it was much worse than she was going to tell me. She wanted to talk about Kate, that was obvious.

"The Empress of Russia herself has been taking a great interest in Miss Marsden's mission and has furnished her with letters and papers securing escorts and protection and access to prisons and other public institutions."

"Miss Field, what I really want to know is how did Miss Marsden come to take up this work in the first place?"

I knew that this was what my readers wanted to hear. There had been much discussion at the suffrage meetings about Nurse Kate, everyone was full of admiration – but she puzzled them on her motives. Most people felt she would never return from her present mission.

"Miss Temple, Miss Marsden says herself that the call came to her when she was engaged in nursing the sick and wounded in the Russo-Turkish war. When she was only eighteen she was present in the field hospital of the Russian army. Her services at Sistovo and Schipka are gratefully remembered by the Russians whom she nursed, along with eight other nursing sisters."

Ada's soft voice trailed off – in the reflective moment that followed I found myself following her gaze; a light breeze rustled the azalea planted under the window; the painting of the Madonna and child above the fireplace, and her hands clasped securely on her lap. She'd spent many weeks alone with Kate Marsden on a harrowing journey, I was quite sure she was reliving dark experiences in her mind; including being very, very cold.

"One day during the war she was seeking a place of refuge for the sick and wounded and strayed into a deserted barn, the sole inmates of which were two wretched lepers who had already taken refuge there . . . it was impossible to say if they were men or women, so utterly maimed and disfigured were they as to have lost all resemblance of human beings.

It was the sight of these poor miserable creatures, Miss Marsden says, which inspired her. She felt that here lay her work."

She is so admirable, a great woman for our reader's to look up to and admire I thought, "Did she start her work for the lepers at once?"

"No, circumstances prevented this. At the end of the war she returned to England, and later was obliged to go to New Zealand with a dying sister,[*] after whose death she took the superintendence of a hospital in Wellington. It was here she came upon an article on leprosy by Sir Morrell Mackenzie,[†] which deeply impressed her, and confirmed her resolution to take up the work at once.[‡] She returned to England and applied for permission to proceed to India as nurse in the Leper Hospitals of our Indian Empire."[§]

[*] Ada Field was obviously confused here because, as already documented, her sister was already there but died within 6 days of Kate's arrival with their mother.

[†] Sir Morell Mackenzie, in an article entitled 'The Dreadful Revival of Leprosy', which appeared in the 'Nineteenth Century' in December, 1889, after referring to, its diffusion in Europe and America, says :— 'In almost every other quarter of the globe leprosy is rife at present, and wherever it exists it seems to be slowly but surely extending its ravages'.

[‡] Once again, Ada's facts are slightly wrong. Kate left New Zealand in 1889, Sir Morrell Mackenzie's article was published in the UK in December of that year, Kate had already left and had announced her departure some months earlier.

[§] This is what is printed in in Chapter 15 'Self–Devotion to Lepers' in Leprosy and Vaccination by William Tebb in 1893, which suggests she never really had a clear line of action:

'Miss Kate Marsden's labours among the Maories in New Zealand, and her extraordinary journeys through Russia, and among the wild tribes in remote parts of Siberia, with a view of learning the condition of the outcast lepers in districts where the disease is prevalent, are well known through the reports in the Times and Pall Mall Gazette, which have been extensively copied in English and colonial journals. Miss Marsden's object is to learn by personal observation the condition of the lepers; to discover, if possible, methods of mitigating their sufferings, and to collect funds for the establishment of leper hospitals. Some time ago, Miss Marsden consulted M. Pasteur to see whether inoculation as a cure of the disease might not be resorted to. M. Pasteur held out no hopes of amelioration in that direction, nor did he suggest any other. It does not appear that Miss Marsden has made any inquiries regarding the effect of vaccine inoculation in disseminating the scourge, although, in districts like Dorpat in the Baltic provinces, the lepers are reported to be rapidly increasing, and already form as large a portion of the population as 17 per thousand. The

Ada saw me scribbling furiously in my notebook and went into the kitchen to make us some tea, it was her mother's house and I could hear some discussion in the hallway. She returned with a tray and smiled, although I could see that it belied a great deal of concern and sadness. "My dear, while Miss Marsden was awaiting for a response from the authorities in India her friends advised her to try for an interview with the Queen, which was generously accorded, her Majesty expressing much interest in her work. Miss Marsden was also presented to her Royal Highness the Princess of Wales, who upon hearing of her services in the Russo-Turkish war asked to see her medals. Miss Marsden explained that although entitled to the medals she had not yet received them, whereupon the Princess told her she should certainly have them and most graciously wrote a letter of introduction for Miss Marsden to her sister, the Empress of Russia, explaining the object of her mission. Armed with this Miss Marsden travelled to St Petersburg where she had an interview with the Empress, received her medals and also the necessary letters, her Majesty adding a gift of £100 towards the work. The Empress was quite ignorant that lepers even existed in Russia and was deeply interested in Miss Marsden's proposals to assist them. In May, 1890, she started on a tour through the leper hospitals of the Caucasus, Palestine, Cyprus, Constantinople and Batoum."*

I knew I had a very good story here for 'The Women's Herald' and as Miss Field was showing no signs of wishing the interview to be over – I pushed on.

"Can Miss Marsden speak Russian?"

---

growth of the disease has been co-incident with the development of the Jennerian practice. Miss Marsden's knowledge of the Russian language, and her earnest desire to get at the root of the evil, would enable her to break through official apathy, so obstructive of truthful research, should she be induced to undertake such a mission. It is surely as laudable to arrest one admitted source of the mischief as to prosecute an almost hopeless search for remedies.'

* In Georgia.

The Empress of Russia, Maria Fyodorovna

"Oh only about two dozen words," she replied heartily, "but I have lived many years in St Petersburg and can speak it fluently. I joined her in Moscow and from thence we went to Samara. While there we were told of the one man who could tell us about the Siberian lepers, he was the Archbishop Dyonesius of Ufa. The Governor of Samara gave Miss Marsden a letter of introduction to the Archbishop, which proved invaluable when we called on him. He gave us terrible accounts of these poor lepers in the wild districts beyond Yakutsk. I must tell you they are scattered widely over the districts, and lead a wandering life amongst the forests and lakes far beyond reach of all human habitation. Their main food is the fish they catch in the lakes, and these very fish actually contain the germs which produce the taint of leprosy.* They lead a terrible life amidst indescribable conditions of filth and immorality."

I couldn't help wondering what Miss Marsden intended to do when she reached that part of the wilderness of Siberia and it seemed to me she had relied on Miss Field to interpret, but I wanted to hear more from the sweet lady at my side, pouring more tea.

"But surely life amongst them will be impossible to Miss Marsden?" She paused and looked at me.

"Yes, it will, but she rests in the strength of Him."

Of course she does I thought; God travelled in the sledge with this pair, there were 9,000 New Testaments in there too.

"You've heard about the herb I presume? At Tiflis Miss Marsden heard rumours of a wonderful herb which was said to cure leprosy."

"Yes, do you know more about it?"

"The Archbishop† confirmed this report, but no opportunity has been given to test the healing power of the plant. I would like to tell you something else – I left Miss Marsden at Omsk, as you know, I so regret that illness prevented me travelling further; but before I parted with her I could see that the sick people we saw

---

* This is an interesting piece of guesswork. There is no other written account the author could find of this view.

† Presumably she is referring to the Archbishop of Ufa

WOMAN'S HERALD.

Edited by HELENA B. TEMPLE,
Offices—86, Strand, W.C.
Registered at the G.P.O. for transmission abroad.

The only Paper Conducted, Written, Printed,
and Published by Women.

WOMEN'S PENNY PAPER.

| I WAS THE CHOSEN TRUMP WHERE-THROUGH | COME CHAINS! COME DEATH! THE STRAIN I BLEW |
| OUR GOD SENT FORTH A WAKENING BREATH | SOUNDS ON, OUTLIVING CHAINS AND DEATH! |

No 165. Vol. IV]   DECEMBER 26, 1891   [PRICE ONE PENNY.

regard all doctors with great mistrust, and will not reveal their secrets. When Miss Marsden's imminent arrival was telegraphed to the peasants of a village through which she passed, although a doctor had passed through the day before, they flocked to see her, bringing people suffering from various ailments that she might be able to help them, so great was their faith in her."

"Will this herb prove a cure though?"

"Miss Marsden hopes to discover that."

Miss Field looked at her hands for a moment, I wondered if she missed being on such a great mission; had she wished to cover the whole distance with Kate?

"Bishop Dyonesius wrote to the priest at Yakutsk to have a certain quantity of the herb ready for her. It is called by the natives 'Kutshukta'. Its effects were discovered by a leper whose state was such he could no longer live with his family. He lay in the fields and day by day his people brought him food. He was so prostrate he could only lie on the ground, but after a few days he found to his surprise his sores were healing, and it was discovered to be due to the efficacy of a certain plant with which he came in contact. Experiments were made with the result that it healed leprosy."

This perplexed me slightly, this was no basis for medical evidence, but Ada was sharing Kate's dream and I was glad to listen.

"Miss Marsden now hopes to collect sufficient funds to establish a hospital where the patients can have every attention and care possible."

I had a feeling I was witness to a moment of great female endeavour, women building hospitals, forging into unknown territory, medical experiments . . .

"Where is Miss Marsden now?"

"I cannot tell you exactly," Ada broke off reflectively, "somewhere in the extreme north of Siberia."

"Is not travelling dangerous for ladies in these lonely districts?"

"It might have been but for the kindness and forethought of the Empress and Governors. In consequence of this Miss Marsden was always provided with a strajnik (police official) who drove his own troika behind us."

Oh dear, I thought, it sounds so dangerous, but I knew the readers would enjoy tales of such adventures – but these are very religious women, I wasn't sure that Ada Field wanted to be seen as an adventuress!

"Where did Miss Marsden intend to go after you left her at Omsk?"

"First to Tomsk, then to Irkutsk, and on to Yakutsk. But Irkutsk is the last portal of civilisation. After Irkutsk Miss Marsden must go on by boat, and beyond that she will have to ride."

"Are you happy to be back in England Miss Field?"

"My dear, by the time you print this article I will be gone! I start again for Siberia within a few weeks to join Miss Marsden."

"Have you no subsequent news from Miss Marsden?"

"Oh yes, I was going to mention that I had received a letter. At Krasnoyarsk she met a young Englishman, who acted as her escort to Irkutsk, where she arrived April 28th. At Irkutsk the telegraph line ends. She writes,

'I go to Yakutsk by the first cargo boat there. The Governor kindly gives me an Ispravnik*, who knows within a few hundred miles where to find the lepers. And here is another, written a few days later:

'Dr Alexeeff and myself are now on the banks of the Lena, waiting till our cargo boat starts. We have found out that we must ride on horseback from Yakutsk to Velnisk, 1,000 versts†, then ride about finding lepers, which may mean another 2,000 verses. I have had to have trousers made, and very high boots over the knees, as I must ride like a man

Miss Field and I looked at each other. This letter showed just how tough and determined Kate really was.

"This is all the information I can give you," added Miss Field, "for it is all I have myself."

---

* Russian official
† A verst is an imperial Russian unit of length. It is defined as being 500 sazhen long, which makes a verst equal to 1.0668 kilometres (0.6629 miles; 3,500 feet).

It was time for me to depart as Miss Field was delivering a lecture at The Old Hall Hotel in Buxton within the hour to a group of local businessmen who she felt may help the cause of the lepers. I still had more questions – it is such a deeply interesting expedition, but I had my interview and it was going onto the front page with the previously unpublished photograph that Ada had given me.

I hope Kate Marsden returns safely and when she does I hope she will give her own account of her experiences amongst the lepers to our paper.

Chapter 3

As Jacki, modern day author and now biographer of the enigmatic Kate Marsden, I wanted to talk to her myself, to Kate as a young woman. If I was going to paint her with words, I needed her help in unravelling her complicated life.

We arranged to meet at the footbridge in Pymmes Park in Edmonton; this was close to where she had grown up at The Parade on Silver Street.

When the Marsdens left their family home in the mid-1870s, the fifty acres were still owned by the Ray family and would have been largely a private garden, having once been the curtilage of the Tudor mansion Pymmes Park House. Kate and her siblings would have contented themselves with playing in the nearby fields, glimpsing the chimney stacks of Pymmes Park House through the trees.

If I had done my homework before asking to meet Kate, I would have known this: that the estate was only bought by the borough in 1899 to provide open space for its rapidly growing population. Edmonton was fast becoming a busy urban village. Kate had lived on Silver Street itself from 1859 until 1875 – so she would never have been inside the gates, nor known her way around the park.

It formerly opened to the public in 1906; in the seven intervening years the lovely kitchen gardens had become a walled pleasure garden (Grade II listed,) with an ornamental pond, herbaceous borders and flower beds, the Pymmes Brook flowed through the park into a large boating lake and a set of fine gates welcomed the visitor.

The grey metallic roar of the busy North Circular greeted me as I ran up the steps of Silver Street tube station and across the flyover towards Pymmes Park. The traffic was deafening; vans and lorries were queueing nose to tail up the slip road while another four lanes'- worth of dual carriageway traffic hurtled by. I was glad to find the entrance to the park, imposing wrought iron gates hung from stone piers with ball-finials, because they heralded an escape from the worst elements of my modern world in the twenty first century – noise and pollution.

The sound of birdsong grew stronger as I strode into the park, and soon the traffic roar faded under the shouts of children as they ran around the trees. I found my way to the bridge over the lake, to where I hoped Kate Marsden would be waiting for me.

There she was, in her mid thirties, sitting ramrod straight on a green park bench. I quivered with excitement, and held my hand out.

"May I call you Kate?"

"Miss Marsden would be more fitting, I think, my dear."

That's it, I thought to myself, that prickliness that is mentioned, that air of arrogance. Damn it, I thought, I'm not being very fair; I am in an era of propriety now – she is being polite, she's a Victorian, after all.

"Are you a modern journalist?" she quizzed me.

"I suppose you could call me that!"

It was a mild morning in early October, but Kate had on a black overcoat over a navy skirt. Her hems were long. Just then, ladies' dresses were showing a cautious change with imaginative use of colour, cut, lace and ruffles; but the Kate I saw wasn't embracing change. She clutched an old black leather handbag with unreliable clasp. When it sprung open, I briefly noted the contents – a sheaf of tattered cuttings, a tube of mints, pair of brown leather gloves and a little tweed purse. She saw me looking and snapped it closed again.

Something wasn't right; she seemed bothered, even uncomfortable. I looked again for that magnetism in her personality, the shine in her eyes that drew people in and coaxed generous contributions from them, the passionate tone of the spokesmen for lepers and the bearer of their pain. She looked hard at me and I detected a wretched sadness; the things those eyes had witnessed were an unfathomable place I couldn't go to, not least because, whatever we were doing here together in our prime, she had been born in May 1859, myself 96 years later.

In the only way I knew, I tried to put her at her ease. I offered her a chocolate digestive biscuit from the packet in my shoulder bag; I had thought hard about what I could offer her that she might enjoy.

"What have you been writing about me?" she barked. I flinched at the sudden touchiness.

"Good things, really good things, Miss Marsden. Do you know what's meant by a fan? Well, I'm yours. I must be, because I recreated your journey across Siberia; well I tried. Things have so changed that I couldn't keep to the exact route, that was impossible. Anyone who could do that journey in winter, like you, has my full respect."

"Good things? Well, that does make a change. What newspaper do you write for?"

"Miss Marsden, I'm writing your biography, nobody has written one, not since Henry Johnson when you were still a young woman. It should be published in 2017."

She positively paled in front of my eyes and stared hard at me, trying to make sense of what I'd said.

"But I am still a young woman, even if I am a spinster."

Time travel baffled us and we munched our biscuits and listened to the wind rustle in the tree tops. An army of sparrows flocked around us searching for any crumbs we might drop.

"I grew up near here, you know; our house was in a row called The Parade, just over there. We had a beautiful long garden where I used to play there but sometimes our nanny brought us here to look through the gates and we could see the big house; as you see, we are sitting in its garden."

I turned to look behind us and there was Pymmes Park Mansion, large and lofty, rising behind a beautiful cedar tree on a lawn dotted with white marble goddesses on plinths. Three giant chimney stacks towered into a blue sky above a semi-circular portico. The neat sash windows had more panes of glass than you could count.

"Well, what a joy to see that, after so many years of peeping through those gates without catching a glimpse! Oh, and over there are the lovely Pymmes Villas with views over the park; that were being built about the time I joined the Deaconesses. And over that way is the workhouse."

I hadn't the heart to tell her, yet, that the mansion and the lovely houses she talked about would be bombed flat in the Second World War. But the workhouse – I hadn't heard about that, that must have been absorbed by the North Middlesex Hospital. Perhaps growing up so close to it, watching the wretched residents live out their sad lives, imbued in her a resolve never to be poor and down on her luck.

"Miss Marsden, if we could change the subject, to Russia – would you tell me why you set out from Moscow to travel East in the winter. Wouldn't it have been better to do the bulk of the journey in spring and summer?"

I felt I knew the rationale, but I just wanted to hear it from her – and I was interested in how accurate advice would have been in the 1890s. Did anyone know in Moscow know how cold it would turn out to be?

"My dear, I needed to arrive in Yakutia in the spring so that I could ride out to the lepers in the forest – the Lena is only navigable by boat from June, I had to time my arrival to coincide with the first cargo boats leaving just north of Irkutsk after the thaw. That was the last tarantass ride I had to make, thank heavens, till the return journey."

I watched a group of boys, maybe eight or ten years old, throwing sticks into the lake; they wore large white collared wool shirts over little buttoned jackets and knickerbockers, while a group of smaller ones wore sailor suits. All wore smart rounded caps, cheekily pushed back on their heads. They splashed lake-water over one another and, as they shot off out of sight, their laughter lingered long after we'd gone . . .

Chapter 4

'At the inn where I was staying the maid, when giving me a spoon, wiped it against her backside.'

Anton Chekov

Among new friends in Tomsk, while waiting for a tomato salad and glass of wine to arrive at the table, I unfolded the map I'd brought and the Russians crowded excitedly around it. They had never seen such a thing before, this copy of an 1871 map I had found in the Royal Geographical Society library called 'Post Map of Asiatic Russia'; it was about as near as you could get to the one in the photograph of Kate in 1890 standing in her extraordinary Jaeger outfit designed for the Siberian cold.

The buzz among them showed me their excitement, they were loving each new revelation about the Victorian nurse who visited Russia along with its accompanying magical story and its strong Tomsk connection.

Now Yuliya was leaning over the map and saying, "There will be local journalists eager to meet you, they will be waiting at the places we want to show you, firstly we would like to show you where the city was founded back in 1604 and take you to the monastery that has relics of our founder Bishop and the local Siberian saint who was became the Russian Emperor; after that perhaps the Museum of Local History and our Bishop's Palace because of the current exhibition of Siberian trade routes there."

Yuliya was determined to show us as much of Tomsk as possible – particularly those parts likely to have been visited by Kate Marsden, not least Tomsk State University, already (as Elena, her colleague, pointed out) a proud entity within the city by the time of her visit, while Kirill made a case for Kate having made a professional excursion into the Tomsk countryside to the convent run by the Sisters of Mercy.

The doors of the department limo was held open for us, and we were off, allowing me to gather my first impressions of the 'Siberian Athens'. The name came courtesy of its important component of university students and the easily identifiable buildings serving them. What consistently caught my eye was the concentration of refined timber houses generously decorated with intricately carved 'wooden lace'. This, for me was quite unexpected, but as my friends explained, Tomsk is one of the oldest cities in Siberia and strategically 'planted' in the early 17th century on a hill above the River Tom, where it continued to grow. All its early houses had to be hewn out of the forest and the tradition persisted till the time of the latest tsars.

The city's central cultural and conservation area is dominated by it's mighty pink cathedral of the Bogojavlenskij or Epiphany. My first impressions were of two domes, like immense bell jars, one of them sprouting an improbable black spire that pierced the cloudy sky. The giant burgundy-coloured timber door dwarfed Father Victor, the young priest who was to host my visit, who was waiting for me, bearded and serious, looking the epitome of Orthodox piety.

I stuck by his and the translator's sides, intent on understanding all that father Victor was explaining about the Bogojavlenskij. I felt the VIP status I had quickly gained clutching at me and I didn't dare turn round and look for my travelling companion Ellie, because by now the TV lenses were following me and I needed to fill my appointed shoes. Now, as the cameras closed in on me, all I could do was concentrate on, and react to, Father Victor's earnest, smiling face, while inside I was all female worries: was my summer dress inappropriate? In the shadow of the Bogojavlenskij, was it showing too much cleavage and if he noticed would he be offended? I snuck a quick peep and noticed the top button straining. I was mortified at the thought of it bursting and my godly guide never recovering from the shock.

I was led inside his vast temple, followed by my own cultural entourage, along with sound men, cable-carriers, producers with their clip-boards and the entire tourism department.

"This cathedral was founded in 1777," Father Victor continued softly and unabashed, "but it wasn't fully completed until 1901." "The wooden church has repeatedly suffered from fires, but every time it has been restored; after the revolution in the 1930s the temple was closed . . ."

Kate must surely have been here. I pictured how she would have loved all this media attention! She was, after all, still pumped up from having met her Imperial Majesty the Empress of Russia. If they'd had TV cameras, then she would surely have played up to them with her legendary personality.

Now, we had reached a long room with gold painted wooden caskets, ornately carved and labelled in Cyrillic script; our party formed an intent quadrant, watching in hushed silence, where I stood with Father Victor, I was aware of all eyes following him as he reached inside his black robes, pulled out a great bundle of keys and unlocked his treasure chest.

"The chief treasure of the Bogoyavlensky Cathedral is the relics of the sacred great martyr and healer Panteleimon who lived in the 3rd century. The Lord endowed him with the special gift of being able to cure human diseases and infirmities."

Everyone seemed to feel the tension as he lifted the ancient box out of the cabinet and held it towards me. Everything in me willed him not to place it in my hands which were shaking; what if the Englishwoman dropped it on camera? I was saved by a thought of the Antiques Roadshow – there, they never seem to drop anything – but they're used to it. It allowed me to smile at him, and nod – and he gently replaced the box.

"Every Wednesday" Father Victor went on, "after evening service, a wooden ark of holy relics of God's Saint Acathistus is displayed and opened and each person can touch the relics, praying before them for themselves or for relatives."

I wasn't sure what relics: had he said the right arm of the saint? I hadn't liked to ask in my ignorance. He had mentioned the Holy Books the Saint had inscribed and the Miracle Objects, of which five are lost. But now we were being led out of the inner shrine and onto the stone steps of one of the bell-jar domes; up and up and up, with the camera man squeezing ahead and filming my ascent. Once more I worried about the top button of my dress and I desperately wanted to refresh my lipstick and look less travel weary for whatever TV channel this was; after all, do many guests on TV spend the night before they are filmed sleeping on an airport floor? I wasn't sure I liked celebrity status.

We emerged out onto the wide decked platform surrounding the giant cathedral bells: our arrival sent all the fat pigeons perched on the stone sills of the deep windows flying off across the city. Unaware of what was in store for me – my eyes were straining past them to the statue of Lenin erected on a square which the traffic drove round, his arm was held out with a finger pointing past the green Taiga stretching out to the horizon beyond, all this reinforced my realisation that I really was in Siberia.

Father Victor gestured me up to the platform and in his soft godly voice, invited me to ring the bells.

Everybody was staring at me. "You want me to ring these bells" my inner voice recoiled, "they are massive, I will disturb the whole city of Tomsk, a place the same size as Birmingham!"

Many feet below, in the busy street, the traffic was queued at traffic lights; I looked across to people wandering peacefully in a park and beyond that, to office blocks and apartment buildings. I thought of all the people enjoying the calm of a Tuesday afternoon.

"Please, we all want you to ring the bells, you are our guest." said Father Victor, smiling.

I hesitated, and then stepped onto the platform, and as I pulled at those heavy ropes attached to the enormous bells over Tomsk, the camera man focused his camera and the lady with the microphone with its long trailing lead began to speak into it in Russian and I couldn't help thinking about all the poor people down below that I was now disturbing. I sensed them stopping whatever they were doing and looking up, and thinking,'who is ringing the bells so badly on a weekday afternoon?'

But the faces around me indicated that they were happy with my performance on the bells. Tomsk and it's representative people held me – unlike poor Anton Chekov, Kate's near-contemporary, as he stopped off on his way to the far Eastern Sakhalin Island in 1890, the year before Kate. The great writer undertook a similar journey to hers by train, horse-drawn carriage and steamer to the penal colony on Sakhalin Island, Russia's largest island in the North Pacific Ocean. The purpose behind his arduous journey was to spend three months interviewing thousands of convicts for a census. He wrote detailed letters to his sister along the way and he wrote to her that nobody in Tomsk smiled; the only nice thing to be noted was its food. "Tomsk is not worth a wooden nickel. It is the most boring of cities, and the people are the most boring." He wrote in his diary. "The city is not sober, the lawlessness is Asian. The dirt is impassible, but there occur the rudiments of civilisation — at the inn where I was staying the maid, when giving me a spoon, wiped it against her backside. The dinners are excellent, unlike the women who are hard to the touch." Tomsk took its revenge in a bronze statue depicting him tipsily gazing through his pince-nez towards his favourite restaurant, in long overcoat and with exaggerated large bare feet; or are they flippers?

Crowning this lovely city sits Resurrection Hill. Here I was to be the guest of the Museum of Tomsk. I jumped out of the car, looking forward to stretching my legs with a run up the old cobbled street called Obrub – only to run into another cameraman 'lying in wait'! So I walked calmly on up, past the police station, a Czarist presence that the visiting Chekov would have noticed, to the breathtaking onion-domed museum, its crafted timber walls all silvered by the passing of time.

Once the original cameraman, the man holding the cables, and the slightly-built woman with the distinctive mannish haircut in charge of the microphone had puffed their way up to meet me, they seated me on a sort of exterior wooden dias. I was doing my best – with wild gesticulations – to answer their questions, to try and compare and contrast these two journeys, Kate Marsden and mine, and explain why I thought she had put herself through so much.

As we were winding up our interview, and as if to move things on, an antiquated black BMW, came chugging up the hill, with a heart made out of pink and white roses adorning the radiator, and pink ribbons knotted to the mirrors, bumper and hub caps. It was still only early afternoon, but the wedding parties were arriving to take advantage of the one scenic shot that has Tomsk written all over it – carefully angled or cropped to exclude the giant grey cement works blocking the downhill view. Up here in front of the museum, the happy couples began strolling hand-in-hand through the dazzling orange of the marigold-beds, while their friends emerged from a rummage through the Museum's dressing-up wardrobe, strutting to pose with bride and groom; the young men in full length Cossack coats of burgundy brocade and crimson velvet trimmed with ermine and gilt and chimney-like fur hats, the young women in pink bonnets and matching velvet skirts. It reminded me of my school productions of Shakespeare in England, and as I revelled in the exuberance and broad smiles, I thought of all the vodka shots they would be downing for the rest of the day.

The pretty museum marks the place of the founding citadel of 1604; there is a stone monument to Tomsk's foundation, and close by stands the faithful reconstruction of the timber Golden Gate tower. My brief sojourn in Obrub Street, round which Tomsk first grew up, was enough to awake a sense of it's history, proudly corroborated by my hosts from the tourism department and my colleagues of the film crew. As we were leaving, the spontaneous farewell gestures of all the cossacks and brides and grooms and their gaiety, momentarily brought back thoughts of my own farewell all those hours ago at Heathrow – and what that might lead to. But now we were whirled back into Kate Marsden's likely itineraries, between the prison and hospital visits she made there in 1890, the Art House, the Bogoroditse-Aleksievskij monastery and Tomsk Imperial University.

This kept us busy until early evening when, exhausted but culturally invigorated, we crowded into one of the booths with red vinyl seats of a celebrated Tomsk eatery. At last, with a big glass of Georgian white wine in my hand I could begin to unfold for my hosts my understanding; up to this point, of the strange woman who was still sparking so much interest a hundred and twenty years on.

When now I reread Kate's book, its awkward structure and wilful lack of key information almost validates the criticism it received on publication. It frustrates my hopes of a greater understanding of her motives, and the rationale behind her call to travel East. I want her to explain why she chose Siberia in the first place, what in her early training determined on leprosy as the focus of her mission and what inklings had she got before setting off to this vast and little known semi-continent? Had she the faintest apprehension of the cold she would have to endure, of the vast distances that she would have to cross, of the seas of wild forest and innumerable lakes? Did anyone warn her that she would be travelling in an eight-month long winter, in days that only get light for a few hours round either side of midday? Who could advise her that her destination was the coldest spot on earth? There is nothing in her pages to account for the advice she must have received, nothing to illuminate the steps taken in preparation for her successful enterprise. Of all the women whose heroic journeys I have followed, in this respect she remains frustratingly opaque.

We know that she was unwell on arrival in Tomsk, and lay low. But once back on her feet she went straight to the city's hospital to monitor patient-staff relations. Next, armed according to her own account with sugar and New Testaments in Russian, she braved Tomsk's prisons, dark and wretched places where she was doubtless witness to terrible suffering. For all its optimistic beginnings and its growing academic renown, Tomsk had been for at least a century the place of judicial exile and political oblivion, and among the prisoners Kate was likely to have encountered would have been political idealists, among them internal Decembrists and Polish partisans. By her own reckoning, she distributed around

2,000 testaments among Tomsk's overcrowded convicts, of both sexes, as well as sugar for the tea she handed out.

My hosts from the tourism department helped my musings, by introducing me to the 'Russian Joan of Arc', as Maria Bochkareva has been called. A native of Tomsk, she would barely have been two during Kate's sojourn. Elena cited her as the one Russian-born woman of the last century, who was a match for Kate in valour. We don't normally think of pre-Revolutionary women choosing a military career, but Bochkareva earned several decorations for heroism in the Tsarist army; and in the wake of two failed abusive marriages, she heard a voice calling "Go to war to help save the country!" And when the Romanovs fell, the democratic White Russian government under Alexander Kerensky gave her permission to create an all-female brigade called the 'Women's Battalion of Death'. "Come with us in the name of your fallen heroes," Bochkareva entreated Russian women in June 1917.

According to her memoirs, her loyal "tigresses" continued fighting after peace was announced. She did not adapt to the idea of the new Soviet government, and the feeling was mutual: her battalion was soon disbanded and it wasn't long before she took a steamship into exile in America. Yet she returned to the continuing civil war, and ensured her own downfall: in spring 1919, she went to the Russian Urals to try to form a women's unit under the White Admiral Kolchak. But she was captured by the Bolshevik forces in Tomsk and sentenced and executed by firing squad on May 16, 1920.

"Wow", I exclaimed, "some feisty lady!" Elena nodded in agreement. "She's buried in Tomsk, quite close to here."

For such a tough trip I was glad I had found a suitable fellow adventuress. I had met Ellie at a pre-arranged meeting at a London hotel, for an hour, a few weeks earlier in the month. I went there full of apprehension about the choice of any one person as a companion mindful of those on previous expeditions who had broken ranks: trying to change the route, skipping the day's journey to go shopping, undermining my leadership, or pleading exhaustion. What made it for me about this personable, South

African social worker was her track record and her assurance that she was quite willing to sleep on a sack of any nameless ship's cargo on the Lena under a sky blackened with swirling insects! Also, she had made many long, overland journeys; I had met my match, there wouldn't be a hairdryer lurking in the depths of her ageing rucksack, and she would be up for anything. By now the two of us had camped on an airport floor, and – fully embracing the purpose of our journey – Ellie had performed wonderfully for that morning's TV interview in front of the museum.

The next morning we were off together with our team into the Seiluzhki countryside, through which wound the old Siberian Road or Tea Route. Here along the ancient way to Irkutsk which Kate had traversed by sledge, there would be more performing for cameras, singing of songs, ringing of bells, trying on costumes and swapping knowledge of our heroine Kate Marsden.

There was a buzz of excitement inside the car as Paval, the historian, and Max, our interpreter, answered our eager questions and explained that the road had been driven through in the 1730s – principally as a postal route along which letters were carried monthly. At the same time, as the only road connecting the eastern and western parts of Russia, it allowed embassies from St Petersburg to the Chinese and Mongolian courts ready access, and opened a gateway into the vastness of Siberia. From the start, the Russian judiciary saw this forest wilderness as a place of detention and exclusion, and summer and winter, the streets of Tomsk rang with the footfall of convicts being marched to the camp settlements.

In the cool breeze from my open car window, I pictured men and women marching in chains, with their heads bent, their feet dragging, and their futures bleaker than anything that Charles Dickens could conjure up.

But the new road doubled as a well-used trade-route, tea, first presented in 1640 to the Russian Tsar in Moscow by the early eighteenth century, was becoming popular among Russians and Tomsk was one of the first Russian cities to trade in tea, brought by land caravans and water. Along the new road, for the next two centuries, passed eastwards animal furs and skins, leather, iron, copper and wheat in exchange for the tea from China and Mongolia; the trade was so successful that the tea plantations in China expanded to match the demand. Thus, the busy route expanded the culture and socio-economic status of the region and other permanent settlements emerged along it.

At this point in my journey, the roadside pines, silver birches and larches had, in the Siberian sunlight, the charm of unfamiliarity; – but even I would come to long for an old oak tree or a gracious elm. It was a jolt to come upon a petrol-station among all this ancient nature, and the modern world intruded again when Paval's phone rang in his pocket. Staring at the straight summery road ahead, I thought of Kate swaddled mummy-like in the back of her freezing sledge, unable to move her head and she rolled about amidst her cargo of tea and Bibles like a rotating giant sea-slug.

At this stage in her mission, this quote from her book suggests the following scenario:

'I could see little gleams of light which we passed coming from tiny hut windows in the forest.

"Driver", I shouted, "Can't we stop a minute at one of those huts?"

"Eh, what, madam?"

"Those huts where the lights are on, can't we rest there?"

"Lights? They're not lights! They're wolves".

"Oh, my goodness me!"'

That funny little plaintive 'oh'! The voice of an Englishwoman with a stiff upper lip, alone, because her travelling companion Ada Field had had to quit at Zlatoust, out of her depth, and comfort zone, colder than she could ever have imagined, and fearful of what might turn up next.

I turned to Pavel, sitting behind me in the car, "In the book, Paval, Kate talks about wolves and bears and as she travels a lot at night you get the impression that the wolves are practically nibbling at her ankles! Are wolves and bears a problem today?"

I could hear Paval saying "Da, da," and Max assured me that the driver sees wolves, and bears, and moose on the road from time to time. I thought at once of Bram Stoker's Dracula, published in 1897, five years after Kate's book with its thrilling gothic prose:

'I saw around us a ring of wolves, with white teeth and lolling red tongues, with long, sinewy limbs and shaggy hair. They were a hundred times more terrible in the grim silence which held them than even when they howled.'

Eighty miles into our journey to Novo-Kuskovo, there was no let-up on the wayside forest wall. But finally, we drove through a settlement of log cabins with corrugated metal roofs, grey picket fences behind which stacks of wood, chopped in preparation for winter alternated ahead with rows of cabbages in carefully marked out vegetable patches. The driver slowed to turn off, we came to a rest opposite a pretty compound with baton-shaped lime green fence posts.

In answer to Paval's mobile, there stood two women dressed up for our benefit in full regional finery. This trip would hold many surprises for me and not least the Russian love of spectacle, pomp and dressing-up accompanied, wherever possible, by national music relayed at full blast and we were about to experience that here in spades.

No sooner had we got out than Russian music peeled out through the Siberian forest from high-set speakers. Only that, and their clip-boards, betrayed the present time as with evident warmth they greeted our party in Russian, one in royal blue, four long panels attached to a bodice, the other one in a similar outfit in cherry red. Both wore white muslin blouses with elaborately embroidered sleeves and round embroidered hats with sashes down the back completed the colourful ensemble. I loved the way the one in blue completed her speech with a wide balletic arc of the arms and a deep bow. Now they were walking out from the gate, the lady in red looking straight at me and proffering a new newly baked brown loaf on an embroidered cloth. What is the etiquette here? I whispered to Max, remembering the potential embarrassment of having been asked to ring the city bells of Tomsk. "You need to break off one small piece of the bread and then dip it into the salt before eating it."

The ladies were talking and Max translated as they spoke, "so that you may live long and prosper, so that your house will be full for guests and staff and you may always have enough bread and salt."

It was admirable beyond any amateur-dramatics level the enthusiasm and sincerity with which these two played their parts, their speech, sometimes unison, sometimes antiphonal, spiced with similes and descriptive arm-gestures. Eating the bread as instructed, I wondered if I would ever have staff; I remembered that I did in a former life have a Polish lady to clean my house once a week. The thoroughness of her vacuuming still remains a wonder and mystery to me.

The doorstep of bread and salt was washed down by a fizzing white drink that I sipped from a three-legged ceramic cup held out by the lady in red. Max told us, it was sweetened and fermented mare's milk; this unique culinary experience would become quite familiar to me as my journey unfolded. It tasted good.

"If you come in you will live for the whole year without misfortune because we are going to take you first to the Pine Tree of Wishes." At that they gave us all yellow and cyclamen pink ribbons, and led us towards a magnificent and clearly ancient pine-tree within the compound. Max told me what to do next.

"You need to make a wish as you're walking towards the tree; then, tie your ribbon on the tree, to make it come true."

I am not normally superstitious but that large looming pine made me wrestle with my thoughts. One wish, a very special wish, – a wish to be used wisely – what should it be? There were two very clear contenders and my fingers played with the smooth satin of the ribbon as I neared the tree.

My head filled with images – the departure gate at Heathrow, my grown-up son out in South London on his bike, his camera in his back-pack. In my fifties I could still believe not only that the love of my life was out there, but that the man who had chosen that airport rendezvous to tell me, in his softly compelling voice, that he loved me was IT. But, feet from the tree, the mother in me was recalling every last detail of my son's conversation with me before I left – the good work he hoped to get next week, the room with damp that he was looking to exchange for a proper flat. I tied my pink ribbon to the old Russian tree. Before the journey was over it had woven its magic.

And now, from the energetic gestures of our hostess in blue towards the adjacent glade, I deduced that we were now obliged to dance. From speakers, concealed in trees either side of the big pine now aflutter with yellow and pink wishes, blared out loud Russian music with a disco twist. She signalled to us to hold hands, and led round in a snake pattern before forming us into a circle; I found myself running to keep up with our boisterous hostesses as they turned us this way and that, dodging under arms and changing hands with one another. It was only when the music stopped that the Blue Lady welcomed us – officially – to Novo-Kuskovo village, home to the first county hospital in Tomsk District. It had been founded in the first years of the previous century by Dr N. A. Lampsakov. The first Director's house is now the museum; nearby is the building where the horses were kept, and you see it – she told us – exactly as it looked in 1903.

Not with that music churning out, I thought, but the spirit of our reception was irresistible. At once, Blue Lady grabbed Ellie and me by the hand and led us off down a timber boardwalk, with the happy swagger of one having so much to be pleased about, and led us away from the main wooden house along a wooden broad walk.

Paval, our gentle moustachioed historian, was at our side. "Of course there are many layers of this wooden path under here," he said, "when one surface rots, another one is just built on top." Of course! I thought; for more than half the year this ground is deep in snow and ice.

As September's sun warmed the Siberian noon, out came the mosquitoes. As we were shown the log-built buildings among the trees and their varied uses, I stooped to scratch at an ankle, and even our colourful guides were snatching at the air around them. Maxim was pinching his earlobe as he relayed to us the surprising information that this country hospital had been the first establishment in the county supplied with electricity.

Relief from our torturers came when at last we ducked inside one of the log buildings, its interior dominated by a great black stove; a reminder that summers here are short and lives are geared to staying warm in winter. The adjacent building, Lampsokov's house, was devoted to pre-Revolutionary rural life. I was curious to note that the men's area displayed, along with the usual array of carpenter's tools, a loom and spinning wheel. Opposite it was the kitchen area, here our Red Lady proudly pointed out butter churns, held up pewter and pottery vessels for us, and tapped the iron sitting on the hob. A baby's crib hung from the ceiling above a colourful string of handmade felt dolls, "What are they for?" I asked.

"Oh," she said, "that's to protect the baby from evil forces".

On a white tablecloth sat, ornate and resplendent, the samovar, so much a feature of Kate's book, with its stack of charcoal underneath for heating the water and cracker holder round the rim, for her the token of a destination reached.

"You have a vague idea that the appointed place for halting cannot be far distant. Jehu* begins to want his vodka; you long for the sight of the singing samovar, and a nice, snug, warm room, with feather bed, well aired sheets, and, perhaps, a warming pan; and the horses seem to sniff their supper from afar, so on they wildly go, snorting and foaming, until, at last, at the post-station you pull up sharp."

What a treat it was turning out to be, this special reception at Novo-Kuskovo. For me, and no doubt for my companion, this was my first immersion into the nation's culture. My only previous experience of Russia had been a ten-hour stopover at Moscow Airport over twenty years previously, my then four-year-old son and I had made en route to Kenya! Now, in the Siberian sunlight, at leisure to move and stretch, I recalled the terminal's severe shortage of seats, so that I had to perch in the only space I could find, with my boy sleeping on my shoulder. I had all the time in the world to look up at the vast ceiling and what arcane purpose

* Jehu the legendary furious chariot driver from the Old Testament.

was served by all those brown metal bins attached to it. The only relief came when, after several hours, I collected a voucher for a free meal and we trailed into a large canteen where I was handed a slice of white bread from a trolley and brown gravy was ladled over it by a large lady who looked like an Olympic shot-put thrower.

Here I was, years later, being led on an exclusive visit, all recorded for local news by a photographer who followed us everywhere. Even at this late stage, our Red and Blue ladies were giving 150 per cent: Paval had already nudged me to look at the old horn gramophone, and here was Blue Lady winding it up and dancing to an urgent male voice singing against a crackly military orchestra to fill this room of 1903. Ellie and I, in ancient 1910 nurse's bonnets clapped while our hostesses spun and leapt to the exultant folk-dance.

Poignancy and reflection occupied the last rooms of the museum; it was here that we heard about Dr Lampsakov, the founder of this country hospital, his long directorship and his sad demise. Black and white photographs in a glass case supplied the backdrop. We heard that this area had been heavily fought over during the Russian Civil War: when the Reds were in power, he treated their troops; when the whites briefly took over, likewise* – but concealing the presence of his Red patients. Here, Red lady invited Paval to pull the ring in the floorboards, which revealed a substantial trapdoor. We stared down into the black hole.

"It led into the forest," Max translated, "and its course was only rediscovered when the new road was built in the 1970s."

---

* The Russian Civil War (November 1917 – October 1922) was a multi-party war in the former Russian Empire immediately after the Russian Revolutions of 1917, as many factions vied to determine Russia's political future. The two largest combatant groups were the Red Army, fighting for the Bolshevik form of socialism, and the loosely allied forces known as the White Army, which included diverse interests favouring monarchism, capitalism, and alternative forms of socialism, each with democratic and antidemocratic variants.

After a lifetime of service, Dr Lampsakov was investigated, under Stalin, for anti-Soviet activities in 1937, and summarily shot; though his widow, until her own death in 1953, was permitted to continue running his pioneering forest hospital. For the remainder of its useful life, it was administered by the local community; and now, wonderfully unchanged, it is a vivid museum to heroic times. If only Kate could have seen it.

It would have been churlish to refuse a cup of tea with water heated in a samovar and so I drank my first-ever cup of tea in Russia, (although I am still not a tea drinker). Large square biscuits were served with it, (they looked like dog biscuits but I'm sure they weren't!) and I tucked in while Max showed us photographs of the 'Saying Goodbye to Winter' folk festival that is held here every year. Now it was Ellie's turn to shine; helped by our friends into regional costume, she posed for our photographer and did twirls for international relations in a stunningly embroidered full length dress, complemented by a bright red shawl decorated with roses and topped with an ornate peasant headdress. There was a swing nearby, and for our final open-air shot Paval motioned me to join her sitting in it.

But it was Kate Marsden – the inspirer, after all, of our journey – who crowned our visit. With Max to help me out, I told our two enchanting hostesses a little about her life and mission, and my aim in traversing Siberia and in my other adventures.

"My whole purpose in recreating her journey is to bring their names to the world's attention."

I held up Kate's book and handed them postcards that we were carrying with us to celebrate Kate and then they posed with our famous, soon-to-be-well-travelled plum pudding we'd brought form England. I couldn't help noticing it, but they both had a bemused look, as if they hadn't quite expected to have added to the history of their Tea Trakt, with which they were so familiar, a completely new snippet from an unexpected source. We all hugged three times – the Russian way and they asked me to come back again. "Why don't you come back in winter?" It was rhetorical – I couldn't conceive of coming back in winter!

ХУДОЖЕСТВЕННО-ЭТНОГРАФИЧЕСКІЕ РИСУНКИ СИБИРИ.

The Tea Track by Kosharov

Back on the Tea Trakt, with the sun still high, we drove with a sense of shared fulfilment throughout the Semiluzhki countryside, between grassy verges dotted with colourful wild flowers.

Now our eyes took in again the sleepy villages, the ubiquitous heaps of winter fuel, dogs barking behind aged wooden fences obscuring pretty rustic houses; some of the older ones had ornately carved windows painted pale blue and white, and their bright tin roofs seemed to grow out of the deep vegetation surrounding them. The ominous tree line of the Siberian forest was never far away; that gateway into the dark world of danger and the unknown.

I was aware that our hosts hadn't eaten since breakfast, apart from the square biscuit at the hospital. Even so, they were game enough to spot a photo-opportunity when in one village some bored-looking teenage lads came loping up and, discovering two of us were anglophone, dared each other to practice their schoolboy English on us. "My name is Nikolai – Nik." Nik's friends made faces into the camera behind him and we all laughed and set off again.

In the village of Semiluzhki, our driver turned off the dusty road where a woman was hard at work on top of her winter log pile, and the sides of our car scraped lush vegetation as the track

The Tea Track by Kosharov

narrowed. A lone bird plaintively sang as the car pulled up at wet sawdust in puddles and a pointed heap of soil. The workmen sawing huge logs didn't look up as we got out of the car. "Where are we now?" I enquired in a perplexed tone.

"This," said Max, "is the one-man village of Vladimir the Cossack."

I saw him standing there. Obviously forewarned of our arrival, (but I am not sure how because this was not a man inclined towards a modern device such as a mobile phone), he was a man whose sheer imposing height dwarfed those men working around him. Dressed in khaki combat trousers, t-shirt and big boots, Vladimir had thick black tightly-curled hair and a thick beard. I couldn't help thinking he was Peter the Great in the years he apprenticed himself off to the ships' carpenters at Deptford!

And now, beyond his broad shoulders, I spotted the timber fort this retired policeman had been instructed to build by St Nicholas in a dream.

Maxim introduced us, and told him why I was there: Kate Marsden's story once more being told on the dusty road she had once travelled. This bear of a man looked straight at me and spoke at me in loud Russian. Most of the translation got lost in the wind, but I gathered that a Prince had come to this place at seventeen, and prayed all night. At one point he turned to our driver and ticked him off roundly for smoking.

"Russians," he said, "should have a healthy spirit." The fierceness of this remonstration made me laugh with delight. He turned back to me, clutching the Kate Marsden postcard we had given him. "She couldn't have missed this place: it's on the road. She would have stopped to pray at the chapel that I have rebuilt."

I nodded in agreement, "She probably gave out Bibles here."

"Da, da, da, da," said Vladimir the Bear, "this is the only road she could have come on, and Siberian saints used to pray here."

I immediately caught the depth of his faith from the way he spoke about the saints. His status in the community had allowed him free rein in building his castle or fort unhindered; his work was endorsed, he explained, by professors in Tomsk. My question to him translated by Max – turned out to be naive, "So this work is your passion?"

"Niet," he answered firmly, "passion is a sin." I was put in my place and we moved on, further into his life's work.

The log chapel, which he had evidently rebuilt in the style of the original, was compact with many roof levels and a diminutive tower. The imposing steps leading up into it gave it a stately presence and a centre point of the fortress, ringed by many rough-hewn structures that formed its perimeter. There was an emptiness that negated any sense of present purpose, though some had the look of cattle sheds, granaries on stilts or log stores there were no cattle or horses present to add to its authenticity. Other buildings with towers or long enclosures or open-sided sheds looked forlorn too, it felt like he was building a museum.

Vladimir led me into his chapel, and told me to cover my head with a silk scarf from the collection at the door. Then he broke into an unstoppable speech, asking me my religion, and standing me on the spot where, in the old chapel, he insisted Kate Marsden would have stood and he recited a prayer for all travellers. I felt I was sucked in by his powerful, bear-like personality, transformed by the depth of his personal religion; but I couldn't help thinking that he recited the traveller's prayer at such a lick that surely God must have missed it.

"Would you like to go up my bell tower? I have built it to look the way it was 400 years ago."

Oh, no! not again, I thought; he'll go and ask me to ring the bells!

"Okay," I politely answered, "let's go for it."

The log tower was accessed by a rickety, seemingly home-made ladder. I went up first, increasingly aware that while Vladimir had been at great pains to provide scarves to cover lady visitors' hair on holy ground, there was nothing to mask the sight of my bare legs as I negotiated his rungs in my knee length dress!

From the top I could appreciate the impressive scale of this hand-built fortress. With a tower at each corner and its expansive ranges of cart-lodges and byres, it left the only modern object on view – a red tractor at our feet, completely dwarfed. The same went for the village of Semiluzhki scattered sleepily over wooded slopes beyond Vladimir's ramparts.

My friendly Cossack then rang the three bells hanging at our eye level, bursting into loud song as he did so. Then he turned and laughed, his eyes positively alight. I could see a school beyond the fort; were they too having their busy Wednesday disturbed by my visit, like the residents of Tomsk the day before?

There was so much more that he was eager I should see, and, with me in his wake he strode off towards one of the corner towers. Here he laughed at my reaction to a stuffed brown bear, poised, to jump, inside the dark doorway; he gave me a brief lesson in loading an ancient pistol and placed some sort of evil metal knout into my hands, so heavy that I almost dropped it, before pulling on a helmet with nose guard and chain mail hanging from the neck and asking me to hit him over the head with the truncheon! How could I? Vladimir didn't mind – he was in his element. For all his life's pious calling, what shone out now was his genial Cossack playfulness. I was overcome with a sense of safety in his company.

In a dark and dusty corner, he led me towards a shelf-full of framed religious icons, becoming serious again he lifted one of them down, placing it in my hands. "This one weeps tears every year, and the people from the city come out to see it. I had it from a priest in Irkutsk. Now, this one here is a very rare item representing Sofia, the Wisdom of God. It is the only icon in Tomsk like it." I wondered whether we'd just stumbled upon one of the five Miracle Icons, long since lost from the cathedral.

His final act of kindness was to hold up his box of Russian fairy-tale toys, picking out first Coco and the Fish, a beautifully wooden carving of a fish granting Coco his dearest wishes, and then a witch on a broomstick, each in turn a masterpiece.

Something awakened in me, while in Semiluzhki, of the wonders achievable by the woodworker's art.

Now, back in Tomsk, pretty tree-lined streets with wooden houses carved with beautiful ornamentation greeted us. The earliest wooden lacework that embellished them dates from the mid nineteenth century, and no two houses were in any way similar. With new eyes, I marvelled at the craftsmanship.

It was good to rest in the Hunter's Lodge that night. It had been an exhausting day and Ellie's and my visit was coming to an end with only a television interview to do before we left in the morning. With more time we could have got to the convent where in 1892 Sisters of Mercy were sent by Princess Shakovskaya, with the assistance of a Tomsk bishop, to nurse the lepers in Yakutia; this post-dated Kate Marsden's sojourn, but she writes about the nuns that were sent out from Tomsk to the lepers she'd identified in Yakutia in her book. We could have visited the Memorial Museum Remand Prison or even eaten at the restaurant "Vechiy Zov" housed in a former transit gaol with, my friendly guides assured me, an indescribable aura of pre-revolutionary Russia. As for the Tomsk Hospital, the State Medical University, the local branch of the Red Cross Society and the Museum of Wooden Architecture,these would all have to wait for my 'winter visit'!

At the start of recreating this great Russian journey, it was time to bid farewell to our generous hosts from the Tomsk Region Department of Culture and Tourism and leave for Irkutsk via Yurga, where Ellie and I would change onto the Trans-Siberian railway.

THE PRINCESS SHACHOVSKOY, THE THREE SISTERS WHO ARE ALREADY
AT WORK AMONGST THE LEPERS, AND SELF.

The Princess Shachovskov, three sisters and Kate Marsden (centre)

Chapter 5

The map of Kate Marsden's route taken from her book

I may have been 'slightly inconvenienced' by being diverted, because of fog and arriving four hours late – but Kate Marsden had to do that journey to Tomsk, all 1,793 miles from Moscow, by train and then on a sledge through temperatures averaging -50 fahrenheit!

Kate's journey from Moscow had only been the second leg – she had already been travelling for some months after setting off in November 1890 from Constantinople. When she arrived in Tomsk she was ill from severe motion sickness: 'I was groaning under the almost intolerable pain caused by the constant lurching of the sledge', and it took her two days to get her strength back. In comparison I obviously had little reason for complaint, I'm quite certain I would have been sick for a month had I arrived in Moscow on a sledge from Turkey!

Travelling across Russia in her footsteps was one way for me to try and understand why she undertook so difficult and dangerous a journey. I wanted to know what sparked her passion to help lepers; her vision was incredibly sure since she never once wavered. But, surveying her childhood and teenage years, we may begin to pick out certain elements that played an important part in forming her admirable dedication to leprosy.

Firstly, her mature persona as a natural nurse with an urgent desire for people to be healthy may well seem to be rooted in her childhood. She was born the youngest of eight children, and despite its evident affluence, the whole family lived under the terrible shadow of consumption. It had blighted the previous generation of the Marsden family and Kate and her siblings had evidently vowed never to marry and therefore not have children, the only way to stop the genetical track of the disease, they presumed.

'Consumption' is the wasting disease tuberculosis, which does exactly what the older name suggests: eats away at the body. Tuberculosis can infect any part of the body, but most commonly affects the lungs, it was the most widespread disease of its day, almost always proving fatal. The first widely practiced remedy was care in a sanatorium where patients were surrounded by nature's greenery, fed with nutritious food and exposed to fresh air. It has its literary evocation in Thomas Mann's 'The Magic Mountain' of 1924.

Kate was different to her four brothers and three sisters in being the tomboy of the family; her feisty independence and outdoorsy spirit probably saved her from her siblings' fate, who all died of consumption before reaching maturity; only she and a brother were the sole survivors.

Mr Marsden was comparatively wealthy, having practiced for many years as a solicitor in Cheapside in the City of London; the family lived comfortably in Edmonton which, in 1859, was still a village of 'stabling, hayricks, fields and large gardens where flowers and fruit trees mingled in delightful confusion'.

Here, Mrs Marsden was left to bring up her large brood; Johnson's account of her is anodyne, if a little ambiguous: 'Her mother, who bore the chief responsibility of training a large family, was a woman in whom the gentleness of her sex was strongly developed combined with strict ideas of family discipline.' what is this meant to mean – that she was a severe mother, but had charming good looks?

Young Kitty Marsden chose to hang out in the garden with the gardener, to climb trees and run about till exhausted and if a punishment was to be locked out of the house, she revelled in it, particularly if there was sewing with her sisters to be done inside. The genteel accomplishments expected of young ladies in the mid-nineteenth century were anathema to her and this carried on, too, into her school life which she put up with as a necessary evil. For Kate, as at home, schoolroom punishments were an almost daily occurrence.

It is not hard to imagine how the inflexible education system of the 1860s and 1870s would have been totally unsuited to an inquisitive child living in a world of her own. Children were expected to listen in lessons and answer a question correctly when asked, but to ask a question was an impertinence and Kate was the sort of child who wanted to know the why and how of everything she came across. It would be another hundred years before the education system began to accommodate itself to children like her and, indeed, to recognise that an enquiring mind is intelligence-building. Understandably, Kate made little progress in her Margate school and her naughtiness and its consequent punishments increased; and while Mr and Mrs Marsden do not seem to have been harsh parents they really didn't know how to deal with this little earth-spirit who loved to be aloft in a tree and regarded animals as her friends.

They do, indeed, seem to have allowed her to have pets and, from some undocumented source we know that the young girl acquired sufficient carpentry skills to create for these animals a hen-house, a rabbit hutch, a dog kennel and a coffin for a dead kitten, giving them an enviably competent finish. These pets she regarded as her special friends, and if she felt unwell she would shut herself up with them; and if one of them died, she would bury the creature with the ceremonial of a funeral service. When the dreadful day arrived that she had to go away to boarding school, she went round and informed the cats, rabbits, chickens, cows, donkey, horses and even the plants; and, in case they hadn't understood, did the rounds a second time with her goodbyes.

The death march of consumption had already swept up the lives of her brother James, who died at eleven when Kate was two and Alice at thirteen when Kate was eleven. Next, dropsy or oedema, took up the breadwinner of the family: Mr Marsden died in 1873, when Kate was fourteen and away at boarding school.

On his death the family discovered that he had made little provision for them and so the agreeable house and garden in Edmonton with its servants and horse drawn carriages and expensive furniture had to go. For Kate, though, there was a silver lining as her schooling came to an abrupt end and she went back to live with her mother in a new house, where nursing sick brothers and sisters siblings became a way of life. As if by magic, for a girl so accustomed since she was a baby to being told off, so much so, that she had come to believe that was her nature, the gratitude of her nearest and dearest as she cared for them, came as a revelation. Now she was growing up, the gentle manner practiced on her animals and dolls matured into empathy, and she knew herself loved for her kindness.

That early life of roaming around the garden, running after the animals, climbing the orchard trees and feasting on fresh raw fruit and berries had an effect on her own physique and morale that outlasted her tomboy-Kitty years. It was indeed the healthy lifestyle prescribed for patients in the Sanatoriums; and, for all the illnesses that would beset her in her long life, she alone of the eight Marsden children survived into old age and she was tall, strong and most of the time, robustly healthy.

It soon became clear that the teenage Kate would have to put her energy to good use, to help her mother in her immediate financial distress and, in the long term, not to be a financial drain on the limited family resources. The solution was obvious, to become a nurse; but all the hospitals she initially applied to turned her down as she was too young.

It is now that we encounter the tenacity and nerve that characterise the mature Kate Marsden. She refused to give up, and at the age of sixteen she received a letter from Tottenham Hospital, then at Snell Park near her old home in Edmonton, accepting her as a probationer.

In 1875, nurses were still unsalaried. Theirs was a vocation and, like nuns, they worked in a religious environment in which their lives were rigorously controlled and it was extraordinary that Kate flourished as a teenage trainee nurse at the Protestant Deaconesses' medical training institute in Tottenham, because life there was austere and already, for most of her adolescence she had been a fighter against many of the conventions expected of her.

This tough regime was the brainchild of a German physician, Michael Laseron. A Jewish convert to Protestant Christianity, he had established the institute in north London in 1868. In their book 'Sister Janet, Nurse and Heroine of the Anglo-Zulu war 1879' Best and Stossel wrote:

'Dr Laseron exuded goodness and he attracted a local philanthropist named John Morley, who asked him what project he would most like to see fulfilled. Without a pause, Laseron replied he would like to establish a hospital built on the same lines as Kaiserworth in Germany to train young women, not only to be nurses, but also to be devout Christians. He outlined his plans to create a Protestant equivalent to the Sisters of Mercy, where his nurses could, by their Christian example, spread the word of the Lord.'

Mr Morley donated £6000 (nearly half a million pounds today) and the Deaconesses' Hospital was built.

In Dr Laseron's appeal for women to join the Institute he suggested that their lives in society as single young women was only 'ornamental' and that by joining them they would 'raise themselves from the indolence of their useless lives and enlist in active, healthy service for Christ'. He told his new recruits that their lives would thus become spiritually uplifting, invaluable and useful. Did the use of phrases such as 'useless lives' raise eyebrows in the 1880s among the emerging 'new women'; or was patriarchal dominance, with its stifling, patronising attitudes, par for the course?

That this should be the path by which Kate Marsden chose to enter adult life shows how limited the options were for someone in her position. She had been living with an impoverished mother; few of her seven siblings were now alive and she chose to leave home to become a virtuous, angelic being, treading softly among sick and dying as a trainee nurse in a stiff and unflattering uniform.

This selfless act was never intended to help support her mother: in order to attract only the most altruistic and dedicated girls, Laseron proposed not to pay them salaries, but give them only enough to buy new undergarments, with a little pocket money over. He set on record that the Institute sisters found the seven guineas a year it amounted to 'sufficient'.

The happy and carefree tomboy Kitty who had played so freely in the garden had become a teenager in a white cap and apron, a dark coloured dress and a bonnet, to be addressed as 'Sister'. The Institute's order committed her to five years service and to remaining unmarried: love was frowned upon, as it could lead to distractions, engagements and defections.

The free-spirited Kate seemed to flourish in this disciplined atmosphere and despite the challenges of domestic nursing, after only eight months training she responded to one even greater,requesting to join the small group of older, fully-trained nurses leaving to tend the wounded soldiers in the war between Russia and Turkey, it was an impulsive act of imagination, astounding in a sixteen year old girl in mid-Victorian London.

Janet Wells and Kate, her junior by three months, trained together at the Deaconesses' Institute; they went on to serve in Bulgaria together. 'Sister Janet' was a brave and dedicated nurse, who not only nursed in the Balkans in 1878 but went on the following year to become the only nurse to serve on the front line in the Anglo-Zulu War. She left many notes and scrapbooks but frustrate ingly, there is no record in her biography of a friendship with Nurse Kate although they spent a few years living side by side.

What compelled the teenage Kate to ask to join the highly dangerous mission to Bulgaria? Perhaps it was the carefree Kitty clashing with the life of an austere nurse, but she was one of only nine women who left the Institute and travelled out to Bulgaria in 1877. They left from Dover, at Calais they boarded a train which for five days conveyed them through Munich and Vienna to Budapest and finally to Bucharest. From there they were escorted to Vardin on the Bulgarian side of the Danube, which they crossed on a pontoon bridge. Unbelievably, she was still only eighteen and had no previous experience to match what faced her when she got there; here there were serious maimed and wounded men. She arrived with her older nursing colleagues in a rough wagon with crude bales of straw to sit and lean on; and their eyes widened to the sights and sounds of the war which Bulgaria was experiencing.

Grivitza by Henryk Dembitzkye
One of the key battles of the Russo-Turkish War of 1877–1878

The war that was raging left a legacy of death and life-threatening wounds. In 1877, news from Bulgaria of terrible atrocities and massacres at the hands of pro-Ottoman militian fighters had been widely reported in the British press, galvanising British public opinion against Disraeli's generally pro-Ottoman policies and sparking demand for practical medical aid.

It was an auspicious date for the country: through the Treaty of Berlin, signed at the war's conclusion, it became an autonomous state, though parts of it would remain under Ottoman protection, it functioned independently, with Alexander of Battenberg as its princely Head of State and achieved full independence in 1908.

Even the more experienced nurses among the group were unprepared for the chaos: facilities were minimal, and in addition to the war-wounded lying on the ground, for whom they did their best, providing proper nutrition to enable them to fight off fever and infection, comforting them and cleaning their wounds, they had a typhus outbreak and other epidemics to cope with, as well as a constant stream of refugees from the war. The sisters had between them, at Vardin, to look after some six thousand sick and wounded.

In the face of the enormous hardship and dangers that the nurses had to face it is reported that Kate coped well and showed genuine sympathy for her patients and that considerable personal courage was tested daily.

One day she and an older nurse were sent out from the camp to a battlefield site to search for any wounded soldiers who may have been overlooked. Wandering into what she took to be a deserted barn, she encountered, inside, two men scarcely recognisable as human beings. They were lepers. This, beyond doubt, was her first encounter with sufferers of the disease.

There is no record of the outcome of this encounter. Perhaps she was instructed to leave well alone, since there was nothing that could be done. Perhaps her whole soul rebelled against such doctrine, but she was disciplined and humble enough to bite her tongue. But something happened: it was a traumatic event in her young life and it fostered in her the lifelong determination to do something for leper sufferers and to understand more about the disease.

Their primary care may have been for wounded Russian soldiers and they were attached to the Sixty-Eighth Hospital Regiment, but it can't have escaped their notice – and moral conscience – that it was the Russians who were directing the mass slaughter of their opponents. Long before the League of Nations established rules for the humane treatment of prisoners-of-war, it can be taken for granted that the Russians disposed of their Ottoman captives on the spot, or marched them Northward through the snow, where their frozen bodies were reported as littering the roadsides.

The Siege of Ottoman-held Plevna took place less than eighteen miles from the nurse's base at Vardin. This major engagement of the Russo-Turkish war was initiated by the joint armies of Russia and Romania to end the 500-year domination of a key Balkan city by the Ottoman Empire. The siege succeeded at the fourth attempt, when the Ottoman forces under Osman Pasha attempted a break-out, and were comprehensively defeated. Osman Pasha – to quote Noel Barber from his book 'The Sultans'* – 'was treated as a hero by the Russians. When the Grand Duke Nicholas finally came face to face with him, he shook his hand and cried, "I compliment you on your defence of Plevna. It is one of the most splendid exploits in history." The immaculately booted Russian officers echoed, "Bravo!" And when Osman Pasha first met the general in white uniform and realised it was Skobeleff, he took his hand and said to him, "One day you will be commander-in-chief of the Russian Army".'

However, a very different fate was reserved for the soldiers of the Ottoman line. Despite repeated Russian promises that prisoners would be well-treated, nearly 45,000 Turks were interned in the bitterly cold open air of Plevna for two weeks. They received minimal food, let alone essential medical aid; and as for drinking from the River Vid, this was already contaminated by hundreds of floating corpses. Three thousand men died before the rest set off in the snow to various internment camps. Of the men who started, many barefoot, on the long march to prison, a mere 15,000 reached Russia. A fate as terrible awaited the seriously wounded left behind in Plevna. The Bulgarians, conveniently ignoring their promises,

* The Turkish Defeat at Plevna, 1877
From The Sultans, by Noel Barber (Simon & Schuster, 1973), pp. 189-191:

dragged them from the hospitals and massacred every man. In the late 1880s a small paragraph appeared in a Bristol paper: 'Thirty tons of human bones, comprising thirty thousand skeletons, have recently landed in Bristol from Plevna'. They were then ground up, and used to fertilise the city's parks.*

It is still shocking for me, writing this in Bristol in 2015, that local gardeners could unquestioningly rake the bones of men who had fought bravely against the Russians and died far from home, into flower beds gracing Brandon Hill or the elegant lawns of Queen Square.

In his account 'Under the Red Crescent: Adventures of an English Surgeon with the Turkish Army at Plevna and Erzeroum, 1877-1878' Charles Ryan seems oblivious of the existence of the British nurses attending to the Russian wounded:

'Although we had no female nurses, still I found that the Turkish women, whenever they had an opportunity, attended to the wounded with the devotion of a Florence Nightingale.'

In particular ways which were beyond her imagination, Kate Marsden's experiences in this harsh battleground were equipping her for her future journey across Siberia: firstly the deep snow and cold they encountered; then the lack of accommodation deemed suitable for a Victorian lady, and having to spend nights in open carts huddled together to keep warm. Then there was the ominous presence of wolves prowling in the night; lastly, the large, flat open distances to cover by cart and the sight of prisoners and sick people.

The nurses began to fall into bad health and two of them became dangerously ill of typhoid; so they returned to England and Kate, the youngest, was left to nurse the sick girls and to help the wounded. She returned to England after almost six months in Bulgaria, 'The Girl's Own Paper' reported that: 'the intense strain upon body and mind would have broken down anyone less brave and fearless but she went on from November to April fulfilling her duties, and carrying with her brightness and consolation wherever she appeared'. Not broken perhaps, but it changed her, still in her

---

* Sister Janet by Brian Best and Katie Stossel (Pen and Sword 2006)

teens, she was a woman of the world but was not to remain mentally robust and its direct aspects had given her a different perspective on life and an increased self-esteem. Her compassion in her work drew kindly comments and – at the end of that first crucial year a testimonial survives to show it:

'Deaconesses Institution, Tottenham

May 13th, 1878

Miss Kate Marsden was one year in training in this Institution, and showed great aptitude for nursing. She was an intelligent, willing pupil, and was very kind to the patients.

During the four last months of the time she was in Bulgaria, at the seat of war, in company with other Sisters from the Institution, she showed great readiness and address, and untiring patience and perseverance, in spite of many difficulties and discomforts.

Any further particulars that may be desired will be gladly furnished.

Christian Dundas, Lady Supt. of the Deaconesses' Institution'

And there is a postscript written by Christian Dundas:

'She assisted vigorously in nursing the sick sisters, and also did her part exceedingly well in hospital, showing decided nursing talent and ability, and treating her patients with true interest and kindness of heart.'

Henry Johnson commented in his biography of Kate Marsden* that 'her sympathy was genuine'. I can see where Kate's drive to help lepers might have come from: her innate aptitude for nursing siblings dying from another, but similar, illness with no cure, resistance to having been perpetually written off as worthless, the burning desire for a cause that would reverse this opinion of her, (or to reach the greatness and possible celebrity status of Florence Nightingale), and now, the shock of the lepers in the barn. Kate had by now also resolved not to marry, which meant she had the time and freedom to forge her own choices as to her life's destiny.

---

* The Life of Kate Marsden by Henry Johnson 1895. Little is known of him except that he was a family friend who wrote his short autobiography to offset the criticism that Kate was receiving at this time.

Kate returned to England from Bulgaria in April 1878. At the age of eighteen she immediately received great accolades for her work in the field. Henry Johnson blandly wrote: 'The selection for a work so arduous and perilous was a distinct and eloquent testimony of the estimation in which her qualities were held', in my eyes she showed pluck, had an adventurous spirit and most importantly was willing to flout convention.

I am baffled. Why did Kate Marsden promptly leave the Deaconesses Institute and the friendship of the other sisters that she had just endured so much hardship with? Rather than forging close bonds with each other had they, God forbid, actually fallen out? Particularly Sister Janet, who never mentions Kate in any of her writing, as already pointed out?

Dr Laseron had personally selected the girls on the promise that they would stay for five years. The only thing we do know is that she moved for a short time to Westminster Hospital, now long gone, which stood next to Westminster Abbey. A description of it in 1878 reads:

'Close to and in connection with the hospital, an institution has been opened, styled the Westminster Training School and Home for Nurses [established 1873], having for its object the training of a superior class of nurses for the sick, for hospitals, and private families. An agreement has been entered into by its managers with the Westminster Hospital to undertake the whole of the nursing there. A limited number of probationers are received at the home, and to those who may be accepted is given the efficient training and practical instruction required.'

Before 1878 was out, she had moved again. This time to Liverpool; here she gained, at the early age of 20, a post as Sister-in-Charge at the Woolton Convalescent Home.

It's idle to speculate whether Kate was an early victim of post-traumatic syndrome, or whether such a young and independent woman was advised, for her own well-being, to offer her unique and valuable skills to Merseyside.

It seems that she found some sort of peace at the convalescent home. Uniquely, perhaps, Kate's Balkan experiences had equipped her with what we would now be called colour-blindness for the racial melting-pot of Merseyside. The superintendent at Woolton appealed to her with her high standards in his expected system of nursing and medical regulations and Kate liked the 'high state of perfect' that was maintained. She took breaks in most of the up-and-coming British resorts from Ventnor to Windermere, though some of these trips may have been to visit ailing siblings, whose deaths continued to challenge her beliefs and question her life as she grew older.

Unfortunately it was, perhaps, post-traumatic stress that intervened. After four years she resigned on health reasons; a lung complaint, or mental illness, we don't know for sure. It hadn't affected her work: she had made so lasting an impression with Woolton, that on her departure in 1882 the Board and staff gave her a cheque for £100 (a year's salary), 'a handsome tricycle', (an apt embodiment of burgeoning late Victorian freedom), and a 'beautifully illuminated address' as a sign of their appreciation.

Did Kate Marsden ever ride the 'handsome tricycle' presented to her in 1882? We will never know!

The Chairman of the hospital Board spoke of her as 'Both by birth and education, a lady. She discharged her duties in a most efficient manner, possesses considerable administrative as well as nursing ability.'

Around this time her older brother, Joseph Marsden, died at the age of thirty. Now she had just the two sisters, Eleanor and Annie Jane and a brother Frank. Eleanor would die in Hastings later in 1883, with Kate nursing her through her final month.

In 1884 Kate's mother, Sophia, received a desperate plea from Annie Jane in New Zealand. The last surviving Marsden daughter had made her way to Britain's healthiest colony in an attempt to throw off the family curse. Sophia and Kate therefore set sail from Plymouth, travelling via the Suez Canal. Including the many provisioning stops, it took forty-two days, which must have seemed painfully slow. Sadly, Annie Jane died just six days after they arrived in Wellington, on 16 January 1885, aged thirty.

Her death reduced the once large Marsden clan to three. After the burial, they both elected to stay on; Kate took the job of Lady Superintendent at the Wellington Hospital. She was well qualified, the Wellington Evening Post reported on April 1st 1885:[*]

'Miss Marsden is a young lady aged 26, who recently arrived in Auckland from England, and possesses the highest testimonials of qualification for the office to which she has been appointed.'

She accepted a salary of £100 a year and a room at the hospital.

Ironically, it was the New Zealand press that would ultimately become her enemy: and within a few short years it would be regularly filing accusations about her conduct and querying the events in her life.

Though doubtlessly grieving for Annie, and still disturbed by what she had witnessed in Bulgaria, Kate settled into colonial life with her mother and approached her new role at the hospital with her usual rigorous efficiency. The Evangelical Deaconesses' Institute, for all its harsh rules and insistence that its recruits were missionaries first and nurses second, had given Kate a good enough grounding in practical nursing and social work to enable her to supervise the hospital and the training of nurses.

[*] New Zealand Papers Past Evening Post, Volume XXIX, Issue 76, 1 April 1885, Page 3

She started first-aid classes, and rallied the New Zealand ladies to form a branch of St. John's Ambulance Brigade and was elected Secretary, inviting applications from women willing to receive instruction in the art of nursing. This gave her the opportunity to mix with the Wellington elite, leading to frequent accusations of social climbing.

The president of the committee, Lady Jervois, was the wife of the Governor of New Zealand, Sir William Francis Drummond Jervois, and the vice-president was Lady Vogel, wife of Sir Julius Vogel, the colony's former prime minister. Kate also met the distinguished ex-Governor, Sir George Grey, in his youth a friend of her uncle, Captain James Raymond Wellsted (1805-1842), a noted Arabian explorer. It could be said that in these first five months she had gained a firm foothold in Wellington society.

'The Girl's Own Paper' writes: 'It was while matron at Wellington she became conscious of the great sufferings caused to the miners and people living far away in the hills from their want of knowledge of ambulance work. They would bring a man many hours' journey to the hospital who had broken a limb without touching it, and naturally on arriving at the hospital the arm or leg would be so swollen, bruised, and ulcerated, that it was almost impossible to treat it.'

One day she heard a loud noise outside the hospital, and one of the doctors said, "That must be an Irishman" (an extraordinary presumption).

"No," said Kate Marsden, "it sounds more like some one in pain."

Down she went in a second, and found a poor man who had been kicked by a horse, and had sustained a double fracture. His poor leg was hanging straight down, the people not having bound even a handkerchief round it, not from want of thought but entirely from want of knowledge. They often came enormous distances with broken legs unset and suffering intense pain, and it was this state of things which first suggested to her the idea of giving ambulance lectures."

Then, in the course of her duties, came a mishap which would have lasting effects.

The Grey River Argus (Grey River ad Grey Mouth named after Sir George) reported on the 25 September 1885:

A SERIOUS ACCIDENT

Miss Marsden, Lady Superintendent at the hospital, was standing on a step ladder taking down some linen from a high shelf when the steps gave way. Miss Marsden fell heavily and sustained serious injury to her back. She now remains partially paralysed.

It is generally agreed that Kate's physical injuries weren't the worst of it. It seems to have induced a severe nervous breakdown. Johnson states that 'for several months she was dangerously ill' – and she felt impelled to resign her post. The conditions under which she left were entirely favourable: Sir William alluded to her 'excellent service' and put it on record that she was 'most highly esteemed'.

In lieu of notice she was given one month's pay and a nurse from the hospital accompanied her and Sophia to a new home in Nelson, south of the Cook Strait, to aid Kate's recovery. Another account states that she was granted six months salary by the government, (not bad considering she had only been in post for five months); and it is this 'golden handshake' which may have begun to colour the public's view of her, especially when it was circulated that mere days before the accident Kate had taken out two medical insurance policies. To this imputation were compounded rumours – from the hospital itself – of her high-handed dismissal of a doctor, leading to her being ostracised in her final weeks, and whispered about as a bossy-boots.

The Golden Girl image was for the first time tarnished, she was also, perhaps, experiencing a backlash against the religious training she had been subjected to as a young woman. In her own written account she refers to this period as a time when she took 'many backwards steps and turned away from Christ'. Middleton diagnoses the 'suggestion of a guilt complex, a desire to atone for something.' There are no documents that exist that tell us what this behaviour was.

Once, in the stillness of Nelson, Kate's mind had regained its equilibrium, it engaged on a new mission – or, rather, the mission of her months in Bulgaria reborn and reinvigorated. Perhaps the horror of finding the two lepers in the barn had revisited her during her breakdown; but with the sense of life returning came a desperate urge not only to improve the conditions for victims of leprosy wherever they might be, but also to find the cure for the dreadful disease.

The end of May 1886 saw her re-elected Secretary of the Ladies' Committee of the colonial St John's Ambulance Association and began to give lectures on first aid. These proved particularly popular in the Nelson area. She had attended many injured miners while working at Wellington Hospital and she saw the need to instruct people in immediate assistance in accidents down the mines and elsewhere. Since gold had been discovered in 1856 on the West Coast several mining settlements, notably Greymouth, Hokitika and Westport, had come into existence. Interviewed in the Pall Mall Gazette, Kate explained:

"I heard of the miners in the South Island, many of whom lived several days' journey away from any place where they can get medical assistance in cases of accident . . . In order to enable them to help themselves and each other till medical assistance can be obtained, I went among the miners all over the island and gave ambulance lectures. It was a strange experience. Sometimes I had to travel four or five days to get to them; then I gave my lecture, sat with them by their camp fire, slept in a tent which they had specially put up for me, and rode off again next day to another place."

She also says that she saw Maori lepers; later on her observation was disputed; she was even called a liar in the press.

On May 9th 1889 she visited an antimony* mine at Endeavour Inlet to give one of her 'ambulance lectures'. Press notices state

---

* Antimony was known from ancient times; the naturally occurring black sulfide was used as the cosmetic kohl. The element is used to create durable alloys, (usually with lead,) such as pewter, type-metal, and Britannia metal.

AMBULANCE LECTURES AT WAKAPUAKA.

[FROM A CORRESPONDENT.]

MISS MARSDEN, who has had a great deal of experience in nursing and attending to the sick and wounded, having belonged to the Red Cross Society, and as a member of that

three European wars, rict with two most her first, she in the to deal with accidents of various kinds, such as we are liable to have in a place like this, where the axe is in such constant use, and so many are liable to be injured from falling trees, vicious horses, &c, &c. She also gave the gentler sex some most useful hints as to how to make the sick one's room comfortable, and make their time of trouble as pleasant as a careful nurse can. She also dealt with nursing in serious illnesses. In her second she went a little more into detail as to dealing with accidents, giving us hints as to the best way of roughly setting a broken limb until the doctor could be reached, how to make a rough stretcher out of a coat and two poles, how to deal with burns, and foreign matter in the eye and ear. She also gave us some of her experiences on the battle field when before Plevna with the Russian army. The people turned out very well, filling the schoolroom at Hillside on each evening. She will be returning to us again, I understand, to give us some more simple lessons in bandaging, &c, and also some more of her experiences on the field of battle. I understand she is going to give lectures in Motueka, Brightwater, and Nelson, and I am sure if they only knew the great value of them, they would crowd out to hear her. She has certainly been a great help to us, and has given us hints which may be the means of saving many a valuable life, and easing the sick bed of many a weary invalid.

that 250 people packed a hall and heard her recount her battlefield experiences, and promote her programme for home nursing, a formula guaranteed to appeal to both halves of her audience. But, aged thirty, Kate Marsden's thoughts on leprosy had matured; and it was to this audience that she first confided her immediate plans, and they were invited to contribute towards implementing them, which they did, generously. She was returning, via England – where she would leave her mother – to visit Louis Pasteur, no less, in Paris, and from there it was her resolve to continue on to Hawaii, and there assist Father Damien at his Molokai leper colony.

In June 1889, five years after their arrival in New Zealand, Sophia and Kate were on their way back from Nelson to England. The six weeks at sea marked the end of Kate's fifteen years as a nurse, and the beginning of a new chapter, her years of celebrity.

'Since the beginning of Miss Marsden's nursing experience it had been her wish to help those least cared for, and after her return to England, she obtained her mother's sanction to devote her life to the leper. Believing them to be the most outcast of all God's creatures'.

Henry Johnson, 1895

Was Kate dishonest in pocketing Endeavour Inlet's – and presumably other subsequent contributions? Only in this respect, that Hawaii dropped off her map once she had visited, and discussed her plans with Dr Pasteur, which she did in early 1890.* In confirming with him the nature of the ailment, she learnt from him that inoculation against leprosy was not possible: Pasteur, indeed, used the word 'incurable'. This should have put any ordinary person off; in Kate's case it conspired to fire her up.

---

* **Louis Pasteur**, December 27, 1822 – September 28, 1895) was the French chemist and microbiologist renowned for his discoveries of the principles of vaccination, microbial fermentation and pasteurization, and for remarkable breakthroughs in the causes and preventions of diseases.

As for her improvised methods of funding her project, among the miners and those that would later ensue, we may assume that much of the murmuring against Kate came from people in settled employment. Kate had no ostensible income, inheritance, husband or other 'legitimate' funding at her disposal. This is an important biographical factor extending into her later life.

In the 1890s there was no state pension; many people, particularly the elderly, ended up in the workhouse. So where was Kate to get money from to live off and to pursue her altruistic wish?

Evidently, by now, reports of lepers being cast out of their villages in other parts of the world had overtaken Hawaii in Kate's agenda; but what probably put the Hawaiian enterprise on hold was an unexpected invitation to visit St Petersburg in May 1890 and to receive a medal from the Russian Red Cross for her services as a teenage nurse in Bulgaria. It was not to be refused: such an accolade would be key in her mission to help the lepers. From now on she would have to use every opportunity to let people in the right places know what she was attempting to do and to raise funds.

Before sailing from New Zealand she had already acquired help from an unexpected quarter – she had applied for presentation at Court, and she was presented to Queen Victoria herself on March 5th 1890. She would write that 'I sought this honour, knowing that it would help me in carrying out the work in foreign countries'.

An unexpected upshot of this reception was an invitation or 'command' from Her Royal Highness, the Princess of Wales to a 'Drawing Room' at Marlborough House three days later. Princess Alexandra as sister of the Danish-born Tsarina of Russia had particular reason for wanting to hear what Kate hoped to achieve; Kate herself must have played her cards right: 'Alex' was as good as her word in writing to solicit the approval of Her Imperial Majesty and her assistance in Kate's enterprise, a project well in line with Alex's self-appointed role since marrying 'Bertie' in 1863, fulfilling public duties related to charitable work.

Whether through pushing, force of persuasion, or just plain luck Kate Marsden was about to take Russia by storm, with the very best recommendations that anyone could hope for.

Ostensibly, the invitation from the Russian Court to Kate to visit St Petersburg was in order that she might be personally decorated for nursing bravery in that gruesome winter war with the Ottomans a dozen years before. But reports of her hospital work in Britain and one of the colonies came into the equation, as did her resolve to dedicate herself to the plight of lepers. So it was inevitable that this tall, personable and eligible English spinster of thirty-one, the epitome – surely – of equanimity, eloquence and cheery personality, would be a hit in Russia. Kate would use her newly exalted status to full advantage.

Other writers who have commented on Kate Marsden have noted an urgency about her. We are told* of her 'stately appearance' in her 'nurses's garb', of her 'clever way of blending humour with instruction' and, more than once, of her 'cheeriness'. the sort of nurse who enters a hospital ward calling out 'How are we?'

To do what she did she definitely was an unusual and impressive figure for her era, she was unique.

Kate accepted the class system as it was and was intent on making the lives of poor people more bearable and it may be surmised that Kate, in her strict religious indoctrination by the Protestant Deaconesses, had absorbed a sense of the unalterability of the human lot – 'God made them high or lowly, and ordered their estate'.†

This first visit, provided the moment of decision Kate needed. Once back from St Petersburg with her treasured decoration of the Russian Red Cross, she had decided that *her next course of action was to go on a leprosy fact-finding mission to Europe, the Middle East and Caucasus and then back to Russia, where she would cross Siberia.*

Henry Johnson writes:

'Since the beginning of Miss Marsden's nursing experience it has been her wish to help those least cared for, and after her return to England, she obtained her mother's sanction to devote her life

---

* Johnson in his *Life of Kate Marsden* 1895

† (All Things Bright and Beautiful, Mrs Cecil Frances Alexander, wife of an Ulster Dean – circa 1860).

to the lepers, believing them to be the most outcast of all God's creatures.'

It sounds simple, but we should try and imagine her mother, a woman in late middle-age, reconciling herself to one of her last two surviving children, out of eight, embarking on a quixotic adventure which, surely, in her mind, she may never return from.

Kate would indeed return from her intended expedition to Russia; but by then it would be Sophia who would be dead.

'Every now and then in the course of our lives it is our good fortune to become acquainted with men and women who combine characteristics of no common order, whose lives and self sacrificing, and whose determined purpose is, with the loving Father's help, to remove or lessen some of these evils which ruin the happiness of His people, and almost blot out His image in their hearts.'

Girl's Own Paper, December eighteenth 1890*

Kate Marsden in 1890 as depicted by 'The Girl's Own Paper'

* 'The Girl's Own Paper' was a British story paper catering to girls and young women, published from 1880 until 1956.

After very careful preparations, Kate Marsden left England in September 1890 for Alexandria. Before she left she came to a providential arrangement with 'The Girl's Own Paper', which commissioned her to send detailed reports of her journey for printing as inspirational articles; they also agreed to assist in her fund-raising.

The first article they printed in December 1890 began with a long eulogy to strong women, of whom Kate may be seen as the perfect contemporary embodiment. 'Enthusiasm, devotion and courage, combined with simple child-like faith must of necessity be the characteristics' they suggested, of these noble creatures. They suggest that there is 'one with us now', and that she is one who cannot fail to create in us the deepest interest and an enthusiastic desire to help her in her work.

Kate couldn't have hoped for a better endorsement than this, the paper told its readers about the good service she had done both in Britain and abroad among the sick and wounded. Her influence upon the 'rough miners in New Zealand', and the instruction she gave them in ambulance work, 'should fill our hearts with thankfulness that God put it into the heart and power of a woman to be of such service to the age in which she lives.'

Kate Marsden was a hero in the eyes of the paper and it's readers are the closest that she ever reached to celebrity status in her own country. They compared her to David going out to meet the giant with a sling and a stone, that she was as fearless as he, that she was 'going out against the giants of disease, misery and oppression in their most hideous forms'. At the dawning of the 'New Woman' in Great Britain, Kate was exactly the sort of person to inspire other women whose lives were full of drudgery and lacked opportunity.

If anyone still wondered why Kate was going to Russia, 'The Girl's Own' laid it on the line: 'This wonderful and dangerous mission undertaken by Miss Marsden is to travel through Russia up to the remote parts of Siberia to see for herself the condition of the lepers, of whom there are so many scattered throughout this awful country, and to find some means of alleviating their misery and improving their physical condition; and further, to comfort the Christian exiles, among whom are delicate women and children.'

This last statement is very vague and probably refers to something that Kate said in passing – we don't hear of this part of her purpose again.

This article then seems to be in need of some careful editing. If the tone changes to innuendo, leaving the modern reader wondering what else was said in the interview, here is what might have happened:

"The Empress was wonderful", Kate enthused, "she bestowed upon me the decoration of the Red Cross Society for my work in the Russo-Turkish war; look here it is."

The medal awarded to Kate, drawn by Jon Harris

"Miss Marsden, we are so proud of you here at the 'Girl's'. we talk about your achievements all the time." Kate beamed and put away her valuable badge safely in its box.

"Well I am so thankful to everyone, the Emperor as well and the Court and high officials. But you know I had to have money to do all this – I hadn't worked since New Zealand."

"How do you get by Miss Marsden? You must need a certain amount lodged in the bank for your use, you would be in an awful position if you, a woman, alone and in the remotest parts of Russia – to be stranded for want of means."

Kate paused, looked at Emma Brewer the reporter with a long stare.

"Well, people help me, you know, those that can afford it." She made a little cough. "Those who believe in me and are proud to be associated with me."

Miss Brewer didn't know what she meant. "So who are these people that help you? If you don't mind me asking? Big businesses? The banks?"

Kate Marsden tried to look demure, but she was a big shouldered woman and it didn't really work, she looked up again at the earnest reporter in front of her.

"Older ladies help me, widows, women of independent means. When I returned home from Russia I met a lady who made me an offer to defray all my expenses and to help me in every way possible. I was so happy because now it was all easy and clear and I could leave straight away – but unhappily, it failed utterly."

"Well, why, . . . yes, why?"

"There is no need for me to state the cause." Kate's answer was final and no amount of pressing could change the situation.

What was Kate suggesting? We are left wondering, and there are no more leads to follow.

'The Girl's Own Paper' was unreserved in its adherence and asked its readers to picture this woman of thirty-one, refined and gentle, 'leaving her home and every one she loved and starting alone for the utmost corners of the earth, for the sole object of learning to minister to the dreadful disease of leprosy.'

Hidden in the text is a wonderful tribute to the early female explorer, as 'The Girl's Own Paper' threw down its feminine gauntlet: 'Surely Stanley in darkest Africa pales before her. He had company, she will have none; and only up to a certain point will there be any decent means or travelling.'

What a pity so lovely a reference was so soon forgotten. How long would it be before society realised that women had just as much courage and stamina to go out and explore the unknown? Many, many decades: men were not going to let go lightly of the male bastion of exploration, men continued to rule the colonies. These were firmly patriarchal days.

The paper then writes that friends presented her with cheques that were sufficient for her to make a start. 'It must be our care to get additional contributions lodged in her bank so that she may have no anxiety about money, and that the object of the mission fail not for want of it'.

Contributions paid in :—	£	s.	d.
Mr. Williams (of Hitchcock and Williams) . .	10	0	0
Messrs. Morgan and Scott .	25	0	0
Mr. George Spicer . .	10	0	0
Mr. Hugh Matheson . .	50	0	0
Mr. Gurney Barclay (Bevan) .	10	0	0
Mr. Benjamin L. Cohen .	5	0	0
E. B.	1	0	0
J. R. B.	0	5	0

* An example of the typical sums money paid towards Kate Marsden's expenses through 'The Girl's Own Paper'

* From 1848 until he died in 1898 the senior partner of Matheson and Company was Hugh Matheson. Matheson & Company was a London-based trading house closely associated with Jardine Matheson of Hong Kong and Jardine Skinner of Calcutta. It arranged finance and handled imports from those two companies of products such as tea, silk and jute. Matheson & Company also became involved in venture-capital, specializing in mining. The company was a member of the consortium that formed the Rio Tinto Company. (Wikipedia). This information is indicative of the interest from the corporate world that Kate was generating through 'The Girl's Own Paper'.

It seems extraordinary now that the paper was collecting funds from their readers for a cause of which the outcome was so unclear, and yet it deposited the money straight into Kate's bank account. What's more, over the course of the next year it printed four articles of her journey, and after each one it listed the contributions paid in:

The above amounts to £111.5.0 and its value today would be many thousands of pounds. When she reached Moscow she couldn't leave until she had raised more money, so what happened to these huge amounts being raised – did she squirrel this money away for altruistic purposes or did she spend it in Europe?

The 'Girl's Own' reporter saw Kate off on the Parramatta on September nineteenth 1890, noting that 'She is full of spirit and hope and has cast fear behind her.'

The Parramatta was a Scottish sailing clipper that plied between Great Britain and Australia and America from 1866 to 1898. She was the second fastest Blackwall frigate,originally designed to carry wool from Australia to the United Kingdom. Her September voyage set Kate on her route to Moscow, dropping her at Brindisi, from where she would continue via Alexandria to Jerusalem, Cyprus and Constantinople. Kate scarcely mentions the voyage in her book, or why she had decided not to travel directly to Moscow on it.

She wrote to 'The Girl's Own Paper', describing the lazy Indian crew and waxing eloquent about the setting of the moon as they sailed into Malta early in the morning, 'a sight never to be forgotten'. She suggested to her young readers that 'gazing upon the whole scene' brought her soul nearer to God.

On the connecting boat between Brindisi and Alexandria a small adventure took place. A crowded sailing vessel, which 'looked lovely in the sun with all sails full set', attracted their attention. The skipper of their boat gave orders for a lifeboat to be 'quickly manned and lowered, and away it went, leaving us all intensely excited'. It was a Cretan boat full of sponge gatherers who had lost their bearings after their chart blew away. They hadn't had water for five days so the captain of Kate's boat ordered their casks to be filled and sent them over two bags of biscuits and several bottles of vinegar and helped find their way back. The crew was so grateful that they sent over six sponges for the captain and the sailors who had manned the rescue boat – Kate bought one of these for two shillings and, a new skill for her, photographed the boat as it set out back for its home port.

'The Girl's Own Paper's Eastern Correspondent reported back from Alexandria as a wide-eyed tourist. That might be taken amiss today, given that she was on a leprosy fact-finding mission supported by her readers, but her despatch was popular and I'm going to stay with her. She makes a point of visiting Pompey's Pillar, 'meeting droves of camels, goats, and donkeys and men carrying skins filled with water'. She was shocked to see women lying and sitting half asleep at the base of the Pillar – stupefied by smoking opium. After that she visited the cemetery, which was filled with wailing women; later on she watched women washing their clothes with stones in a river and thought that 'they did it in a most inelegant manner'. She spent a day at Schutz, outside Alexandria, as the guest of the Andersons, leaving by train after breakfast and having to be carried on a donkey for the last part of the journey wondering 'whether anything with such slender legs could possibly carry me'.

Back in Cairo, she was invited to visit the wife of the Khedive. What follows is the account published in 'The Chicago Tribune', that differs slightly from articles in 'Girl's Own Paper' and in 'The San Francisco Call' of December 14 1890. This suggests that Kate may have been writing many reports to different newspapers of her journey towards Siberia.

Chicago Tribune Dec. 6, 1890
THE KHEDIVA OF EGYPT.

Her Interview With Miss Kate Marsden,

the Leper Missionary

Miss Kate Marsden, tho missionary to the lepers, who is now traveling extensively to collect information about the stricken people to whose service she has consecrated her life, was invited, during her brief stay In Alexandria, to be presented to the Khediva. Her Highness, the Princess Emineh-Hanen, the Khediva, is the daughter of the late El-Hamy-Pasha, and the mother of two fine boys and two pretty girls. She is a fine-looking woman of about 80 years, with bright eyes expressive enough to interpret the thoughts she could not put in words to her English visitor. She has an imposing figure, which was on the occasion of presentation draped to advantage in a well made black gown. The palace of the Khedive is a peculiar structure, painted entirely white, surrounded by a court prettily decorated with green creepers, and paved with a peculiar mosaic made of stones in two colours on their sides. The maids in attendance in the inner hall were all simply dressed alike in plain black and white dresses. Not a man was seen about the palace, whose furnishing is extremely plain and simple, the only pretty room being the central one, in which were lovely mirrors and candelabra and beautifully inlaid and floors.

The royal lady graciously welcomed the plainly-dressed woman who came before her in a costume unlike anything ever seen in the presence-chamber before, for Miss Marsden, to quote her own words, was limited to choice 'three severely plain uniforms, one of which was crushed, the second very creased and the third on my back, its freshness all gone, likewise some of its buttons. Besides, they all so warm, being intended for rough traveling in Russia, and by no means suitable for royal receptions or for the hot climate. My bonnet had already done good service in London for six months, and, its original colour being black, it was then a rusty brown. Gloves, fortunately, I had, but my only pair of boots were thick traveling ones, made for Siberia. Fancy my clumping into the presence of her Highness with such boots'.

But the meeting was pleasant. Tea was served in the little exquisite cups with no handles, and the plain woman in the travel-worn gown and heavy boots was made to forget, by the courtesy of her royal hostess, that she was not in full court dress.

In 'The Girl's Own Paper' version, we learn that the Khediva was most welcoming and pointed her to a seat on her right where they sat for a while. We don't know if there was a translator to hand at the time, so there may have been awkward silences. The cups without handles, were filled with an unidentified warm liquid and Kate didn't know what to do. 'It might be perfume or coffee', she writes, and it wasn't until 'her Majesty took one up and drank its contents' that Kate could do and did the same.

While enjoying the warm weather and hospitality, she devoted a day to a careful inspection of the German Hospital in Cairo. Then she left for Jaffa on a Russian steamer.

Despite the complete lack of material, so far relating to lepers and leprosy, contributions to Kate's campaign coffers showed no sign of drying up, (the proceeds of the sale of 'Mrs Brewer's needlework' of eleven shillings is an example of the individual as well as corporate support she was receiving).

So why was there so much generosity towards her? Was this because Kate was becoming a phenomenon of fashion, and her singular undertaking as riveting to her supporters as that of a contemporary campaigning celebrity is to us today?

She arrived in Jaffa at six in the morning and hired a Cook's agent to assist her, writing that wherever a Cook's agent is stationed a traveller is safe, whereas 'the rabble surrounds travellers and confuses them with their frantic talking and gesticulation.' It was an eleven hour journey by carriage to Jerusalem. Here, and in other parts of the Holy Land – she told the paper – she could at last acquaint herself with the condition of the lepers. On the way she met rows of camels and donkeys, all moving one behind the other and heavily laden. Passing through Ramleh, she went up the tower of the old mosque; Ajalon, she noted, was very stony and dusty, 'but full of interest, to every Bible reader'.

'My first sight of Jerusalem,' she wrote, 'was a row of lights, and when I called to mind that Christ the Saviour had Himself been over this ground, I again dedicated myself to Him to work for His poor afflicted ones.' As a pious afterthought to her readers, she added 'may He grant me strength to persevere against all and every obstacle'.

Kate was entranced and spiritually moved by Jerusalem and used its Biblical connections to overcome her anxieties and long-ing thoughts of home. Knowing that her 'feet were treading where the Master's had so often gone before,' at the Jaffa Gate, she took off her boots and bowed her head. After that, every nook and cranny became sacred. On her first morning, she called on the English Consul for a stamp in her passport (passports being a recent innovation) and then visited the Deaconesses' Mission Home, 'one of the coolest, quietest houses in Jerusalem'. The next day she was off to the Moravian Leper Hospital accompanied by the Bishop of Jerusalem and Mrs Blythe, travelling – since it was two miles out of the city – on donkeys, 'making an odd procession, headed by the Bishop's servant in native costume,' and followed by Kate's donkey-boy. The camels that met them on the road proved vicious, snapping at her legs as she rode past on her little donkey.

Her first encounter with a recognisable group of lepers was just outside the city walls. In her despatch, she seems to adopt the eyes and manner of someone who has the medical and social knowledge to sound like an expert. Surmising that these people had chosen to be beggars rather than be cared for by the hospital, she asks 'Could anything be so unwise as this freedom?' She realised that the coins they collected from passers-by were contaminated by their hand-contact before being redistributed amongst the population. In addition, their lesions attracted flies which immediately settled on the passers-by, and Kate relayed her understanding of how the leprosy germs spread in these words:

'The result of this freedom to the poor lepers is disastrous, not only to them, but to the people around them, and it is time the authorities should awake to the danger.'

On her return to the city and she headed for the Jerusalem Hospital. Her impromptu hospital assessments would become a staple of her Russo-Siberian visit. In this large and substantial institution, the Jerusalem lepers were well looked after by sisters who devoted their lives to the service of 'these poor afflicted ones'. The extremity of illness of some of the patients rekindled Kate's longing to be 'among them with some effectual remedy'.

More than anywhere else so far on this journey, Jerusalem made Kate restless, disturbing her sleep patterns. She had to be constantly on the move, to see everything she could in this holiest of cities. No print survives, but she photographed the rugged paths of the

Mount of Olives; she was riding out to Bethany, 'always associated in our minds with the only peaceful moments our Lord knew when on earth in the house of Lazarus, Martha and Mary'.

Her camera accompanied her to an Anglican contact, outside the walls, Miss Crawford, at the Deaconesses' home that she had built, and after lunching with the two resident deaconesses, joining in their prayers that God would bless their work, she went up to the flat roof and took four photographs of the wonderful scenery below. Her ride back to the city took her right over the Mount of Olives. Once again, no prints of her photographs seem to have survived.

On one of her visits, she was incensed to see a donkey left to die on the roadside. On another, at night, she observed her friend the Bishop's daughter at work among destitute Jewish women; here she suffered a double mishap when she tripped and fell, and the lad hired to carry the lantern for her dropped it and fled, leaving her in pitch darkness. In Bethlehem, which she reached without accident, she took in all the biblical sights, commenting that 'Bethany and Bethlehem are both very much as they were thousands of years ago when once you get away from the recently-built houses', a comment that could easily be made today!

On the way – at Jerusalem 'The Girl's Own Paper' June 3, 1893

Before returning to the port of Jaffa, Kate visited the Wailing Wall, reacting to it as the saddest thing she had ever witnessed. Perhaps in reaction, she had herself photographed both as a Bethlehemite and a Jerusalem woman. The one printed here, published in 'The Girl's Own Paper', is extraordinary. In no other image still available to us do we see Kate Marsden as anything but an austere nurse. Here, the features are most definitely hers but the half grin on her lips suggests she was having fun, as if back at the dressing-up box of her childhood, scrabbling for costumes with her brothers and sisters.

Kate's departure from Jerusalem, made on an unsprung cart, and so presumably with no help from Thomas Cook's agent, brought her to Jaffa in the middle of the night. In the morning she witnessed a Turkish funeral, commenting that 'the whole spectacle formed a curious and interesting picture to an English woman!'.

Further descriptions of Jaffa's ancient port, the southernmost and oldest part of Tel-Aviv, eluded Kate's readers, along with any record of what must have been a lovely journey along the Mediterranean coast of Turkey to bring her to Constantinople.

It would have been interesting to know her private reaction to being in Turkish waters. Fifteen years before, as a young nurse tending Russian soldiers in the Russo-Turkish war, she knew the Turks as the enemy. Now, as she sailed into harbour at Constantinople her first impressions were of an earthly Paradise but such comparisons stopped at the quayside. To her nurse's eye and nose, as she told the 'Girl's Own' readers, the city and people were a picture of dirt and wretchedness. Besides, leprosy was everywhere in evidence, lepers were openly in the streets; Kate was horrified by their condition and treatment. She was dismayed at the lack of care provisions for them which consigned them to a life of buying, selling and begging in the markets of this thoroughly depressing capital.

Kate paid a boatman and guide to take her to the Asian side of the Bosphorous where she heard there was a formal leprosarium established in the middle of a cemetery. The long and arduous boat-journey was followed for Kate and her guide by a long carriage ride. On arrival at the cemetery gate the wind howled through the gloomy cypress trees, and her first sight of the poor lepers standing shivering to greet her was truly pitiful.

How could any nation, 'however barbarous' treat its fellow citizens so badly? She went among them and on her departure they sang her the traditional 'Leper's Song' which sounded to Kate like a dismal wail which stayed with her, her 'whole being quivering with agony at the depths of misery she had witnessed'. During all the long journey back her guide, who had taken her there, would not look her in the face or speak to her because she had gone in among the lepers.

These sights reinforced her resolve to find a cure for leprosy or at the very least make its victims' lives more comfortable. As she prepared to leave for Russia she prayed, 'for the swift help of heaven and of men in my mission of relief.' Though Kate is not necessarily the most reliable witness to her motives, I think we may accept her assertion that the fire raged inside her even more strongly after Constantinople, and her subsequent acts of altruism caused her to be seen as one who had left her mark on the world through a great deed.

In Kate's writing, sincerity sweeps in and out like the tide and we, the readers, are left stranded on the beach, begging her to tell us what really was going on in her mind. Occasionally, though, in bright moments of Kate's writing it all seems very clear:

'I may be called an enthusiast, or a woman who bids high for the world's applause. I care not what I am called, or what I am thought of, so long as the goal of my ambition be reached, or so long as I may see before I die that the work commenced, though faultily, is on its way to completion.'

It is surely from this time on that any doubts among her subscribers through 'The Girl's Own Paper' were satisfied as to the work she had set off to do.

The Ottoman Empire had inherited a vast and growing burden of leprosy from its Byzantine predecessor. From small beginnings in Anatolia, the disease had spread through the Byzantine empire and sufferers were generally well treated, subsisting on alms from their neighbours, and five leprosariums were constructed in the vicinity of Constantinople itself. When in 1453 the Ottomans under Mehmed II took over the Byzantine lands, it is estimated* that there were upwards of 600,000 lepers within the population. The rulers, for all their investment in palaces, mosques and universities, paid less and less attention to the leprosy question, and by the time of Kate's visit it seemed that nobody cared any more.

Finally, before embarking, she enjoyed the privilege, rarely accorded to foreign visitors, of glimpsing the Sultan himself reviewing his troops. How could she resist, having already been face to face with her own Queen? Perhaps she had let slip that particular honour when she met an American attaché to the Sublime Porte, because it was him that told her where to be, in order to have a clear view of Abdul Hamid II in his finery. With her experience of nursing in Bulgaria, she would have a clear opinion of this sultan, ready-formed, but compounded by the state of his capital and by the rumours of what later be called pogroms, and of state-sanctioned massacres of Armenian Kurds and dependent Bulgarians; occasioned by the increasing fragility and loss of influence of the Ottoman Empire. She arrived early for the grand tattoo, made all the more colourful by the soldiers' uniforms of red fezzes bound with green cord, white gaiters, red waistcoats and blue coats; one cavalry mounted on grey horses, flourished red banners above the heads.

The ceremony was heralded by a bevy of small carts filled with sand or 'clean dirt', as Kate slyly called it, which was quickly shovelled and raked all over the square. Then, a bugle sounded, the soldiers presented arms and the Royal carriage and its entourage appeared; in the intense silence a 'weird cry was heard, which was the signal for the troops to raise a shout of welcome, a shout that travelled away and away, and echoed from every hill'.

Seemingly oblivious of the crowds, the sultan, merely raised his hand from time to time in acknowledgement. Throughout the

* (The International Federation of ILEP Anti-Leprosy Associations) www.ilep.org.uk

entire tattoo, he remained in discussion with one of his most powerful henchmen, Said Pasha, and Kate noted his palpable anxiety and fragility. Kate said 'There was no ray of sunshine in his worn face, and he looked wretchedly ill'.

This is how 'The Girl's Own Paper' reported it:

'All the old generals, who were drawn up on either side of the door of the Mosque, bowed low and saluted him, while the soldiers turned their faces to him the whole time. He remained there about an hour, and then returned, driving himself this time. He whipped up the horses, and as they dashed off all the old generals scrambled after him as best they could; for, strange as it may seem to us, they are not allowed to drive or ride, but must always follow on foot.

It seemed rather an undignified ending to such a grand spectacle to see these old and tried generals fairly out of breath endeavouring to keep up with the Sultan's carriage.'

She put it on record that she would rather be a beggar in England than a Sultan in Turkey, since for him there could be neither freedom nor liberty, as we understand it.

Kate's last day in Constantinople was spent at the English cemetery in Scutari where 7,000 British soldiers are buried. It is likely that she had based her stay in the city in a hotel in Istiklal Caddesi, or Independence Avenue, because to catch her ship she travelled through the Tünel, an underground funicular railway a third of a mile long built in 1875, with two stations linking Karaköy and Beyoğlu. It runs down the northern shore of the Golden Horn, yet despite it being the second oldest passenger underground line – after London's District Line of 1863 – in the world, its charms were lost on Kate. For her, it went down hill too fast, an unpleasantness aggravated by the men standing, smoking and spitting, and the women jostling their way into the carriage with their elbows.

She left Constantinople on a Russian steamer to cross the Black Sea to the Georgian town of Batoum, or Batumi as it is known today. What we know of this voyage comes from 'The Girl's Own Paper', not from her book.

The Russian Red Cross medal, demonstrated worn, seems to have worked wonders: on boarding, the stewardess kissed her hand and asked leave to touch the medal; and on the basis of her audience with the Tsarina she was allocated the best cabin in the vessel.

After her revulsion over Constantinople, Batoum, with its pretty houses and backdrop of mist-cloaked hills came as a pleasant relief. But her hotel, 'kept by a Frenchman, was so awful in its sanitary arrangements that she wondered the whole family were not dead of fever'.

But it was only for one night, because the next day she embarked on the eighteen hour train journey to Tiflis (Tbilisi). In her book she comments that her height made the overnight journey – presumably in a seated compartment – cramped and uncomfortable. From this point on, though some months in arrears, her progress is being monitored by that most innovative of national prints, The 'Illustrated London News', accompanying its reports with photogravure images. The first coverage comes in late February 1891, by which time Kate had already left Moscow, having arrived there in November 1890.

'A benevolent English lady has lately set forth on a very long journey of some months over the vast distances of the Russian Empire in Asia, having previously visited Syria and Turkey, on a purely charitable mission. The task which Miss Kate Marsden has courageously undertaken is that of visiting all the establishments for lepers, collecting knowledge with regard to their miserable condition, and striving to learn how the disease can be prevented or mitigated, or what can be done to relieve its suffering victims. From Constantinople, in the autumn of last year, she made her way eastward to Erzeroum, Batoum, and Tiflis, in the Russian province of Georgia, whence she travelled, quite alone, across the Caucasus into European Russia, arriving at Moscow to complete her arrangements for the Siberian expedition.'

The paper would run a further article about her travels; clearly her movements had, by then, sufficiently tickled the public's imagination. But let's continue with that first pleasingly thorough and cheerful report under the title 'Miss Kate Marsden's Travels in the Caucasus' published 28 February 1891:

'At Tiflis, Miss Kate Marsden was courteously received by the Russian Governor*, and was allowed to visit the hospitals and other public institutions. After a brief sojourn there, she started in a four-horse carriage, attended by a native man-servant, on the road northward over the mountains. The cold in that season of the year would be very severe. Her nose, she says, suffered most: it ached and smarted till her eyes watered, and the tears were frozen on her cheeks . . . Ivan, her man-servant, accompanied her, fully armed with sword and dagger, and many other warlike instruments. The four horses of the carriage were harnessed side by side, the two outer ones being trained to keep their heads turned outward. In this way she started, the tinkling of the horses' bells giving a cheery sound. On the first day of the journey she could scarcely see the way for dust, but this was changed as she approached the mountains. She met thirty-two carts, drawn either by oxen or buffaloes: in some cases two buffaloes were yoked together, with two oxen yoked before them. After having left Tiflis about fifty miles behind, she began to encounter all kinds of strange wild-looking men who belonged to the mountain tribes. The journey was a constant ascent, with sometimes a large river dashing round a curve below, and at others massive rocks standing hundreds of feet above, looking as though they would fall upon the traveller. Going on farther, everything changed: the view in front would be completely hidden by some lofty mountain, so that the road seemed to have come to an end.

Each time the horses were changed she went into a wayside house and had tea, if possible, looking round at the unfamiliar people who came in to look at her, then again into the carriage, and feeling that each stage was taking her farther from civilisation and deeper into the grand mountains. As night came on she wrapped her clothing more closely around her, and felt rather afraid of the dark. Still, she enjoyed the life in those beautiful mountains – the fresh air, the sparkling snow, the clear ring of the

* Once more, she is spared any difficulties in meeting these people by the magic wand of her Imperial Majesty's favour.

horses' hoofs on the hard ground, all made her feel, as she said, fifteen rather than thirty two years of age. When writing in these wild spirits she was on Mount Kasbek, one of the two grand crowning points of the Caucasus range, the other being Mount Elburz.'

By the time Kate reached Moscow in September 1890, 'The Girl's Own Paper' had collected a further £180, a huge sum in modern value. So again I wonder – how much of it had she already spent and why did she arrive in Moscow so determined to raise more funds? 'The Girl's Own Paper''s last bulletin on her reveals that the Empress gave her £100 towards expenses and some wealthy Russians a further £50 and she was encouraged to give a lecture at the Historical Museum of Moscow outlining her earlier nursing adventures and aims for the future. The entrance fee was a rouble, or about 2s. 5d, and the talk took place under the watchful eye of Her Imperial Majesty and the Governor-General of Moscow and the police formed part of the audience.

By my reckoning, she now had in excess of £330 and the paper states she needed at least £400. And so, as winter took hold in 1890, Kate Marsden was installed in Moscow and applying all her concentration in preparing for the adventure of a lifetime.

'Kate Marsden marches to music and never gives up'
Henry Johnson

The moment she stepped out of the train at Moscow to find the waiting sleigh, Kate Marsden experienced the full force of a Muscovite winter and realised how inadequate her ordinary clothing was. She rose above her discomfort to take in the buildings, notably the churches lining the streets to her hotel. The sledge slid almost silently across the snow, and she noted that since the horse wasn't fitted with bells the driver had to yell at everyone to get out of the way, a self-defeating strategy against Moscovites in high fur collars reaching above their ears!

She gave herself time to recover before visiting Prince Dolgoroukow (her spelling) at the palace in Moscow, who represented His Imperial Majesty, the Czar.

As to which Prince Dolgonukov she sought help from, we have a choice of two, Vasily Alexandrovich advisor to the Russian Emperor Nicholas II and Vladimir Andreyevich Dolgorukov, governor-general of Moscow from 1865 to 1891. From the turn the conversation took, Prince Vladimir seems the more likely.

A dress code was in force, and Kate wished that, as when she had met The Khedive of Egypt, she had the frock she'd worn at the formal Tea with Princess Alexandra, so she would have to wear nurse's uniform again. 'So I brushed it up, and, with a clean pair of white strings to my somewhat worn bonnet, I concluded my toilette and finally set out, not without a feeling of nervousness.'

It seems remarkable to us, 120 years on that she could gain access to Prince Dolgoroukov so quickly and easily, but when she arrived at the palace she was ushered into his presence and was struck by the Prince's 'kind manner and gentle voice' and they must have had a language in common. He asked her what he could do; she outlined to him her mission to seek a remedy for the suffering of lepers; and with his blessing, it was her objective to locate a herb with potential healing qualities and investigate rumours of outcast lepers in the Yakut region. When she asked his permission to visit the hospitals of Moscow and make a record of any lepers that might be there, 'His face took a still kinder expression as he drew closer, and questioned me about my proposed work, seeming rather bewildered that any woman should attempt it.' He wasn't the first to think that, but more than anyone she had so far encountered, Dolgoroukov knew what her proposed journey would entail.

He instantly summoned the Inspector of Hospitals, and instructed him that Nurse Marsden be shown everything she wanted to see. As she prepared to leave his presence, he inscribed to her a book about Moscow in an exquisite binding. Though this is now lost, unlike her Russian red Cross medal(now in the safe keeping of the Royal Geographical Society alongside her brooch from Queen Victoria), it was with Kate on her return to England; she would later write of it as a loving remembrance of one who 'readily exerted himself on behalf of the poor, suffering lepers.'

Prince Dolgoroukov's firman applied to the institutions within his jurisdiction, and we can be sure, on the basis of the thoroughness and inquisitiveness with which Nurse Marsden inspected other hospitals along her route, that she made good use of it. But one from the Tsarina herself, granted at the end of April at an audience just as Kate was about to leave, was crucial in opening doors for her right up to her final Eastward destination, Yakutsk.

'Her Imperial Majesty showed the utmost kindness, entered heartily into my plans, and gave me an invaluable letter, requesting Russian officials to facilitate my wishes in visiting hospitals and leper settlements in the empire.'

Here it is, translated for 'On Sledge and Horseback to Outcast Siberian Lepers':

Dated St. Petersburg, April 20 [Russian calendar, May 2], 1890.)

'The bearer of this, the British subject, Miss Kate Marsden, is proceeding to Siberia with the object of devoting herself wholly and entirely to the care of the lepers. Before her departure for Siberia Miss Marsden visited St. Petersburg, and had the happiness of being presented to Her Majesty the Empress. Afterward she inspected some of the hospitals here, and has now the intention of inspecting the like in other towns and places of the empire. H. I. M., estimating at its worth the highly Christian and sincerely philanthropic significance of the journey so undertaken by the traveller, and also all its difficulty, has been pleased to command me to hand to her these lines, that she might show them to all persons in authority in such hospitals as she may desire

to visit. H. M. the Empress will be extremely grateful to the said authorities if they will give Miss Marsden their co-operation during her inspection of the hospitals in charge, especially those in which occur patients suffering from leprosy.

(Signed) Prince Ivan Golitsyn.'

This document is useful to us, too, in providing a précis of Kate Marsden's mission as it matured in her mind. It took into account the visits and observations she had made in the Ottoman realms. By now, as she explained to Prince Golitsyn, who was also involved, her concerns had gone beyond palliative care; and she was now intent on finding a cure for leprosy. Thus her expedition to eastern Siberia would have a second purpose, beyond visiting the leper colonies – she was hoping to locate a herb rumoured to have powerful curative properties. It is a legend that Henry Johnson suggests she first encountered in Constantinople and subsequently as she travelled through the Caucasus. Finding this unknown herb became the second pillar of her commitment, 'so that the lepers of India and every country might be benefitted and delivered from death.'

And Johnson suggests – it was in Tblisi that she resolved that in crossing Siberia she would establish whether this plant was legend or reality. She was still anxious for the funding that would create the new hospital, but with her medal pinned to her chest and the Tsarina's letter safe in her hand, Kate Marsden was ready at last to embark on her greatest adventure.

Chapter 6

"Game over!" The young Russian, spotting me, proudly yelled out his only two words of English, then walked past me in the gangway. "Game over, game over". The other passengers in the platzkart, all men, turned round to see what was going on and laughter rippled through the carriage.

Game Over was a cheerful young man with learning difficulties and uninhibited by convention. He evidently sensed his life's purpose in making people laugh and playing computer games.

There was no way our inauguration journey on a Russian train would now go unnoticed. We were travelling in third class, platzkart and Game Over Boy had successfully announced us to the entire carriage.

Travelling the thousands of rail miles that comprised the motherland can quickly cement bonds between the unlikeliest of travellers and the platzkart is a great leveller, fostering a special camaraderie on long journeys. In Russia it's known as the 'hostel carriage' – an open-plan saloon furnished with short, uncomfortable bunks for which you have to pay for the privilege of hiring linen. These happened to be the only seats available to us on the first short hop of our journey from Tomsk to Irkutsk. We would be linking up with the main line from Moscow at Yurga, two hours away. The smiling provodnitsa pushed past Game Over Boy to check our tickets. Among these men, she was boss: starched white shirt, short stylish hair, peroxide top and auburn beneath, smooth shiny skin with kohl-rimmed eyes, and a smile revealing gold incisors.

Among the bags scattered round my feet I delved into the smart one given me by our new friends in Tomsk, emblazoned with the city crest. My hand slid among a host of gifts to reach the tickets, gifts as yet unopened and un-assessed; but if every parting along the way was this generously celebrated, our hand luggage was going to become a real problem.

As we rolled into Yurga, there were many kind hands, including our provodnitsa's, to escort us off onto the platform. We stood amid our reef of luggage and waved back. 'Do svidaniya!' cried Ellie.

"Do svidaniya!" waved our friend, as the grey and red train door slid closed; I wondered whether she was smiling at the isolation of two girls, who must somehow find the right platform, among the multitude surrounding us, for the Irkutsk train. We were only too aware, that we had three minutes to board, and that we had the minimum of Russian to get the necessary instructions.

The last doors to slide shut framed the provodnitsa of each carriage, standing impassive as the imposing grey and red train picked up speed. Faceless hands waved at us through tinted glass; the last carriage became a blur, revealing a lemon station building crisp and neat in the sunlight, grandly built with white pillars and tall oblong lozenge windows. Ellie and I stood there bemoaning the fact that our luggage made rapid platform-hopping impossible. My big bag at least had wheels. When a yell, and a gesture in the right direction came from a man – who looked vaguely in the know, I grabbed its handle and we legged it.

A stately babushka grinned and watched us haul our luggage up the three steps onto the Irkutsk train. We threaded cumbersomely from kupe to kupe looking for the numbers matching our tickets. Our new provodnitsa lacked the warmth of the earlier one and we smiled innocently while she jabbered at us, until we realised that we were being asked to purchase our sealed plastic bag of laundered bed-linen from her for the thirty-six hour journey. Our four-berth kupe was unoccupied, so Ellie and I squeezed our luggage into the rack and eased back on the turquoise velour seats, luxuriating in the space. This was going to be a long journey; there was no way of knowing who might join us along the route, woman or man, nor what unsavoury habits they might bring. I wondered if I should celebrate the opportunity for a cultural exchange with a random stranger! But my sheer tiredness eroded the explorer in me, and I dearly hoped we would be left alone.

Ellie decided it was about time we learnt to read a Russian ticket. We spread ours out on the table. Russian tickets are clever; they have a great deal of valuable information particular to your journey couched in that baffling cyrillic; train number, date, departure time, carriage number and class – luxury, kupe or platzkart, seat number. With a little help I could identify the personal information printed on the ticket – name, passport information and – good heavens – my father's name! Buying a ticket for the Trans-Siberian Express is a challenge, but once you've got one the Russians make damn sure you can't exchange it with another traveller, or re-sell it.

Thanks, to Ellie's modest Russian, I could now at least point to all the relevant bits – and say Da or Nyet – when the inspector came round.

Intriguing as the last train had been, with all the men crowding round, I was glad The Trans-Siberian was quiet and that – so far –we were alone. In case an invasion took place we selected the upper two bunks and made them up with our boiled sheets. They came from their bag stuck together, but as smooth and starched as Nurse Marsden's apron. (That way, she would explain the lice slid straight off!) I lay on my bunk, with my head at the window, watching the vast, dark forest slip by; and when an inward curve came in the track, I could glimpse the beast of a header engine, red, solid and indomitable, pulling its snake of carriages.

I was the Trans-Siberian virgin, and readily tapped into Ellie's experience. She told me that in the course of a long solo journey from Mongolia to Moscow in a kupe, somewhere beyond Ulaan Baator, just as she was getting accustomed to having the compartment to herself, a Mongolian family crammed themselves in. "What was it like," I nervously asked, "to suddenly find yourself part of a crowd?"

"They had loads of bags, I couldn't believe they had so much, but they managed to stow them away. They were very nice actually, but we couldn't talk to each other; I'm not even sure what language they were speaking."

I thought of the small window-table between the lower bunks, where, when we weren't lounging on the narrow bunks we sat and wrote or read. It was a quite a business balancing a cheese sandwich and a bottle of water on it, but Ellie's companions managed gravity-defying feats.

"They had a leg of fatty meat wrapped in newspaper, and started carving bits off and eating them with their fingers." That made me stop and think. As a traveller, adventurer, pursuer of the world's most esoteric voyages, I concede that the reality is that this is life, their life, their normality. But hey, what a challenge to a vegetarian like me to share a tiny space with a carnivorous extended family, whose numbers swelled or depleted as the journey went on, odours of meat and sweat filling the air, and greasy fingers invading anything at hand height. (That's me – but you, dear reader, may substitute smokers, snorers or those with flatulence . . .)

As I contemplated our two pristine bunks, and the two lovely lower ones that we lounged and read at, our new butch provonista popped her head in to vacuum the small grey rug between the bunks. Then, as evening set in, we broached the bottle of red wine we had stowed; we felt its magnificence; blessing our journey, so we drank to Kate Marsden who had travelled in such dire discomfort on the rough road through the forest – still, today, parallel to the train. I treasured the private moment, knowing that at any stop, in the middle of the Siberian taiga, there might be company.

While on our own we felt it was time to see how 2,500 postcards look. Stacked up on our little table, they became a purple mountain that our friend Vladimir could have made use of in his fortress. We had at every opportunity handed them out with their Russian-language translation pocket biography of Kate Marsden on the back, to bemuse fellow-travellers. Some even took them as souvenirs. Looking at our card castle, my companion exasperatingly observed.

"These cards are multiplying not decreasing." Somehow, we had to unload them. Spreading our story, and Kate's, across Russia was going to be harder than I'd originally thought.

"Do you know what? I damn nearly ordered 9,000, I'm glad I didn't now!"

"That's just silly, why on earth would we need that many?" Ellie said.

"Ah, but, that's the number of New Testaments that Kate took with her in her sledge. I expect whole boxes of them kept falling on her and Ada as they rattled along in those sledges!"

"But, Jacki, 2,500 postcards – I mean LOOK at them – is a ridiculous amount; how on earth are we going to give them all away – or carry them, for heaven's sake?"

And so, from then on we made a point of offloading a sheaf of them into any eager hand. Imagine the purple trail that followed us across Russia, until, at our final destination, we at last ran out. It's gratifying that they may still, today, be adorning remote Siberian living-rooms, perched on reindeer antlers or an empty vodka bottle.

Mercifully, we were spoilt for privacy. No new guests arrived in the night. In the morning, with my penknife, I cut our old plastic coke bottles into ersatz cups and then filled them with hot water from the galley samovar and coffee. The grounds rose to the surface like plastic debris on the ocean; Ellie seemed content with her breakfast of black bread and Russian beef jerky.

After this simple breakfast, the train's motion induced a mood of self-questioning. How well prepared was I for this journey? How did I feel this re-enactment measured up to my absorption with Mary Kingsley on Mount Cameroon, or with Isabella Bird in the Southern Himalayas? I had done my best to put my physical self at the disposal of those two wonderful women; their 1890s journeys had given me the chance to exert myself with hours of exhausting walking and climbing. In responding to Kate Marsden's tug at my imagination, I was painfully aware of the downside. I was not exerting myself as she had. I took stock of myself – sedentary train travel, with a diet of plastic cheese and white-bread sandwiches, made me feel a lard mountain screaming for a gym! How could an expedition be made entirely sitting down?

How had she and Ada fared at this distance from Muscovite civility? What evidence of life caught their eye? The rare villages we passed had the same grey Soviet blocks, abandoned factories, pylons lurching unevenly on poor footings, the identical wooden dwellings with unpainted picket fences, perhaps a glimpse of a river, a black lake, or a road winding its way through the trees. By the train track there was a profusion of summer flowers, yellow, mauve and dusky pink amidst banks of thistles and clover, bringing beauty to the ugliness. No obvious wildlife, no eye-catching building, no soul-stirring monasteries broke the serial monotony of larch, silver birch and pine, some tall, some fallen, some majestic, some struggling to exist. From where we watched, these trees formed an ocean, our train was a ship penetrating its dark interior, snaking on and on into the black heart of an interior smarting of centuries of misery and deprivation.

'Can it be wondered at that, when I retired to rest at night, after visiting day by day these scenes, my dreams were haunted by desperate convicts, threatening murderers, awful looking women, poor, starving children and ever clanking chains ? And the faces of those exiles haunt me still'.

Kate Marsden

A Siberian tarantass c. 1885

Kate Marsden writes that the day before she left Tomsk the police chief of Krasnoyarsk paid her a call. This was a city over 360 miles to the East; but since he was in town, and hearing that she was there, he came to warn her of the dangerous condition of the rivers and roads through the region – the very area that Ellie and I were even now traversing in our safe, comfortable Trans-Siberian train. He told her that the sledge he was travelling in had gone through the ice, and narrowly escaped drowning.

Today's Krasnoyarsk, after *Novosibirsk* and *Omsk*, is the third largest city in *Siberia*, with a population of over a million. This important junction on the *Trans-Siberian Railway* combines being a prime producer of aluminium but also, with outstanding natural attractions applauded unreservedly by Anton Chekhov himself and subsequent visitors, its beauty deriving from the convergence of two great rivers and their associated lakes.

In Kate Marsden's itinerary, the Krasnoyarsk superintendent made it his business to escort Kate from Tomsk to Krasnoyarsk. They travelled in a heavy tarantass, used in place of a sledge once the thaw or 'breaking-up season' had started.

Kate detested the tarantass and describes it as a 'nerve shaking and bone trying contrivance'. The tarantass was a carriage peculiar to Russia, built with two well-separated axles, above which a boat-shaped body was suspended on two long timber poles in place of springs. A leather awning stretched behind and overhead, and three horses hitched into the traces.

In snow, the wheels could be removed in order for the body to be mounted on sledge-runners. The prime disadvantage for Kate was that seats, as such, were non-existent.

By this stage in her journey – April or early May – Kate was fully acquainted with the perils of travelling in Siberia. The rivers could only be safely crossed when the ice remained many feet thick, or, once the ice had melted, when a ferry link re-opened. Eager to push on, Kate gladly accepted the police chief's offer of protection.

There are two great rivers to cross before reaching Krasnoyarsk: the Kiya and the Yenesei. On the banks of the Kiya, it was obvious that it was touch and go with the ice, so the superintendent halted the tarantass and sent his man out onto the ice to test its condition. It had begun, by day, to melt and crack, but the night frost froze it again. She was bound by the superintendent's local knowledge, and judgement. There would be no one to rescue them if they got half-way across and found it only semi-frozen.

The Kiya crossing, for me, illuminates Kate's stamina, and dauntless pragmatism as a traveller. What did she think, staring out across those frozen wastelands and the thawing rivers – that many, many people had died (as they still do) trying to cross? What thoughts assailed her, with her burden of Testaments, packages of tea and plum pudding? Should she press on? Or hang about till the ferry re-opened? How did she balance her own mortality against the mission on which so much depended? Who would care if she drowned in an unknown and remote country so many thousand miles from the pretty gardens of Edmonton? Would there only be Ada Field, who had left her earlier in the journey, to mourn her if she died? Her family were all gone; (her mother too died at about this time in 1891, though it would be many months before she knew that).

When the tarantass descended the river bank, straw was laid over the partly melted ice to bond it with the next frost. The superintendent's serf returned from his reconnoitre of the ice with a discouraging report. At this, the police chief offered Kate the chance to transfer to a lighter carriage, and she accepted. This indicates his concerns that the laden tarantass might not have made it, and they would have all gone under, horses, Testaments, Imperial medal and all.

'As we drove in the carriage', Kate wrote, 'premonitory cracks were heard below, which created a little uneasiness. On landing safely we found, in a few minutes, that there was an old, shaky bridge to cross, which we were told was more unsafe than the river, and which was studiously avoided. However, the bridge must be crossed, and we tried our best not to think about danger. The crazy thing shook a great deal, but we got over without an accident, thank God!'

The hazards redoubled as they approached the Yenissei River, the largest of three great Siberian rivers flowing North into the Arctic Ocean. (The others are the Ob and the Lena.) Rising in Mongolia, the Yenissei drains much of central Siberia*. Kate wrote that it was one of the broadest she encountered during her journey, and as she began to cross she couldn't see the other bank at all, and she was understandably extremely nervous, venturing onto the moist and cracked ice surface. Straw had been laid, as usual, but to no obvious effect.

'Sometimes, when a feeling of dizziness came on, I shut my eyes; but I knew I was in God's hands, and felt sure that no accident would happen, and that He would allow me to reach my final

---

* Yenissei – 5540 km, navigable only in parts, is the longest in Russia, the Nile, the longest river in the world is 6600 km and the Amazon is 6480 km.

destination among the lepers. When the other side was safely reached my feelings of relief and gratitude may well be imagined.'

On the Siberian Express, I had been aware in the night of the change in the train's incessant rumble as it traversed a long bridge. Some time later, the train's forlorn whistle heralded our arrival at Krasnoyarsk. And so at daybreak, from the Krasnoyarsk side, we looked out across a river basin that stretches to beyond Lake Baikal. The Krasnoyarsk Railway Bridge that carries the Trans-Siberian Railway across the Yenissei is a kilometre long:one kilometre of safety for us, one kilometre of hell for Kate, alert every second for the cracking sound, and the inevitable ditching into the freezing river and instant death.

Immediately North of Krasnoyarsk the Taimyr tundra begins. Here reindeer, in the largest herd in the world, migrate to grazing pastures in Evenkia and the Putoran Mountains. The main subsistence of the nomadic Tundra Nenets, to the north, and the Southern Khandeyar or Forest Nenets, developed since the ceighteenth, is reindeer hunting and herding. To help in their herding, they have bred the renowned Samoyed dog, whose docility and strength in pulling sleds and adaptability to Arctic conditions, has endeared them to the leaders of countless Polar expeditions. The Nenets and their Samoyeds follow the herds, camping in conical yurts, fending off the Siberian wolves, and sharing a diet of fish and reindeer. For these nomads, as against the settled communities of Siberia, there seemed to be no particular incidence of leprosy, which kept them outside Kate's concern and therefore mine.

I stared out of the train window, musing surprisingly about love. I can only guess at whether Kate Marsden entertained such reveries, that woman's head seemed to have no space for frivolity; filled, as it was, with hospitals and prisons, procedures and cures. Yet, the Siberian version of Kate's story, written as a play, goes this way: as a teenage nurse, she fell in love with a man she was nursing in the war in Bulgaria; he had contracted leprosy and, desperate that he wouldn't survive, she promised to go out and find a cure for him. By the time she returned he had died. Lovely story, lovely sentiments, but pure fiction.

Our bold Miss Marsden arrived in Krasnoyarsk after negotiating the River Yenessei, to Kate herself, the Yenessei crossing must have seemed the major milepost in her mission.

Once arrived in Krasnoyarsk, and with the major milepost of the Yenessi crossing behind her, Kate Marsden had no compunction in showing her letter of introduction and requesting access to the city prison. Like some modern Ofsted Inspector of Schools, she collated her notes and gave it high marks. 'The prison is in admirable condition, well managed, with good ventilation, and proper sanitary provisions.' Her matronly comments extended to the hospital: 'All the appliances of the latest scientific discoveries, as well as the best systems of nursing, are here in operation'.

Despite giving no clues as to her Krasnoyarsk lodgings, Kate couldn't disguise the fact that she had a pleasant stay, and that the people she met were supportive of each other's well being. She had time to note a difference between 'metropolitan' Russians and her first true Siberians. The latter, reminded her of British Colonials in their frankness, honesty, uprightness, truthfulness and loyalty.

'They will give a welcome to every stranger, and help all in need. They have a great love for the Czar, but a natural antipathy to officials, who put a wrong construction upon Imperial orders and carry out such orders in accordance with their own private interpretations rather than in harmony with the Emperor's wishes. But neither this, nor anything else, shakes their allegiance and devotion to their Czar.'

For the next leg of her journey Kate decided to buy her own tarantass, that way, she reckoned she could choose one that wouldn't be quite so uncomfortable.

The tarantass dealers weren't quite as virtuous as the Siberians she had described. A series of men with vehicles in differing states of maintenance presented themselves to her, all intent on fleecing the foreign woman. She stood up to them – literally – and turned them away, one and all. A crowd of townsfolk gathered to see how this English nurse would do business. All this must have tickled her: 'There was a great deal of whispering and talking, and then, when the owners of different vehicles began quarrelling and fighting, the hubbub was immense!' So began her experience of negotiating with Siberians and Russians. It would stand her in good stead in the coming months.

In the event, for thirty roubles Kate closed on one that she had made a point of testing for safety, soundness and capaciousness, but in the event, not, as she would find, for comfort.

But this time of year was no time to be setting out. With a rise in the temperature the deep snow and ice were melting – the first signs of the Siberian spring. Unfortunately it didn't ease her journey but rather made things much worse. The unpaved roads, were as deeply rutted as a ploughed field.

'When a thaw commences the soft, pulpy state of affairs begins; then there comes a slight frost and a thin layer of ice, frequently misleading the traveler. When he thinks he is going to glide along in tolerable ease, he suddenly bumps down through the ice into a great hole of sticky, pulpy mud, or if there has been a very severe frost during the night, all the roads are turned into solid blocks of frozen mud. I know the roads are in excellent condition in some seasons of the year; but it was not my good fortune to travel at such propitious times.'

And so in her final days in Krasnoyarsk she packed her tarantass carefully, aware that its lack of springs could make the long journey to Irkutsk a misery. She laid out bedding on top of carefully placed packages, and left, having made up her mind to be 'brave, patient and resigned'.

This resolve soon faltered: the journey to Kansk was a nightmare and left her ill. A tarantass isn't designed to carry people. With neither seats nor anything to hang on to, whenever the horses jolted, the passengers slammed against the side-boards and their feet hit the sharp wood of the head-board. As soon as Kate had scrambled upright again, another lurch would pitch her forward; and eventually she buckled to, resigning herself to being tossed about like a sack of straw. After a mere couple of hours her limbs, muscles, head and insides ached unbearably. 'Tarantass rheumatism, internal and external, chronic, or, rather, perpetual, is the complaint from which you will have to suffer during that thousand miles. At the end of the first day you would like a feather bed for about a week.'

I defy anyone, especially her self-appointed chief critic, Isabel Hapgood, trading on her own experiences of Russian travel, to accuse Kate of exaggeration or invention. It stands against Hapgood's own integrity, knowing at first-hand the conditions of travel at the extremities of the Russian Empire, that she should teach her stuffy late-Victorian readers to pooh-pooh Kate's motives and question the truth of her despatches and her sincerity – and yet she continued to flay her victim well into the Edwardian era, and at that stage was seen to be winning.

Looking down from our kupe onto the flanking forest trail Kate had once bumped along, I gratefully compared modern expectations of comfort for travellers with those 125 years later – even as I strained the coffee grounds through my teeth as I drank from half a plastic bottle, I thought what was an absolute pleasure this was compared to what she went through.

At the end of her second day of travelling, Kate was ill enough to be no longer aware of wind or weather, and had to be carried into her night's lodgings. She wrote that she could have slept for a month. Arriving in Kansk, she could no longer remember the consecutive order of the events of her past life, particularly the most recent ones! She may even have been wondering what she was doing in Russia in the first place.

A wet dawn had broken by the time our train slid into Kansk, but the dark sky and drizzle did nothing to enhance the grey concrete drabness of the standard Soviet station; with nothing of the pastel prettiness of Krasnoyarsk and Yurga. Umbrella-toting Russians swarmed across the open tracks to change platforms, spurning the concrete bridge over their heads. Ellie nipped out for more pot noodles at the kiosk, leaving me having kittens: what would I do if the train left before she got back?

At this point there are at least ten tracks to the Trans-Siberian railway; six of these sidings holding stationary wagons, oil bowsers and heavy machinery transporters. The lines of wagons were so long that their ends were half-lost in the Siberian drizzle.

But I was well aware that this functional dreariness masked the real Kansk. Had visa restrictions given me more time, or train tickets been more flexible, a rewarding day could have been spent here. Kansk is an old city with a vibrant contemporary culture. The annual Kansk International Film Festival of Avant-Garde Cinema runs through the end of August into early September, and gathers all those involved in experimental and contemporary video art from across Russia and beyond. But, despite my own interest in film, we had timed it just too late! Here came Ellie with her stash of pot noodles; perfect timing as a spasm ran through the carriages and the train began to haul us ever Eastwards.

What was she like, this Kate Marsden, my ghostly companion along the Tea Trakt down to our left? First, there was that direct gaze that drew people to her, and easily persuaded them to part with money for her charitable purposes. Tall, not pretty as such, but striking in her nurse's uniform, she had a presence, and an urgency that signalled that she wanted things done immediately – taken the wrong way – as in Wellington – a bossy-boots trait; and, of course evidence of the empathy and compassion that marked her childhood and years of nursing. Her charisma as a speaker persuaded her audiences to listen, and to identify with her cause. Her middle class upbringing gave her an acceptance of existing class structures, and a belief that nobody could transcend out of the poverty they had been born into. I am sure that if I had gone with her on her Russian prison and hospital visits I would have jibbed at her patronising bearing, and shared her detractors' sense of her inflated self-importance. Among the free citizens – and indeed the incarcerated – of Kansk, her evident elevation to near sainthood by her visit to the city prison, gave her critics a field day; nor does it help that Kate lacked humility in her own accounts.

Whether in feather bed or on horsehair hotel mattress, it didn't take long for her to recover. Soon she was outside the city's capacious prison buying up all the bread and soup that the women vendors had for sale at the gates. She entered 'rich with her gifts' and noticed that 'every tiny window was crowded with numerous heads, all trying to have a peep at me.' She was brought before 186 men in chains; on seeing Kate, with her laden baskets, among the accompanying warders, they all called out to her. As she walked amongst them, men took her hand and smoothed it with theirs; they cried, and so did Kate. 'They all crowded as close as they could to get near me, and their faces brightened, often with a smile, as I spoke two or three sentences in half broken Russian.'

The prisoners were grateful for the soup, New Testaments, sugar and tea she distributed. Buoyed up by a surge of confidence, with only a single officer to help carry her provisions and Bibles for her, she entered a cell containing twenty convicted murderers. 'On distributing tea and sugar and the little books their angry, hardened, and almost dehumanised faces slowly softened. On leaving, one of the men, with ready politeness, showed me out of the cell, as it was too dark to see my way.'

But Kansk was a mere staging-post, Kate's journey to Irkutsk, a mere 145 of the 658 miles out from Krasnoyarsk. Woman of the moment or not, she must be climbing back on her tarantass.

I spent the second day out from Kansk peering out at a soggy desolation of electricity pylons, trees and more trees, emaciated and straggly. Occasionally, to mark the emptiness, would be a small wooden house, primitively built, usually with a bench outside, a lime-green field dotted with pink wild flowers, and, if I was lucky an old rusting car.

I wondered what the people did. Few factories, farms, cattle or shops were in evidence, nor any of the people that belonged to the cabins. Now and again I spotted the odd truck on the road flanked by the train track and forest, but mostly, as the sun crept out the train left ominous shadows across the surfaces of dark lakes and bogs, laced with black skeletons of dead trees. In such a wilderness, there was no room for human life: it was the set for the Kingdom of Mordor, coldly unforgiving and hostile. How daunting these endlessly repeated sights must have been for Kate, even as the spring days began to lengthen.

Good news reached my phone as we hurtled onwards. The efficient and vibrant Tourism Department at Tomsk had got in touch with its counterpart at Irkutsk, so we would be met off the train and taken to a hotel. I could sense at last the whole venture opening up, its horizons perceptually changing. There had been many times over the past year that I thought I would never, ever see this inaccessible continent for myself. Now at last it was meant to be, and communities were welcoming me in Kate's name. It was a positive end to a fraught year: whatever pitfalls Kate Marsden had had to face in late imperial times were gratuitously replicated in planning my own trip early in the twenty first century. Twice already my hopes had sustained a near-terminal reversal. Ellie, sitting across from me as we slowed into Irkutsk, could have no idea of the relief I was feeling now.

Sitting in our kupe approaching the next major milestone of the journey, I let my mind race back over the first two attempts to mount my long-cherished expedition, and how both – at the last minute – floundered.

The first thing I had done was to apply for the 2013 Royal Geographical Society Land Rover Bursary. This is an annual award aimed at groups of people who wish to make a challenging journey beyond their usual limits and boundaries. Recreating Kate Marsden's epic journey across Russia would, of course, challenge the team I would put together and the Land Rover would be an integral part of the logistics, to be returned at the conclusion of the expedition. If Kate Marsden were making this journey today, – she would surely opt for a Land Rover, not a damned tarantass, to travel in!

Buzzing with excitement, I approached one of the UK's most respected and experienced survival guides, and asked him if he would be interested in working with me. His response was enthusiastic. Together we put together an exceptional proposal, though it came as a shock that he took it for granted that we would be going in winter. I said nothing; I didn't want to reveal any weakness, and trusted his record, working in the Arctic for a television channel as its survival consultant.

Following Kate Marsden's footsteps, we would be tying in with the 2013 150th Anniversary of the formation of the International Red Cross, whose flag Kate Marsden chose to fly. We would drive from London to Moscow and on to Yakutsk, via the desolate 'Trans Siberian Highway' and the infamous 'Road of Bones', officially the coldest highway on earth, our ultimate destination being the port of Magadan on Russia's East coast. From there, having carried us more than 13,000km, – the Landy would be shipped back home.

The expedition would look into Nurse Marsden's pledge to alleviate the suffering of Siberia's lepers, whilst challenging us and the vehicle in one of the earth's most hostile environments. We would follow as closely as possible part of the 2000-mile circuit she took on horseback to visit the scattered remote leper colonies of the Yakutsk and Vilyuisk regions, difficult enough in our warm vehicle, but for Kate especially challenging: she was not, in the first place, a confident horsewoman, but for the hazardous Siberian ground conditions she found she had to exchange riding side-saddle, (as ladies still did in 1890) for sitting astride. Roads through the forest were unheard of, so Kate's party recruited local people to cut through the forest to the remote groups of lepers, cast out by the Yakuts. To this day, there are no roads or tracks into these areas, and going off-road would challenge both team and vehicle as we endeavoured to push further into the region, past obstacles such as those which at times had stopped Kate and her party in their tracks.

We all knew, as we signed up to the expedition, that the journey would change our lives, testing us physically and mentally in a harsh, unfamiliar environment; and giving us insights into cultures and customs, indigenous and imposed, surviving and sometimes flourishing against the odds.

As we would be self-sufficient, we would, like Kate, be laying up in the forests alongside the route, in tents with wood-burning stoves, eating local food cooked over an open fire. Giving in to expert advice, I agreed that the expedition should take place from December to mid February, assuring of a safe crossing of the frozen

River Lena and giving us the chance to experience for ourselves, and report on the meteorological extremes of the region while gaining an understanding of how the indigenous people cope with an average daily air temperature of -45° centigrade and continue to thrive.

With my experience of previous expeditions, and sensing who would work with who, I recruited a great team – but our survival leader was the key participant. His credentials are awesome, a qualified wilderness guide and instructor; international tracking qualifications that have seen him involved in search and rescue tasks in places as far flung as the slopes of Mount Kenya to the jungles of Borneo; a qualified cross country ski instructor; free-fall parachutist; qualified diver and has medical training to paramedic level.

As a result of his knowledge and experience, he has been called on to work in varying roles with television personalities such as Ray Mears and Bear Grylls and to consult on documentaries with the BBC's Natural History Department.

And then, just as the date was approaching for us to submit our application, disaster struck: Our indispensable leader received personal news that prevented him leaving England; so the application foundered and died.

It was a huge disappointment for applicants and sponsors alike. For me, it was back to square one. But I wasn't giving up. Kate Marsden would be honoured, and in one way or another I would get to Siberia and a motorised, DIY expedition still seemed to me the best way to achieve my aims.

In December 1993 a similar journey had taken place, facilitated by the completion of the Channel Tunnel; television producer Richard Creasey assembled an international team for a first ever attempt to drive continuously from London Eastwards to New York. Despite being written off as a non-starter by the motoring and exploration press, the enterprise was endorsed by the United Nations as a valuable contribution to its 50th anniversary celebrations, and Ford supplied the heavy all-weather Mondoe and Mavericks that they drove.

'The Ford London to New York Overland Challenge Expedition'

'The Ford London to New York Overland Challenge Expedition', if it came off would achieve three motoring firsts: the Channel Tunnel using the service road, the dash across the vast Russian continent in temperatures falling as low as -59°C and finally the 56 mile wide Bering Strait on sea-ice. They were lucky, and from now on in the world's eye.

The snowmobile dash across Alaska, followed by a four day non-stop drive to the United Nations Building in New York City made prime television viewing. As it happens, the ice road they had to take through frozen central Siberia took them, right through Vilyuisk and the town felt this overland expedition had special significance for them. The town's mayor at the time extended a warm greeting to the ice-bound monster trucks and excitedly told the crews about Kate Marsden – a name unfamiliar to all of them.

The diary entry for the day, written by the expedition leader Richard Creasey, gives a vivid insight into ground conditions they were encountering; sadly, it gives no impression of the hospital founded in Kate Marsden's name.:

'25 January 1994

Nyurba to Vilyuysk (Yakutia, Siberia, Russia)

It would be great to film in the leper colony that had now become a mental hospital in the desolate nowhere, and much more important Doc Ford would be able to give some second opinions, so I agreed with Yury that we'd delay our start by going via the hospital.

Victor felt the need to take the initiative. Before I could get a word in he had ordered the Ural trucks to go ahead, as he had at Ust Kut.

The temperature dropped to minus 57 centigrade on, what I now thought of as, this trial stretch of winter road. Soon we would be back on the tarmac and would not again have a chance to see what a winter road could do until we had reached our point of no return.

Our guide for this stretch of the ice road was Vladimir and I spent the time, while Doc and others were in the hospital, talking with him and trying to understand the conditions that would hit us after Seymchan.

There were no clues beyond the fact that we had been amazingly lucky with the weather so far and that the conditions ahead were treacherous. No one, Vladmir reminded me, had ever managed to go the whole distance before.

When the hospital filming was complete Victor ordered the Urals off again, but this time I was waiting and said gently that we should keep as one team and that we'd go when I was ready.

That night we reached Nyurba. Half way on the ice road to Yakutsk.

This time dinner was in a house and we all just fitted round one table. The food was glorious, the atmosphere terrific and Victor, in one of his rare toasts was unnervingly warm. He toasted to a team that he was proud to be part of, that had passed one of the great driving tests of the worlds coldest region and he was convinced that all of us could make it.'

In terms of what I was intending, the 1994 expedition was a mighty motorcade. A single vehicle would do it for me. Thwarted the first time round, I was reviewing my options, when fortune seemed to offer a second chance. I took the train from home in Bristol to Bath and on arrival, took shelter in a coffee shop. The drizzle showed no signs of abating and I was only too pleased to start up a conversation with the large, neatly-bearded, open-faced chap at the adjoining table.

Through the rather good yarns he had to spin he gradually revealed himself to me: a businessman with many irons in the fire, though currently experiencing a dip in his fortunes. I've known others in his position, but was impressed with this man's list of past and present accomplishments. Like others, before and after he reacted with instant fascination to my ongoing endeavour to reclaim the valiant footprints of early women travellers – tinged in his case, I sensed, with friendly envy that I could have found such a great project to be passionate about. We exchanged cards.

I thought nothing more of it; but a few weeks later I had a message asking me to meet for coffee in Bristol. How was the planning for my next expedition going?

"Badly. I still want to drive there, I feel I would understand Kate Marsden better if I went in winter so as to experience her deprivation. I have no idea who would now sponsor me, though."

He raised his eyebrows, "You are an ambitious lady."

I've become one, I thought to myself. There have been times in my life when my confidence has been entirely crushed. Yet my spirited women explorers continue to fuel my passion and fill me with their cool courage. Over time, I've become quite fearless when it comes to exploring off the beaten track. I found myself opening up some of my dearest thoughts;

"I have been thinking, how good it would be to do something that would benefit the community of Yakutia in Kate Marsden's name. I've been in correspondence for some months now with an Oxford professor who is living in Yakutsk, working closely with the forest community where Kate's leper colony was built, and he is emphatic about how much they love her there. Wouldn't it be good to create some sort of lasting legacy?"

"Brilliant," replied my businessman, though I was momentarily disconcerted by the sights of his fraying shirt cuffs. "Any ideas as to what this could be?"

I knew what I wanted, even if it was at this stage a dream. "One thing that might create a lasting impact on the community would be to drive out a Land Rover converted into an ambulance, and donate it to the hospital in Vilyuisk, the nearest town to the leper hospital at Sosnovka. It could be used to transfer and supply patients who live in remote regions of the forest."

I could tell that he had never met anyone quite like me, and was trying to work me out. "That's first class, because it could tie in with the 150th Anniversary of the Red Cross."

Lionel Fields, let's call him, was excited, and so was I.

"Then, once it was delivered, and commissioned in Kate's name, we'd all fly home."

I was already envisaging our Land Rover churning its way through snow and ice in the forest, with THE KATE MARSDEN AMBULANCE emblazoned on its side.

"Of course I will need to raise loads of money, and get a team together, the Landy will need to be modified for driving at sub-zero temperatures."

Lionel responded by ticking off on his fingers the major UK companies that he had dealings with: "I can ask them all to sponsor you." It bothered me: How could one man have dealings with airports, mobile phone companies, pop-up restaurants and healthcare providers? Something to do with computers, he seemed to be saying.

I'm still not sure whether the excitement generated between us wasn't momentarily eclipsing my natural caution, but our meeting finished with a list of tasks for us both to carry out to make the idea a reality.

Now, if there was one thing that Kate Marsden was ace at, it was raising money. While her most productive appeals were, of course, in Royal and Imperial circles, her mercurial and persuasive personality appealed to all levels of society in her request for donations. Who could fail to be stirred by a woman professing to have given over her life to the cause of a debilitating disease like leprosy?

The rumours and accusations surrounding her – that she squir-relled away a proportion of the donated funds for her own comfort and security – later came to blacken her reputation in the West. The reasons for this – as against her near-canonisation in Russia – I will explain later.

Perhaps it was my lack of a starched nurse's uniform or of a life dedicated to the victim's of a horrific disease; or was there a knack to fund-raising that I had yet to learn? Whatever the reason, I turned out to be pretty hopeless at it.

During the next few weeks Mr Fields and I put together a convincing brochure for him, as self-appointed campaign manager to send out to companies he thought would come on board. He had said we should go for corporate sponsorship, and I took his point. From then on I received a daily barrage of emails and phone calls from him, telling who he had had meetings with and how keen they were to be part of it, and so the list of promises grew. But there was still, at this stage, no Land Rover, or other tangible evidence of his efforts.

I was happy to concern myself with the practicalities of the actual expedition, drawing up lists of what and who I would need, and researching the exigencies of driving through a Siberian winter. My chief concern – for the team and the Landy ambulance – was the last 600 km in Yakutia, or (as it is now known) the Republic of Sakha, the largest region of Russian Siberia. The crucial section would be the area of wilderness between Yakutsk and Vilyuisk where we would deliver the vehicle – and we needed to deliver it intact! It was in these pathless forest conditions that Kate had ridden two thousand miles on horseback, assessing the conditions in which the lepers lived.

In drafting my earlier application to the Royal Geographical Society, the experiences of the survival leader had made a major contribution. This time I was reluctant to enlist such a guide until I was satisfied that we were a professional set-up, and sure that the venture would come to fruition. Once I had researched the route and likely worst conditions, my next priority was to make a list of all the kit we would need, carefully costing each item.

Would Kate have preferred more comfort on her journey or was the hardship part of the attraction, part of what drove her? I have already suggested that she would have jumped at the chance to swap her thirty rouble tarantass for a state-of-the-art Landrover. But how much more efficient it would have made her mission!

In the absence of modern transport, she could not avoid travelling for long periods of time in the Siberian winter. She was well-enough informed to know that between December and February the temperature regularly dips from -40C to -60C. It doesn't necessarily snow a lot and the cold is dry, but at such temperatures the frost bites quickly. Besides, she already had experience of a Bulgarian winter, and knew all the shortcomings of nurse's uniforms.

In 1890, the actual year of the Jaegar company's foundation, the outfit they made her would have been the warmest clothing available in the UK.

Naturally, though we don't have records, she will have visited the London showroom to discuss her needs, negotiating with the fitters how best to repel sub-zero temperatures by constructing successive air tight skins so that the air her body heated could be trapped between them. Disarmingly, she describes this Siberian ensemble:

'About the clothing – well, that was a decided burden in more ways than one. I had a whole outfit of Jaeger garments, which I prized more and more as the months went on; a loose kind of body, lined with flannel, a very thickly wadded eider-down ulster, with sleeves long enough to cover the hands entirely, the fur collar reaching high enough to cover the head and face. Then a sheep-skin reaching to the feet, and furnished with a collar which came over the fur one. Then over the sheep-skin I had to wear a ducha, which is a fur coat of reindeer skin. It is not surprising that, when thus accoutred, broadened, and lengthened by a great many inches, I failed to recognise K. M. in the looking glass which a laughing girl held up before me.

But I have not yet finished; some other articles have still to be described. A long thick pair of Jaeger stockings made of long hair; over them a pair of gentlemen's thickest hunting stockings; over them a pair of Russian boots made of felt, coming high up over the knee; and over them a pair of brown felt valenkies*. Then I was provided with a large fur bag or sack into which I could step; my head covering was a fur-lined cap, and the etceteras consisted of

* Felt boots

shawls, rugs and wraps. All this immense load of wool, and fur, and skins to cover a bit of frail and feeble humanity! Yet there was not an ounce too much, as after-experience proved.'

Kate had spent time in London, before leaving for Europe, planning for the Russian journey, socialising, and finding extra support. She was fuelled by 'a titillation of excitement' and some of her friends told her they felt they were preparing for her wedding! This observation may have been closer to the mark than they knew, indeed, as she herself admits, for a while she almost lost sight of the object of it all: the lepers in their outposts, and the herb that might supply the cure.

At comparable stages in our preparations, while I was busy researching double windscreens and extra fuel tanks for driving in the cold in the twenty first century, Kate was pondering whether her sledge drivers would be sober or trustworthy, in the light of the tales she had ben plied with by old Russia hands. Would there be tipsy drivers constantly swigging vodka, who had no qualms about landing their passengers 'topsy-turvy' on a dark night, in the depths of a forest or in the 'solemn stillness of a snow drift'? She mused that, like the chain-mail of a medi-aeval knight, the overlapped cloths and furs of her Jaeger outfit made her into a semi-rigid parcel. Once deposited into the snow, how could she lift herself out of it – let alone walk? At least my modern sub-zero snow suit assured me of manoeuvrability!

My own greatest concern was breaking down in the forest hundreds of miles from help; I repeatedly read the advice that if you accidentally let the engine die, it is impossible to start it from cold again. Now, was there a suitable and safe supplementary heater available for -60°, or would the engine have to stay idling all night while we slept? Having lived in Ottawa for three years in my early twenties, I had seen cars plugged in to houses at night to keep the engines warm when the temperature dropped below -30°.

One morning Lionel e-mailed me: 'Have you thought about a Toyota Land Cruiser? They are brilliant in cold weather, much easier to start and they'll make a far more efficient ambulance. I know the director of Toyota, in fact I've got a meeting with Ian at their offices in Milton Keynes tomorrow, I'll ask him to donate one to us, he's a nice guy.'

Strange, I thought, that he happens to be on Christian-name terms with the managing director of Toyota UK; besides, frayed cuffs swimming before me, what could such a meeting be about?

Though I would continue to puzzle over Mr Field's connection with Toyota's higher echelons till he explained at one of the two meetings I had set up in London: the first with the Press Officer of the Red Cross Association, the second with the lovely couple who carried the flag for Kate Marsden's St Francis Leprosy Guild.

He was right about the vehicle though. According to my own enquiries a Toyota Land Cruiser comes in at between £35,000 and £53,000. A beautiful thing, designed for multi-terrain use, its four-wheel drive makes it brilliant off-road and in challenging terrain, and it is up to pretty much anything that nature can throw at it. Our Kate Marsden Ambulance would be a fitting and enduring gift in her memory – and if it came with a blue light for emergencies – it was now flashing in my head.

The meeting with Toyota had gone extremely well, he reported by phone. They loved the idea of showcasing one of their vehicles in Siberia, and he had persuaded them to donate one to be converted into an ambulance for the hospital in Vilyuisk, it would become as useful as the Flying Doctor's plane for servicing forest communities covering an area the size of India.

A few days later we met in London for the two meetings I had set up. First with the Director of PR at the Red Cross Association, and then with the St Francis Leprosy Guild. Both went well; and afterwards I kept imagining the faces of the sweet couple we had just had tea with, wistfully waving as the ambulance pulled away on its 12,000 km journey across Belgium, Germany, Poland, Belarus and Russia, with the name of their great founder emblazoned on the side in big red letters!

In my elation, I stifled all my questions to him – who was to pay for the 900 litres of fuel, the cold weather clothing, the visas, the flights home, the food and the scores of other costs we would encounter?

We were standing on a traffic island on Oxford Street while shoppers and traffic swirled around.

"That went well," he yelled, shaking my hand over the roar. "I will be in touch as soon as I hear some more from Toyota and the other companies."

Then he went one way and I the other. I never saw him again.

The following week I found out that Toyota's head offices weren't in Milton Keynes but in Epsom. Mr Fields became uncontactable, the flow of emails stopped abruptly, and my website, which he, as the expert, had been working on, crashed.

Kate had met her little spivs on the tarantass-ranks; I had met a con-man over a coffee table. Lionel Fields longed to be part of a great project, an adventure straight out of The Eagle comic; he lied to climb aboard, but he had gone as far as he could, and when he realised that he couldn't keep up he simply vanished, leaving me to clear up the mess.

I rang Toyota in Epsom and asked if they had any record of a meeting with a Mr Fields.

"Who did you say?"

Chapter 7

In the days before leaving London, Kate Marsden was riding the crest of the wave. 'The Girl's Own Paper' announced the gift of the outfit by The Directors of 'Dr Jaeger's Sanitary Woollen Systems', and portrayed Kate's thrill: 'She, who as a rule thinks so little of her own personal needs, is as delighted as a child with each article as she takes it up and shows it, testing the softness of it on her cheek.'

A beautiful little medicine chest was presented to her by Burroughs, Wellcome and Co, which wasn't too heavy and contained everything necessary for dressing wounds and ministering to the sick; while the Editor of 'The Girl's Own Paper' gave her a state-of-the-art combination aneroid barometer, thermometer and compass.

Kate could now turn her attention to the rest of the provisions for her expedition. She persuaded 'a dear English lady friend' to make her forty pounds of her favourite plum pudding, knowing it would withstand any cold weather; and now that food could be reliably packed in tins, she stocked up on sardines and biscuits, along with bread and tea. Oil wicks, which worked better than night lights, couldn't be bought in Siberia, so she bought two dozen boxes, only to be 'calmly' told she had enough there for ten years! Another friend contributed forty pounds of candles, ninety per cent of which got broken in transit. This is the only clue we have that the bulk of her luggage was shipped direct to Moscow, there to await her arrival, several months on from her long fact-finding sojourns in the Holy Land, the Ottoman realms and Georgia.

Once she had arrived in Moscow it took Kate no time to start fund raising and so what should have been a brief stay extended by mysterious means to over four months, punctuated by train visits to St Petersburg.

The stay was worth it: soon Kate received a generous gift, a thousand roubles, towards her funds from Her Imperial Majesty. This was, in todays's terms, more than enough to have fuelled my four-wheel drive vehicle from London all the way to Vilyuisk. Her greatest support at court was perhaps Countess Alexandrine Tolstoi, who did everything in her power to further Kate's plans.

At the same time, something had happened to impair Kate's unstoppable momentum, and it didn't help that on 26 February a New Zealand publication called 'Topics of the Day' printed an article that in short was biased journalism at its worst. They had scrutinised the account from 'The Queen' of Kate's visit to the lepers of Constantinople, which was very close to the one printed in 'The Girl's Own Paper', but 'Topics of the Day' used state-ments like 'it is gratifying to learn that Miss Kate Marsden, after hob-nobbing with the Princess of Wales, the Empress of Russia, and the Khediva of Egypt, has at length got among the lepers whom it is to be her mission to help'. It didn't help that during this time a London journal printed a damaging article which, when read in Moscow, created suspicion that her charitable mission was a cover for potential espionage. If any of her ex-pat acquaintances were beginning to feel unsure about her protracted presence in Moscow, and her seemingly unlikely mission, then the article furnished her detractors with some serious ammunition.

She was only too aware of the changed atmosphere calling it 'no laughing matter,' as her friends began to be aloof and avoid her. She said that she became 'uncomfortably conscious of being decid-edly under a cloud.'

The cold was beginning to get to her too, when she wrote; 'It was not pleasant to drive about in a little open sledge in a tempera-ture about -20° (fahrenheit), the wind and snow driving full in one's face, with clothes (except a shouba lent by a kind friend) only suitable for an English climate.' Did she have any idea what was in store for her when she actually left on her great journey?

Obviously the Jaeger snow suit was held in reserve for Siberia itself, or not deemed appropriate attire for Moscow streets.

Johnson's biography suggests that the idea of Nurse Marsden as a spy may have originated before entering Russia itself when she visited the military hospital in Tiflis. She had applied to the Governor of Georgia for permission to visit, which was granted in the form of a written order; from the Governor of Georgia, but on arrival, she was aware that she was an object of deep suspicion, and that the degree of assistance that she would later receive in Tomsk and Kansk, was being deliberately withheld. In addition to time absorbed in gaining further funds, Kate's book gives another clue to the delayed start, a bout of illness, coupled with what looks to us like depression. She talks of having dark days there, alone in the hotel, and of being sent food by friends and nursed when ill.

Despite this she continued to arouse interest, and I suspect a great deal of gossip, and to raise funds, which was getting harder. She writes in her book about how she did this, 'I fully stated my plans — namely, to find the herb. But, in spite of my plainness of speech (unfortunately, I could not speak a word of the Russian tongue) my motives were misconstrued, and all kinds of rumours were set afloat. Because I stayed at a hotel some people became suspicious, and looked at me askance.'

But throughout these weeks her unfailing friend and companion, Ada Field, stood by her unflinchingly. We don't know how these two ladies met and became friends. She was a missionary, based in Moscow, and fluent in Russian; beyond that, and her later assistance to Kate in North America, all too little is known. Yet she became drawn in to Kate's mission, agreeing to be her trusted companion on the long Siberian journey.

As to the illness, Kate says nothing more. There was the congenital disposition towards consumption, and the hospital fall in Wellington that left her temporarily paralysed; or it could be that the mind of this highly active woman was severely overtaxed. Had Kate become frightened of what was ahead? Were the bouts of illness associated with her nerves? Was it a case of her having gone so far that she couldn't back out, but having also heard and learnt enough from well-travelled Muscovites of the horrors ahead of her in Siberia to have got a severe case of second thoughts?

Her written account gives no clue as who was with her in Moscow and what was discussed, whether a shortfall of funds for the journey or, perhaps logistical problems facing her in Siberia, when 'we all met and discussed matters fully, we decided to go again to Prince Dolgoroukow to seek his help and advice. He offered to assist us in every way, but, in a few days, I fell ill again; and so our hopes were again dashed to the ground.'

But at last wheels began to turn to expedite her departure. The Prince and Mme Coctanda used their contacts to help her, a favourable article appeared in the 'Moscow Gazette', some new English and Russian friends sprang to her support and 'the cloud gradually broke up and drifted away'.

As the ink dried on letters of introduction from one influential person to another, Kate busied herself with final shopping. Within weeks of her period of despondency, everything was ready for the 'perilous, long, and unknown journey', and, together Ada Field and Kate Marsden boarded the train for Zlatoust, the terminus in 1891 of the lines East. She describes it as a few hundred miles from Moscow; it is in point of fact over a thousand, and even on today's Trans Siberian train the journey, stopping at Nizhniy Novgorod, Kirov, Perm and Yekaterinburg, takes thirty-two hours. It was this last city which provided a curious dogleg in Ada's and Kate's journey.

In the style that she enjoyed, Kate was met, (or indeed scooped) off the train at Zlatoust by the Head of Police and twenty police-men, the Colonel of Mounted Police, the stationmaster and a crowd of townspeople. 'It was, I need scarcely say, the letter of the Empress that caused all this attention and deference. The honour accorded was, of course, to Her Majesty, and not to me.'

She loved this fuss and pomp around her; her deflection of praise has its disingenuous side. But fuss and pomp give way to comedy in Kate's recounting of her first chaotic outing in her Jaeger chrysalis on the platform of Zlatoust station in front of so many provincial dignitaries. How, in the snow, was she to make a becoming transfer, with all eyes on her, from train to waiting sledge, when she could barely stand, let alone walk?

Kate teetered down the station steps, just about keeping her dignity, and then stood by the sledge, whose deck was some distance off the road, trying to work out how to swivel herself up onto it. There was no step to help her.

Seeing her predicament three strapping policemen attempted to lift her gently onto the sledge, but even their combined strength couldn't manage Kate in her Victorian snowsuit, so they put her down again. A second time, she tried to get in by herself, gracefully, but once more she couldn't bend her knees; so now in a final frantic and desperate effort, two burly policemen took an arm each and on a signal hoisted her in. Red with embarrassment, Kate just wanted to take off and go, as soon as Ada was deposited in the sledge in a similar manner in her similar snow-suit; but they couldn't proceed until the pair of them were safely wedged alongside their boxes and baggage. Minutes passed, and only once they had thanked the company profusely, Kate gesturing, Ada translating, and the driver and escorting soldier were seated, did they make their escape – back the way they had come. (This will be explained later.)

It was February; the harsh Siberian winter made breathing hard and ice quickly formed on the scarves tied tightly round their noses, hanging like giant fangs from their faces and adding to their discomfort in the sledge. Siberians are used to the cold, and to spending most of the year in wintery conditions, but the two Englishwomen, on the bumping and jolting sledge found their hell compounded by the sudden plummeting of the temperature to -40°.

No smooth progress was possible. The tracks they travelled along had just been traversed by a string of heavy sledges bearing consignments of goods for the Siberian Shrovetide fair, leaving the road a nightmare of snow-lumps and broken ice. The sledge lurched into holes and wallowed among the frozen crests and furrows.

'Your head seems to belong to every part of the sledge.' Kate observed. The women's heads banged against the sides and top of the sledge or were thrown violently forward against the driver, and back on the rebound.

After a few miles they ached from head to foot.

'You are bruised all over; your poor brain throbs until you give way to a kind of hysterical outcry; your headgear gets displaced; your temper, naturally, becomes slightly ruffled, and you are ready to gasp from so frequently clutching at the sides to save yourself.'

Any romantic notions of tinkling sleigh bells were quickly dispelled by her driver's constant yelling, which peaked when they tore through villages, 'alarming poor folk, who clear off, helter-skelter, pell-mell, with knitted brows and muttered observations. All the dogs, roused from their peaceful pursuits, surround you, forming a lively escort, barking, growling, fighting, and jumping snappishly at the horses' heads.'

Long into the evening and intensifying chill, the sledge drove on, never slackening in pace and with no regard for the occupants. Kate thought longingly of asphalt roads and penny omnibuses of home.

At the dead of night they pulled up at miserable huts. I have no idea how the two semi-mummified and ailing women made their descent from their tumbril (or managed to spend a penny in these circumstances). Kate was devoted to cleanliness; she was a nurse, she taught nursing, she was proud of her wards, she appreciated fresh air and the health and wholesomeness of an outdoor life. For her – and Ada while she travelled with her – these squalid shelters, filthy and fetid, can have been little improvement on the sledge; but they promised the pair with hours of stillness and, as I have found, at a pinch you can sleep anywhere.

I wanted to talk to her, and let her have her say. She was always prepared to speak to journalists, because she wanted to have the pious and humane side of her personality on record. I needed to be part of a quirky conversation, with her, to catch her animated reactions as she recreated memories of that long, fraught, exhausting journey. So I flew back through the years to meet her.

Chapter 8

ORDINARY SLEDGE TRAVELLING IN SIBERIA.

November 1892

We met at the Lyons Corner House in Piccadilly Circus, a fashionable place to be seen. Kate seemed to look through me; for all my twenty first century attire and make-up I was just another journalist. Once we had finished our introductions she watched the door and examined everyone coming in. She looked older than her years, though still tall and imposing. I'd expected to see a vibrancy in her, a carry over from that high-energy personality that had crossed Russia, but that seemed missing. My immediate reaction was she was weary; weary of life and wearier accusations.

Kate noticed the book, 'On Sledge and Horseback to Outcast Siberian Lepers', I had deliberately placed on the table, and she picked it up – was this really her? Its full-colour cover design fascinated her, and she turned it over and felt the smooth sheen of its soft cover. Then she read the twentieth century comments on the back cover: 'Kate Marsden tells her story with a passion and determination, at times displaying an endearing vulnerability and a refreshing wit.' I watched a grin break across her face that made her eyes light up. In her world of 1892, the cloth-bound first edition had only recently been published.

I waited for her to replace it on the table and then picked it up myself and turned to the page marked by a fluorescent green post-it note.

"Miss Marsden, I am interested in where you stayed in Russia on your great trip. Accommodation seemed fearfully lacking. You write in your book that you had to have a pocket handkerchief ready before entering one of the 'hotels'. How serious were you when you said that?"

The waitress had delivered a full cream tea to our table by now, I had let Kate order it, of course. She dived straight in while considering my question. I studied her face carefully as she took a good bite from a slice of beautifully moist Victoria sponge.

"You see, my dear, when I entered one of those dreadful sleeping places, the hinges creaked and my first greeting was a gust of hot, fetid air, which almost sent me back outside."

Kate's voice rose as she spoke, she was anxious to impress upon me how dreadful it all had been. The feather in her navy blue felt hat stroked the air as it jerked back and forth.

"I would remember the cold outside and the cravings of hunger, and so I would go in."

Golden yellow crumbs landed on her lap and she carefully scooped them up and popped them into her mouth.

I was enjoying having tea with her, it was a historic moment for me, although the Corner House was busy and among all the other women I stood out because I was aware of calling attention to myself with my short dress and hatless head. Nurse Kate was intimidating but agreeable, she had a well polished medal, and her brooch from the Queen, proudly pinned to her ample bosom. Her stare was impenetrable, as she leaned forward across the tablecloth and enquired:

120

"Will you donate to my leper fund?"

"Well I could do, yes." I replied, concerned as to what she would make of the coins in my purse.

"You do care about lepers, don't you? Shall I describe their symptoms to you, precisely?"

She did so anyway; but I was able to coax her back onto the topic that really interested me:

"Tell me more, please, about those roadside hotels in Siberia."

Kate took a scone from the three tiered cake stand spreading it with strawberry jam from a willow-pattern bowl.

" Ah, well, you see, what we ate for our dinner depended entirely on what we took with us. As everything in that infernal sledge was frozen it was hard to know what was what." I grinned. I enjoyed her stories; I too am an explorer, but I hadn't got anywhere near to experiencing her hardships.

"My dear girl, do you know what it is like to be that cold? At the end of a terrible day in that horrid conveyance my face was barnacled with ice and icicles and my lips and eyes were frozen and I couldn't speak, I would try to mouth a few words but I no longer had any feeling in my face. I thought every night I would die, right there in the Siberian wastelands and my body would be thrown to the wolves."

I stared at her in admiration; as far as I was concerned this woman could eat every damn cake and ham sandwich in the tea shop, or in the whole of London. Surely no other female could have such a story to tell?

"Luckily, Ada and I had the presence of mind to tie blocks of vegetable soup onto the side of the sledge and the driver would retrieve one for us and carry it into the shack of a dwelling and heat it in a pot for us."

"What a great idea." I could feel a withering look falling upon me from the under the plumed hat. It seemed churlish to tell her that these days vegetable soup came freeze-dried in handy packets.

"My dear girl, you do not have an inkling of what we had to endure. Most of the blocks of soup broke off the side, other essential foodstuffs bounced out of the sledge and we left well fed and satisfied wolves in our wake."

I raised a sympathetic eyebrow.

"Most days we had just a few dry biscuits and a glass of tea. Of course there were no waiters to bother us at these 'hotels', we had no fees to pay.

So that should relieve your mind." I smiled at her dry humour, she liked having an audience and carried on.

"There were filthy sheep-skins and rugs laid in the middle of the floor, and that is where we slept, but not on our own. One glance around the walls at the number of moving specks upon them of different sizes and families dispelled that illusion, while the probable arrival of another tardy traveller deprived us of even the comfort of a room to ourselves."

"But, Miss Marsden, at least you were warm, weren't you? You could take off a few of those cumbersome layers you were wrapped up in?"

"Oh yes, the heat of those undesirable premises was grateful and comforting at first; but, some hours before dawn, we longed for the intense cold outside, and we registered a vow that never as long as we lived would we enter such a stifling hole again. But, alas for human constancy! The very next night, or perhaps for many nights, we would eagerly seek the shelter of one of these warm structures, and sleep soundly, until awakened by a sensation of approaching suffocation." She took out her pocket watch and checked the time, I wondered where her next assignation would be.

"Before you go, Miss Marsden, can you tell me what you saw around you, just a little bit about being on the sledge, if you don't mind."

She looked at me long and hard, probably wondering why I wore my thick, long blonde hair in such an unruly fashion, hanging down my back. Surely it should be pinned up in a tight bun – and where was my hat? As confusion played out in her mind her eyes showed here was the opportunity to retell her experiences, again, so as to dispel the unkind rumours that she had made it all up. All the years of being called mad and bad, I could see, had taken their toll . . .

"Sometimes we saw a wolf standing against the dense forest, but they didn't molest us."

What a great lady.

"Sometimes we came to a large lake, which we had to glide over, meeting, now and then, a few men, who had cut holes in the lake, and were lying on the ice, fishing. They were Russian peasants who sat and reclined on blocks of ice as if they were feather beds."

This is great, fabulous stuff.

122

Russian watch belonging to Kate Marsden
Date: 1890 – 1899

"*We passed many dirty villages that had broad streets, and on either side wooden houses, made of the trunks of trees, plastered round thickly with stable refuse. Although this simple method has the advantage of shutting out the wind and frost, it also shuts in all the foul smells. It is a marvel how those villagers exist at all and bring up families in such unwholesome dwellings. As to the cows, from which the people derive their chief nourishment, they are as quiet and as patient as the peasants themselves. They always seem to be in one's way when passing through a village, and endure, with total calm, a sudden collision with the sledge, or the sharp crack of the driver's whip.*"

Poor Kate, she went through so much and then had to spend the rest of her life convincing people, like me, that she had really made this terrible journey. How many other journalists had she met up with and repeated the same stories to?

Suddenly her eyes flashed and she dragged a letter out of her bag. I was impressed by the thick cream vellum envelope and the way she carefully pulled a letter written in the same crisp notepaper out to it. She proudly handed it to me to read.

"Miss Marsden! What do we have here? It's from Her Majesty the Queen!" When I read it aloud, her face beamed with pride and once more she was the tall, exuberant lady who wanted people to like her.

'Balmoral Castle, October 27th 1892

The Queen has taken a deep interest in the work undertaken by Miss Marsden amongst the lepers and desires to recommend her to the attention and consideration of any persons whose assistance she may have occasion to require in connection with her benevolent efforts in the cause of humanity.

Henry Ponsonby

General and Private Secretary to the Queen.'

"Miss Marsden, I am so impressed." I slipped it gently back in its envelope. She continued to beam.

I paid the bill to the waitress, the Corner House decor was so modern, resplendent in its Aesthetic decor, but my eyes were smarting from the smoke in the airless room and I was glad to leave. I was relieved that Kate hadn't smoked, but everyone else had been, even with their children sitting closely beside them.

She disappeared into the crowds and her century in the bustling London street; another assignation accomplished that gave her the opportunity to recreate the past, – but would I believe her, and write favourable words? The milky skin and sad slanting eyes, the way she had smoothed her dress with such vigour, casting her eyes around the crowded room searchingly . . . when she stood up to go, I noticed how her hatted and statuesque figure had turned the heads of men and women in the room.

I knew something that she would never know though, that the very next day after sending her that letter Sir Henry Ponsonby received a letter from Mr Kellog saying *"I am told that the Russians who came across her thought her half mad."* I also knew that Ponsonby would write a second letter on the 29th, indicating that certain suggestions about Kate Marsden's conduct and reputation were not being brought to her Majesty's attention.

Dear Lord Brislow,

'It was very good of you to warn us about Miss Marsden and I hope that financially we shall occur no risk. But H.M. is much taken with her work among the lepers which has indeed induced the Czar to take up the question and has done some real good for those unfortunate outcasts and Princess Christian, advised by Dr Fenwick assures the Queen that the occurrences in New Zealand were misrepresented.'

He then suggests that Lord Brislow concentrate on his ongoing investigation into the Salvation Army instead. "Your arrangement of matters to be explained by the Booths are very well done."

Perhaps, in considering these two Ponsonby letters together, we may sense a growing alertness to potential scams implicating Victoria. Whatever mud was supposed to be sticking to Catherine and William Booth, they stepped out spotless. Kate Marsden, on the other hand, guilty or innocent, was heading into a wave of defamation which would do its best to obliterate her.

Chapter 9

THE LAST STAGE OF THE JOURNEY IN BREAKING-UP SEASON.

To face page 163.

"Sure he was great, but don't forget Ginger Rogers did everything he did backwards . . . and in high heels!"

Bob Thaves, on Fred Astaire 1982

Picture Kate's and my expeditions time-travelling in parallel along
much the same route into Siberia. Mine, that is to say Ellie and my
own, starting from Tomsk, is making its way by train to Irkutsk,
where we'll wait, hoping for Kate to catch us up. But there's a
slight problem, and Kate isn't being entirely helpful.

In her book, she definitively states that she took the Moscow
train as far as Zlatoust, yet in her account of those first few
hundred awful miles in a sledge in the grip of a Siberian winter
she is clearly heading back north to Yekaterinburg or, as she then
wrote, Ekaterinberg, the penultimate station on the line. These
days Yekaterinburg is an important railway junction on the
Trans-Siberian Railway and the fourth largest *city* in *Russia*. The
beautiful dusty-pink station, resplendent as a wedding cake with
its charming chequered roof, dating from 1878, for a few years
formed the terminus of the great line Eastward. Kate had business
to do, and contacts to make, my puzzle long remained, why
hadn't the two women alighted at Yekaterinberg instead of
putting themselves through a hellish backtrack of 166 miles by
sledge? All we get from Kate is a gentle wisecrack, long after the
actual event:

'What is known as the short cut from Zlatoust to Ekaterinberg
a good deal resembles an Irishman's mile. On being asked how
long his mile was the Irishman replied, 'For sure, 'tis a mile and a
half, your honour; but maybe 'tis longer if ye wish it.'

A thoughtful solution, albeit tentative, comes from someone
with a great knowledge of Kate Marsden and her history in Russia.
The man in question is Edward, an intelligent and charismatic
Muscovite whose sleeve tattoos, shaven temples and long-pony
tail would have sent the Victorian spinster spinning. I was instantly
captivated by his thoughtful charm and sheer good sense, as he
explained that in the early days (1890 and beyond) those expresses
on their way to the new rail-head at Zlatoust, didn't actually stop

at Ekaterinberg, also, the Zlatoust dignitaries had gone to some trouble to stage a civic welcome for Kate and Ada, which Kate had been forewarned of and would not have wanted to miss.

Timetables of around 1890 reveal that stopping trains that included Ekaterinberg were few and far between; and that is the reason for the apparently illogical routing. In the event, Ekaterinberg would prove an advantageous detour, though it is a matter of record that Kate's first encounter of travelling by sledge, like her subsequent forays, left her in dire need of recuperation.

On arriving at Ekaterinberg, they stayed at the American Hotel, which Kate immediately took to. She also loved the fuss made of her by Baron Taube, the city's Chief of Police. She recovered from sledge-life soon enough to visit the prison. She was not impressed, observing that it was 'not the best of its kind'. The rattling of the prisoners' chains, extending from their waist to ankles, was a sound she would never forget. In the city she found some old acquaintances, although we don't know where they first met, Mr Yates, Mr Wardroper and his son-in-law who was agent for the Bible Society. It was the son-in-law that recommended that she and Ada travel on via the big trade fair at Irbit,where she would encounter a merchant from Yakutsk with important information about the lepers in that region.

The thoughtful Baron Taube lent the two women a soldier called Popoff, as escort. He 'proved a worthy representative of his master.' For Popoff, the Jaeger travelling chrysalis was no impediment to Kate mounting or descending from the sledge: when they stopped and Kate signalled she wanted to get down, Popoff just let her slide into his arms. If there were awkward steps to be negotiated, he took her by the arm and led her up them, and helped remove her outer furs and high boots before asking what more he could do. She remembered him with affection.

He had a habit of standing before Kate, saluting and saying, 'Slushayous' (I obey your orders). His delicate attention and anxiety to serve her would have touched any woman; Kate was deeply susceptible. After taking his meals, consisting generally of black bread and scraps, he would come into her room saying, 'I humbly thank you.' Kate was very taken with this treatment and wrote: 'Yes, I do love those enduring, hard-working, splendid Russian soldiers; I would trust that one with my life any day.'

When Kate and Ada arrived in Irbit, 124 miles away, they stayed in a strange room that had one bed and two 'crazy' chairs, but no bedding. Considering that Kate's passionate fund-raising was ultimately extinguished by imputations of lesbianism, this should be an opportunity to comment on that. But we have absolutely nothing to stick on her, while Ada remained the squeaky-clean missionary throughout her life. We can never, ever know any such details.

Irbit, in the years up to 1900 the home of the biggest fairground in Imperial Russia has since changed dramatically. With the fairground long gone, it is renowned as a producer of dairy products, cakes and motorcycles for the Russian nation.

When Ada and Kate sledged in, a messenger was instantly dispatched to locate the merchant from Yakutsk. When he was found and informed that a woman was travelling that way he would have none of it. A woman would – for goodness' sake – never be able to face up to 'the sheer difficulty of the journey'. What changed his mind was the suggestion that the woman was going with God, and not relying on her own stamina to get there! The merchant seems to have been overawed, but he told her all he knew about the lepers. As for the herb, he had nothing to tell her.

Kate bought a sledge at Irbit: it was cheaper to own one than to keep hiring at each new stage. The drivers she did hire, stage by stage; she needed their local knowledge. In terms of comfort, owning the sledge didn't make it any easier; she describes the 100-mile ride to Tjumen as the worst sledging she had yet experienced. The main problem was the potholes; her new driver, though, was conscientious, pulling up to examine each major hole before negotiating it. Kate, watching anxiously, reckoned that the situation was so bad that there was a real risk at any minute of driver, soldier, and payload all being thrown out of the sledge in 'chaotic confusion'. It wasn't just the potholes bumping them about; some of the 'snow-boulders' were so big as to resemble the remains of ancient buildings.

The young driver may have been careful, but in other well-known ways he turned out to be as dodgy as a city cab driver. Under the cover of dusk, he diverted them eight miles off the official route so that they eventually arrived in Tjumen in a wretched state. This diversion was made in the middle of the night, when the reliable Popoff saw what had happened and remonstrated with the errant driver, he covered himself with the shirty riposte, 'I shan't charge you anything extra.'

As Kate wrote: 'Remember, please, it was night, with a waste, howling wilderness of snow all round, and no human habitation within many miles.'

Popoff, suffering the same pangs of cold, hunger and confusion as his two charges, replied, 'But we don't want you to make us a present of the extra eight miles. We insist on going where you are ordered to take us.' At this the driver became plain awkward, and when Popoff issued a warning on Kate and Ada's behalf, he threw the reins over the horses' backs, dismounted, and presented himself at the side of the sledge. 'Look here,' said he, 'this is your sledge, and those are my horses; if you don't want to go where I am driving you to, I can just take out the horses and go home.'

'Here was a prospect for two benighted women', Kate continues, 'to find our way on foot into the government road again, tramping through unknown depths of snow, and then walk on to the nearest post-station, or else remain in the sledge all night by ourselves, while the soldier went off for horses.'

Popoff, simmering down, managed at last to strike the right note to bring the youthful driver to his senses: he remounted, shook the reins, and plunged them off in the direction he had been ordered to take.

'On arriving at the village the soldier wanted to report the fellow for his misconduct. Then came repentance. The 'pirate' dropped on his knees, grovelled on the ground, and begged and implored us to forgive him. Then it came out that he was only obeying his master's orders, and that these self employed drivers have a knavish way of taking the traveler by circuitous routes, and charging for the extra distance. We let the youth off, but vowed we would shun the pirates forever after.'

The day got better as they received a 'hearty English welcome' in Tjumen from another Mr and Mrs Wardroper.* Kate refers to the Wardropers as her English friends, but that is we know about them, there is no clue as to what continent they became friends.

'We sat down, travel stained, bruised, and ill, to a hot supper, and were afterward sent off for a night's rest. We tumbled on to the soft and dainty bed just as we were, and soon fell asleep. On awaking a little reflection was necessary before being able to realise our surroundings. What had become of the sheep-skin, the dirty floor, the fetid air, the vermin, and the rest? Ah! indeed, Mr. Wardroper's house as a little heaven, compared to the places where we had usually passed the nights.'

Well rested for once, Kate appreciated the old town of Tjumen with its 'long, broad streets and several churches, generally painted white, with green domes, giving them a bright and fresh appearance.' It set her up for a visit to the hospital, which (obviously back on form) she slated as the worst she'd ever encountered, citing her experiences of 'clean, bright English hospitals'. Once more, in Tjumen, she could assume the authority of a hospital inspector. In an aside she admits the severity of her judgment, but restates her criteria, good level of cleanliness, ventilation, and management; besides, (here, very much the post-Nightingale nurse) she wanted to see precautions were being taken to isolate infectious patients to preclude cross-infection.

News of Kate's arrival quickly spread. Almost at once she found herself involved in an environmental scandal. The Wardropers

---

* In a short article she wrote and reprinted in 'What we did for the Russians' by Michael Skinner, she mentions that Ada and her had a black collie with a white tail with them. The dog is never heard of again on this journey.

took Kate and Ada Field to visit a school they were building in a nearby village (she doesn't tell us its name). This conjures up images of Kate listening to the children reading, but this happy interlude was interrupted by a man running in, having seen the Red Cross emblem on the sledge outside. Through Ada, he begged Kate to listen to him; she sensed the urgency as he implored her to do the village a service. He told her that the river was being so polluted by a paper mill ten miles upstream that the village was doomed. Kate, rising to the challenge, went to the river, tasted and smelt the water, and determined that it was not fit for either man or beast.

'On returning to the village a striking and unexpected scene awaited me. The people cried and implored me to help them, bowed down and pleaded, as I never knew people could plead, saying that the cattle refused to drink the water, that men, women, and children were ill from it, and that they had to walk four and six miles to the nearest village for every drop of water, unless they used melted snow, for men and cattle.'

The man explained that the villagers were dreading summer's arrival: they surmised they would all die. In the gravity of the situation the old men bowed their heads, the young ones looked up to her with appeals in their earnest faces, and the women wailed and gestured imploringly while some families had been established in the village for three centuries, and moving away meant ruin and desolation for them.

'I wonder,' Kate wrote, 'what English peasants would have done under similar circumstances, and with no one to help them. No, I don't wonder; I know what they would do first. The offending paper mill would not have the chance of poisoning the water for another day. But here were some 300 people, apparently being ruined and starved by the despotic selfishness of one man, and they were all as powerless to help themselves as any baby.'

It surprised even Kate that, in Siberia, she had so swiftly become involved in issues involving polluted rivers. Her involvement resonates with me. 120 years on, I would be drawn in to acting to help to save the last wooden hospital in Siberia. The humility with which the Tjumen villagers threw themselves on her capabilities touched her. They crowded round her, begging to see her signed photograph of the Empress, 'peering shyly at the picture, some with open mouths, others in a reverent attitude, with uncovered heads, many with half-starved, weary faces, was a scene which would at least have pleased artistic eyes, and touched tender hearts at the Royal Academy.'

She was touched when they cried as she left with Mr Wardroper to take a look at the offending mill. A friendship had been forged. It was an intensely cold and windy morning, the horses' coats were frosted, and icicles hung from their nostrils and mouths, from the driver's moustache and (Kate noted) Ada's veil. After seven tiring miles they reached the paper mill, where she saw for herself what the villagers had reported. The raw chemicals used to scour the filthy rags were indeed released directly into the river.

What luck to have your cause espoused by someone with Kate's passion and love of action. It only took a group of villagers to arrive, early the next morning, outside the Wardroper's house with a petition to the Governor expressing the depth of their plight to get her, Popoff and Ada packing the sledge for Tobolsk so that she could catch the Governor himself and plead the villagers' cause.

Mrs Wardroper kindly came in her own sledge as far as the river, to see Kate and Ada off; in an unusually wistful aside, Kate wondered whether she would ever see another English face (apart, of course, from the faithful Ada) in 'this vast wild Siberia'.

It is quite beyond our imagination in an age of luxury travel, to picture the depth of these two women's discomfort, their deprivation and sense of danger, and the trust they needed to place in complete strangers in conditions of such extreme cold. Even in a modern Land Rover, (had we had that good fortune), it would have been gruelling. As far as Kate and Ada were concerned, any element of adventure was systematically beaten out of them in the onward course of their journey. The jarring forward motion made them ill. From Tjumen on the Tobolsk trail, the young driver was inclined to give the horses their heads, which made things worse for the passengers. The women were increasingly bumped about in the sledge and frequently hurtled into snowdrifts.

'The snow soon found its way into every corner of the sledge, which, although covered at the top, was quite open in front. Then the snow had a way of settling down the collars of our coats, and, when melted by the heat of the body, trickling down the neck; and sometimes it flew up the sleeves unless we were careful to keep them closed at the wrists. Our good substantial boxes were all stowed away in the 'hold'; over them was a layer of straw, and on the straw we sat, or rather, reclined, with pillows at our backs. The word 'reclined' suggests ease and comfort; but, when applied to sledge-travelling, under the circumstances that we travelled, it means 'Hobson's choice.' You are compelled to put yourself, or get put, into that position; and in that position you must remain.'

The women endured this motion for many hours; but once more it was the driver who gave them most cause for concern. This one, in Kate's eyes was a specimen of 'Young Siberia', and as the approach of dusk only seemed to make him more reckless Kate attributed this to three causes, the biting cold, poor adjustment of the harness to the horses' stature, and the pulls the youth was taking on his vodka flask.

As night became pitch-black the women began to share their worries. Kate had an ominous feeling that something bad was about to happen.

She would tell her friends, the Norris sisters, of this moment, and its immediate outcome, in years to come.

Chapter 10

October 1912

A persistent damp mist crawling off the English Channel along with intermittent rain had kept the two Norris sisters and their lodger, Kate Marsden, inside the large white house, with its ivied walls, all day. Behind the mock tudor gable and narrow windows, veiled by a willow tree were gloomy lamplit rooms where the spinsters whiled away their days with their drawing and writing; particularly letters, because the trio were planning to open a museum, here in this seaside town of Bexhill-on-Sea.

Now in her early fifties, the smooth patina of Kate Marsden's brow was fading along with the brightness in her eyes. Not very often these days did she recall her adventurous past, but as if released by a spell, tonight she had talked to them about the great continent she had crossed, the delighted Norris sisters were quick to react.

"Oh Alice," said Emily Norris, "do let's have a port; and Miss Marsden, please tell us another tale from Russia, I'm in the mood for stories after a day like this."

Kate sat up and removed her gloves. A good sign! The sisters had often sensed that Kate had difficulty relaxing in the house, sitting nervously on the edge of a seat in the parlour wearing her hat, staring out of the window, walking towards the door as if to go out, only to change her mind and sit back down.

"The port has all gone, how about a sherry, let's all have one." A small shock-wave resonated around the room, one of them gave a childish giggle; there had been little to alleviate the tedium of their lives for some months now, and having a small drink in the evening was a secret pleasure; just that little bit naughty in a time of hardships or tedium.

The fire snapped and crackled in the grate. Everything was spotless; even the fire-set on the hearth gleamed to perfection. Alice Norris's water colours, bright and simple, adorned the walls. The pebble-dashed house proclaimed clean and respectable: there was no scurrilous gossip within these walls, no rumour-mongering. Here lived three unmarried women whose lives cannot be faulted. Often the past is another world, one whose door-handle Emily, Alice and Kate don't turn: it gives too many disappoint-ments just sometimes, a seed of intrigue germinates in the still and airless house and Kate's personality can once more shine, her matronly spirit, the recollections of that mission to rescue the lepers, raised its head. Here, between these walls, is, the woman who promoted exacting standards on her wards and lectured training to miners till now unable, with First Aid, to save their injured colleagues' lives. Here is the woman who has seen things that no one else has seen, experienced cold like few other humans, held the hands of brave soldiers as they died in terrible pain. No longer can this tall woman, with straight back and chin held high, walk into polished wards and enquire "how are we all?" Now her thoughts are internalised, and as her shoulders gently slope with age; she has been crushed by the very people who should have believed in her. It has become easier to remain quiet, criticism only ever hurt her, and for all her outward robustness her mental health has always been delicate.

Alice watched Kate sit up and take the small glass Emily handed her, in her hand. There was a glimmer in that gesture of the figure she had once been. Now, quietly clearing her throat, she re-experienced her pleasure in being asked to retell a story from her past, once glorious, buoyed up by passion, but now piously folded and laid in the drawer.

Alice and Emily were kind, they liked to please; the best glasses they delicately picked out from the glass-fronted cabinet would be washed up, dried, polished and placed back on the shelf by fastidious Alice long before Kate had relinquished the hold on hers.

"Did I ever tell you about the horses in Russia? They were treated so badly – by drivers who knew nothing about horses."

"Emily, have you heard about the horses in Russia?"

"No, Alice. Miss Marsden, I'm sure, has never told us about that. I should love to hear."

"I know I've mentioned it, the terrible night drive from Tjumen to Tobolsk; this was when the poor horses suffered so terribly. I wish I could have helped them, but my body ached so badly. I was too cold to move; my *words were frozen in my mouth. We raced so fast, through very deep snow, through the night, it wasn't a good time to travel and I knew that something awful was about to happen, and, I somehow knew it would involve the poor horses. The harnesses were not properly attached and I'd been aware for hours of the rattle of leather and metal banging against the wooden sledge; the two outer horses were in harnesses designed for much bigger horses, and all three of them were in danger of getting their legs entangled in those odds and ends of ropes which were supposed to tie them together.*

Suddenly, the middle horse disappeared, making the driver lurch forward, followed by a bump and a thump against the sledge, as another horse disappeared and we came to a complete standstill. Ada and I . . ."

Emily had leant forward and caught Kate's eye. "forgive me, Miss Marsden, that's Miss Field, your missionary companion who translated for you?"

"Yes, indeed; I do rush on so! Miss Field and I were instantly alerted by an ominous knocking against the side of the sledge and on looking out we found two of the four horses entangled in the ropes on the ground, struggling frantically to get up."

Alice and Emily caught each other's eye, it was inconceivable to their simple suburban minds that this could have happened to such a gentle woman.

Kate continued her story.

"But the driver called out, "Nichivo", or 'it is nothing' in English, but it didn't feel like nothing to us. No amount of "nichivoeing" prevented my feeling very uneasy indeed. Popoff - "

"Oh Miss Marsden, one moment - " interjected Alice, "isn't that the soldier seconded to you by the Provincial Governor?"

"Yes, Miss Norris," Kate replied, "by now our faithful Popoff had jumped down off the box, and there he stood bellowing at the horses, the driver, and the state of the road; then, finding that this failed to help matters much, he began to spit at the horses. Oh, if it hadn't been for the freezing temperature I would have done something; but even our soldier, there for our protection, could only stand on the sidelines, mouthing his curses! Ada translated my rather peremptory order to both men, at least shut off the rain of abuse before it came to blows."

The Norris sisters tutted earnestly; when Alice rose to bank up the fire, Emily put out an arm, to let Kate resume her story.

"By now the wretched horses were upset at being jammed against the sledge and pinioned by the ropes, for their struggles became more decided so the soldier stood on one of their necks, and the driver got its harness free. It was cruel, but it seemed to work; they then untangled the second horse in the same way; but strangely, the driver was too angry with it to drive it any more; and just let it go, and away it trotted, looking very strange in the half snowy half-light, with the harness dangling all around it.

Ada and I laughed at this, although it was scarcely a laughing matter; we were quite vulnerable, it was the middle of the night, deathly cold and we were going nowhere. The miserable driver tugged painfully at the remaining horses, secured them back together and away we went again. But I sensed that something else would happen; Ada agreed.

Sure enough, soon after we had set off again calamity struck. We heard a great deal of shouting ahead and one of those giant long-distance freight sledges loomed out of the night and hurtled straight at us. The driver and Popoff yelled at the top of their voices, but it was too late and we prepared ourselves for a terrible crash! But instead of hitting us the pony leading the other team took fright and swerved, just enough – and so we were all flown into a deep ditch full of snow. Dear me, it all happened in a flash, and there we all were in the ditch, horses, sledge and payload too, unable to move an inch.

Oh, it was horrible, lying helplessly in the snow, to hear the horses, writhing and lashing and tugging at their tangled harness, and on top of that the yelling of the two men. Ada called up to Popoff, what do you want us to do? he replied "Stay where you are, ladies." But it was one in the morning and we had no intention of staying there till another sledge came by, and managed to scramble out, up to our knees in soft snow, and stood shivering; two forlorn, lost creatures, waiting to be rescued.

The freight sledge simply didn't stop – surprise. By now it was just a distant trail of noises in the night.

Being bigger than poor Ada, I stood so as to shelter her from the bitter wind, while the men flogged those poor horses and shouted at them as we looked on. Oh I wish I could have done anything to help, but how could I trussed up in my damn Jaegar, frozen to the bone, and aching all over?

But then the driver ran off into the night to try and find our missing horse; he was gone at least half an hour, but the shrewd animal must have distanced itself from all the human racket. When he got back he hit the horses once more, those blows that fell on their backs went to our hearts. But everything has its ending and, at last, with one mighty effort, horses and sledge heaved themselves out of the ditch. We packed ourselves away into the sledge and set off again, one horse short.

Looking back now, I can't believe it, but things got even worse. Soon we found ourselves bumping over a roughly ploughed field, scantily covered, because the snow had blown into huge mounds. Round and round these mounds we wandered, almost like traversing a maze, only it wasn't funny any more.

Then we came to a steep hill leading down to the river and I woke Ada just in time for her to catch a glimpse of the same wretched horse, who had been the leader in the first mutiny give a jerk and break the harness in three places, thus setting himself free. Then we went full tilt down on to the frozen river with the free horse keeping up us with the harness dangling behind. We expected another catastrophe any moment, and hardly knew whether to laugh or to cry. On reaching the river, the driver got down, tied all the horses back together, abused them some more, and then tore away again.

From here on, we thought we might be "out of the wood". How wrong we were! We weren't to know it, but the driver was nursing an almighty rage, completely oblivious to our comfort. As we raced through a sleeping village, one of the middle horses tumbled, and we found ourselves wedged in other snowdrift. Another war of words arose between Popoff and driver. "They are not horses, but demons!" the youth yelled, as blow after blow fell on the jaded horses' backs.

We got out of the muddle then and we got to our post-station at two in the morning, greeting that hard, dirty floor with exhausted delight and slept, despite the odd baby crying, for a good five hours, dead to the other travellers of all ages and both sexes, prostrate around us.

"Men and women in the same room, whatever next?" Alice remarked, Emily fidgeting with the lace trim on her sleeve reassured her sister.

"What else could they do? There's little in any of Miss Marsden's tales that could be anything like our day to day lives here."

Kate smiled searching their faces. Alice, stared back; wondering how such an extraordinary woman came to be living under the same roof as themselves.

"*The worst thing about those rest houses wasn't sleeping in the same room as the men; that didn't bother us.*"

"*Yes, but Miss Marsden, what was it then?*" Emily asked.

"*Well, can you imagine a room full of unwashed people, wrapped up in grubby sheepskins sleeping and breathing all night without a chink of ventilation?*"

A little suppressed "*ergh*" came from Alice, as with her back to them, she raked the embers. "*The smell, it must have been awful!*"

"*Exactly,*" replied Kate, "*and each morning Ada and I swore we would NEVER do it again, and yet we always did, that very evening.*"

"*Another world; I don't understand it at all.*" Alice said quietly.

There was a pause when no one spoke, the eyes of both sisters falling in pity and admiration on their lodger.

In the silence, the fire sulked and sank, its bright blaze giving way to a cold chill – like the sun going down and winter coming on.

"*Thank you, Miss Marsden,*" whispered Alice "*that was a truly memorable story.*"

One wonders of the dreams of the gentle Norris sisters that night, after such a graphic night-time story.

Chapter 11

"The difficulty is what takes a little time; the impossible is what takes a little longer"

Fridtjof Nansen

It took another day of hard travelling to reach Tobolsk and Kate and Ada arrived at midnight. She must have been as thrilled as we were on our modern journey to be told that the Governor, had booked her a hotel room in the town. She was hoping that something really nice was in store for them and when they spotted a large brick building she said, "Just the thing Ada, look at it." Unfortunately this was the Governor's house and the sledge carried straight on past it. Forever the optimist she presumed something just as nice would loom up around the next bend – but instead the sledge slithered into the dirty yard behind a rambling, down-at-heel wooden structure. This was their hotel. 'Grieving over baffled hopes', as Kate puts it, they were shown upstairs to a stiflingly hot room with just one bed. Evidently, Siberian hospitality took the phrase 'A warm welcome' literally, to the extent that the Tobolsk landlord had concreted-in the window casements, 'in order to destroy the remotest chance of fresh air entering', Kate tells us.

The stifling, airless room made both women feel ill. The single mattress, as grimy as the post-station fleeces, and the lack of sheets hardly inviting; but the first thing was to get some air in. The sound of breaking glass might cause a commotion; luckily, though, there was a ready-broken pane sealed with paper, which she eased off to create a small hole, enough to let a healing stream of clean, cold air into the fetid chamber. Ada and Kate, much perked up, managed a comfortable night's sleep – on the bedroom floor!

Their mission to the Governor, to deliver and back up the villagers' petition about their polluted river, went well. He invited them to stay to lunch, and promised to conduct his own investigation – which, ultimately redressed the villagers' grievance. The 124 mile detour to the North, not part of Kate's original plan, seemed to have paid off; but now they must make up lost time, braving late February temperatures of between 0° to -30°c. To get back on track at Omsk, their route took them via Tyukalinsk, but in the meantime there was a long succession of villages to pass through.

Kate had the Red Cross emblazoned on her sledge to make clear that her mission's connection with the Russian Red Cross Society. In any village the team arrived at for rest or refreshment. 'As soon as they knew that I was a sister of charity, they used to press into the little room where we were having our tea, bringing their sick and suffering for help. As much as I could I ministered to their bodies, while my friend,(Ada as missionary) spoke to them of the great Physician.'

Kate also addressed the eager audience with Ada. 'It was often a motley group: grey haired men and women, bowed with age; young people, looking on with curious, inquiring looks; children in their quaint frocks and tunics, all trying to catch a glimpse of our faces.' They happily accepted the little New Testaments that they were proffered. She revelled in their attention, mediated as it was through shared religion. It made her aware of her uniqueness: 'The thought came to me that perhaps no woman missionary had passed this way,' and tells us that she prayed God to make full use of bringing the people in her path so she could spread the glad tidings of great joy.

Later in the journey, Ada spotted that the sledge-driver, too, could read, and gave him his own copy of the Gospel. Gradually the great store of testaments depleted, lowering the sledge's payload.

Religion was playing an important part in this dangerous journey, the women needed solace in it increasingly as they drove deeper into the Siberian winter and a strange and unknown world. But the Siberian winter and its perils and discomforts were driving deeper into the pair – to near breaking point, in the event. There was no let-up for either of them, such as there would be for us with the suspension, air-con and heaters in a reliable four-wheel drive vehicle.

No amount of praying and preaching was making it any easier and before they had reached Tukalinsk Ada's health was giving Kate cause for concern. She herself was not well; the road seemed to be deteriorating and, psychologically, there was no respite from the vast nothingness of relentless snow-and-ice strewn forest.

At last in Tukalinsk they found it had been arranged for them to stay at a well-to-do peasant's house; the post-station was too dirty for human habitation! They had to be led up the steps by soldiers but were relieved to find a comfortable room, resembling one in an English farmhouse. At first they were too battered to speak, or even undress, but after drinking some coffee they slept like logs – Ada on the sofa, Kate on the floor, out of pity for the younger and frailer woman.

They slept, exhausted into the following afternoon and then, before nightfall, made a tour of the town in a hired sledge. Kate called it 'a queer little place, with the houses all tumbled together, built of solid trunks of trees. The greater part of the population consisted of convicts,' exiled, like later generations in Siberia, from their homes and occupations in metropolitan Russia.

Special visitors were a rare occurrence in Tukalinsk, that evening the mayor held a grand function on their behalf. A man of portly build, he welcomed them in full dress, with Mayoral chain, sword, braided jacket, and white kid gloves, flanked by four doctors. In a former life, Kate would have loved this such an occasion, in the company of doctors; but for her and Ada the atmosphere was marred by the furious smoking of the Russians in yet another sealed room, and after four hours the women's throats and heads ached from the talking, the smoke and the heat. But before they were escorted back to their airier quarters it was agreed that next morning the five gentlemen would escort their guests on a visit to the prisoners.

One of the doctors was actually a vet and he gave her a beautiful model church, which had been crafted by two convicts with an old knife in a dark cell at the prison; it can't have survived the journey back, because it isn't mentioned again.

The snow-storm raging when they visited the prison didn't deter Kate; and she describes what she saw with her usual gusto and critical eye. 'The place was built to hold seventy; but the usual number of prisoners is 200.' The floors were rotten from damp, and there were neither ventilation nor toilet facilities. No English woman had ever visited it before, nor, (in all probability) would again, and memories of Kate squeezing her way through the dark corridors of chained prisoners lingered in the inmates' minds, fading with the years like the New Testaments she handed out. She had no hesitation in describing Tukalinsk Gaol as terrible.

Kate's attitude towards the chained prisoners came from the perspective of a wealthy woman, which is how the Russians saw her. She had somehow assumed the persona of a well-to-do, well connected English lady, who visited prisons and she criticised them as a presumed expert. But privately she was asking God what He would do if He too could witness these terrible scenes, of men chained together in airless and cramped conditions. She decided that He would want their material wants catered for before offering the 'Bread of Life', so she reached their hearts by giving them a cup of tea, or fresh tea leaves and sugar for them to make one, and left with a kind word. She was a memorable visitor, but she wasn't there to change the order of things. This, after all, was their lot, as it was the lepers.

The eighty-eight miles from Tukalinsk to Omsk nearly finished the women off. Apart from their new driver also hitting the vodka, there were no actual incidents; but the journey was long, cold and uncomfortable. But at their final overnight stop, their spirits soared when a soldier arrived telling them that the Governor of Omsk, General Sannikoff, had prepared rooms for them in his own house. This was good news for them and Kate writes humorously about it: 'for we were in no way reluctant to renew our acquaintance with feather beds'. But on a more serious note she writes that on arrival they were both in need of a doctor. They therefore ended up staying two weeks at the Governor's house and were delighted at the way they were treated as members of his family. For Kate, the protracted stay served as a convalescence; for Ada, though, the outlook was different. Even after receiving full medical attention and rest, it became obvious she was in no condition to carry on.

For Kate, losing Ada Field must have been a major blow. What is known of her prior life goes into three meagre sentences: she had worked as a missionary in Moscow, she spoke Russian and she came from Buxton. She remained a loyal supporter to Kate all her life; her respect for her is evident from the interview she gave to 'The Woman's Herald' newspaper on return to England to raise funds for Kate's work in Siberia.

She would accompany Kate on her North-American venture a couple of years later, and she was well – and enthusiastic – enough to be at Zlatoust to greet Kate and accompany her back to Moscow, after the accomplishments of the mission. That in itself constitutes a valiant act of friendship.

> 'Surely Stanley in darkest Africa pales before her. He had company, she will have none; and only up to a certain point will there be any decent means of travelling.'
>
> 'The Girl's Own Paper', 1891

It didn't enter Kate's mind to give up, though without Ada for support she left Omsk with a heavy heart. Travelling east across Siberia was going to become far more demanding: not only had Ada been her interpreter, simply having another woman with her had been a source of comfort, someone to laugh and cry with.

After the vodka-swilling sledge driver from Tukalinsk the Governor-General wasn't taking any chances and he telegraphed the Governor of Tomsk for a special officer to accompany her to Tomsk. He arrived after travelling from Tomsk in four days, Kate used this time to visit hospitals and prisons and perhaps, as Ada Field suggests, encountering her first Siberian lepers. He arrived and Kate notes that 'He could speak French and a little English, and, being also thoroughly well versed in his own language, all fears of future emergencies disappeared.'

Despite the Governor's precautions the 500 mile journey to Tomsk didn't go as planned. The new driver, too, liked his vodka and they hadn't gone far before an incident left her feeling vulnerable. With a sharp crack a piece of harness broke, bringing them to an abrupt stop; the man from Tomsk was ahead in his own sledge and neither noticed or stopped. The soldier with her disappeared with the affected horse and its harness, leaving Kate and the suspect driver together. It was a still, quiet, snowy night. Despite her helplessness, sleep overtook her, only to find, on opening her eyes, another drunken man standing over her: luckily, a Yemstchick, or driver of a freight sledge that had been passing who had stopped out of concern, she expresses her feeling of vulnerability by writing: 'and so, putting two and two together, the suspicion arose that desperate robbers, lurking in the forest, would suddenly pounce upon me. At such times, real and imaginary dangers intermix.I thought that my men deserting me was only part of a conspiracy, and my mind dwelt on the fact that I was in the land of convicts, 40,000 of them being sent hither every year. The hour of suspense seemed six hours; but at last the soldier returned with the horse, with new harness. It was put in its place, and we started off again.'

The full moon revealed a large patch of blood-stained snow where a dead horse lay, sending a shudder through her. It was partly eaten and ripped apart in an ugly way. This was not an unusual sight on her journey; when a horse in this wilderness became exhausted and couldn't go on, it was unharnessed and left for dogs or wolves to finish off, though the drivers did say that if an overworked horse recovered, it would find its way home in due course.

These facts of Siberian life would have been particularly upsetting to the girl from Edmonton who had kept ponies, and loved them as friends.

Kate's sledge was navigating through a heavy snowstorm when they neared Kainsk, which is now Kuybyshev. She had overheard that a party of prisoners was close by and she was keen for them to overtake the party so that she could give them some tea and sugar, 'in order that they might have something to warm themselves with at the next post station'.

This is Kate the ministering angel. I am sure that the Siberian section of her book is coloured by her own view of herself, but it is not without truth. Although in unbearable pain from the sledge, she kept enquiring at each post station if anyone had seen the prisoners, to the point that Popoff himself was becoming irritable with her constant pressing of the subject.

When they arrived at the post station where they were stopping for the night, learning that there were prisoners nearby who would be marching on the next morning, she left in driving snow to bring them comfort; but when she arrived at the cell-blocks she was sharply told it was too late to visit. She was having none of that.

The cold night air pierced through her thick clothes and her heart went out to the men chained up within. 'I knew what comfort a little tea would be to them before they started,' Pointing to her medal, she pushed her way through to the two cells, in pitch dark, and guarded by two soldiers with guns and bayonets at the ready.

Men's voices murmured, chains rattled; for anyone but Kate her situation would have seemed intolerably frightening and perilous. What British woman had ever of her own choice entered a prison cell in the depths of Siberia, knowing that, crowded around her, were desperate men who could lay hands on her and kill her?

The stunned soldiers let her through; stepping into the black hole of a cell, she felt the breath of ninety men in the airless space, led by an unchained prisoner holding a tiny stub of candle, casting evil shadows across filthy walls in the darkness. Gradually the sleeping men became aware of this woman, alone, among them. They stared, dazed as she squeezed through the men packed so tight they hardly had room for their lungs to open.

"Miss Marsden," I entreated, calling out to her through the years, "tell me how you did it, please tell me, where did you find your strength?"

Kate came back to help me understand:

"They put out their hands for the Gospels; but I wondered they did not kill me in their desperation, and how easily they could have done it! Instead of killing me, they blessed my hands for the little gifts. I crept among them sideways, sometimes half stumbling over those who were lying down in the centre, and who had not heard me coming, and so bringing a look of terror to their faces. There was one little hump-backed fellow who looked quite ghastly, and, near him, I stumbled against a man on the floor, only saving myself from falling by catching hold of two other prisoners. How tenderly these men helped me! Their rough hands were as gentle as any woman's. At the end of about three-quarters of an hour I had to leave, for a faintness came over me from the foul air; but, had I fainted, I should have been as safe among those ninety convicts as in my own home in England.

On saying "Good night" I peered into the darkness toward the men beyond in the next cell, and heard the clanking of their chains, and the groans of those who were ill from fatigue; but even their thanks rose in one shout, from end to end, as I went out; and the door was shut and padlocked on those ninety men, lost to their country and to every joy and every comfort of life. May God have mercy! May He bless those little Gospels, and let them be the means of making those sin-laden people look up to One who is able to save, even them, to the uttermost!"

"But, dear Miss Marsden, how did you manage to sleep in the post house that night? You were so tired after your day's journey."

"I went to rest; but could rest come to me, with that awful picture in my eyes, and those groans and the rattle of the chains ringing in my ears? At five the next morning I started on my way. Travelling from place to place, one gets accustomed to meeting the gangs of weary men and women on their way from the capital and large towns. First of all, a black mass is discovered in the distance; then, on getting a little nearer, the soldiers' bayonets glitter in the sunlight; nearer still, you can hear the dismal clank of chains, and soon the gang is close at hand. In order to insure discipline, it is found necessary to shoot any prisoner

who attempts to regain his liberty. An open sledge usually accompanies the party for anyone who falls ill on the way."

Kate saw many more of these gangs of convicts on the last leg of the journey to Tomsk and says that she would walk into the middle of them and put a packet of tea and sugar and a Testament in their hands, noting that the look of gratefulness in the mens' faces was worth everything that she suffered and all that was to come. As her bare hands became numbed from exposure to the cold, and the icy wind went through her, she realised, in some trifling measure, the same physical suffering they were enduring. She gave double measures of tea and sugar to the women, who sometimes were nursing their babies. She writes that she often saw children with them, and open sledges were generally provided for them. Some of the women were convicts and others were accompanying their husbands, from their own choice, into banishment.

Kate Marsden arrived in Tomsk, more dead than alive. From this point, our two itineraries, and our stories, interweave all the way to Irkutsk, the city nestling next to Lake Baikal. I know that Kate was full of anticipation of what that city would hold for her; and that is equally true of myself.

Chapter 12

'Thirty seconds later, Mrs. Cratchit entered, her face crimson, but smiling proudly, with the pudding resembling a cannon ball, all speckled, very firm, sprinkled with brandy in flames, and decorated with a sprig of holly stuck in the centre. Oh! The marvellous pudding!'

Charles Dickens, 'A Christmas Carol'

In London in 1890, ahead of Kate Marsden's departure for Siberia, a kind friend prepared forty pounds of plum puddings. They were shipped to Russia with Kate's heavy luggage and, like the soup, tied to the sides of her sledges and tarantasses, where they swung and bounced their way across Siberia some thrown or swept off to be eaten by wolves, or heated over a stove in one of Kate's dreaded nightly rest stops.

Our own gold-wrapped plum pudding was donated from the Lake District by the 'Ultimate Plum Pudding Company' and promised to be, unlike Mrs Cratchit's cannonball. Described as 'A real midwinter celebration of summer sunshine' family Christmas pudding, light and sweet, with lots of different nuts and fruits.'

Unlike Kate's puddings, ours would accompany us to journey's end, photographed along the way. What Ultimate's publicity didn't state was how frisky it was. It kept popping out of my bag: into the laps of Russian ladies, the less-than-savoury w.c. of the Trans-Siberian Express, on bicycle seats, on my pillow, (god forbid after the first two!) on seats in the mini-buses, it made an appearance on the boat on Lake Bailkal and almost got stolen by a passenger on a train. But this supremely well-travelled Christmas pudding found its proper destination; and a very peaceful one; a glass case in a far-distant museum. Its destiny is never to be eaten.

This single pudding is, of course, only symbolic. There was no way I was carrying forty pounds of puddings, or eating my way through them, like Kate; just as I wasn't carrying 9,000 postcards in my hand-luggage to give out, symbolising Kate's New Testaments. Luggage is a problem, using up energy, and slowing you down. The more you have, the harder it gets to find anything, or go anywhere. Kate was brave to attempt to travel so laden down.

Kate finally arrived in Irkutsk, but for two days she could barely walk. Her body ached and 'smarted as if it had been beaten.' She thanked God for bringing her there safely; nothing would ever induce her to undertake the same journey again, 'except spreading, in a humble way, the Gospel of Christ and helping the lepers'. She was, indeed, anxious to return to the completed leper colony once the painful memories of the journey had worn off;, but she was unable to return to Russia when all support for her personal mission was withdrawn in 1894.

The Pudding in Russia

The enormous red beast of a Russian train we had spent two days of our lives on, slid into Irkutsk station in pitch dark. A young man, we would come to nick-name 'Boy Racer' to us, was there to greet us.

We weren't prepared for the price of the hotel he had kindly booked us, but it was past midnight; the room was lovely and we sank onto our soft beds, luxuriated in our sparkling bathroom, relaxed in the gold-striped living room with real coffee from china cups. Yet at five minutes before check-out next morning we still hadn't heard from our fixer. Everywhere we contacted was booked; the town was full.

"What would Kate Marsden have done, Ellie?"

"Got back in her sleigh!"

And so, the Backpacker's Hostel become our bijou residence for the next few days. The name was enough for me, a middle-aged mother, to conjure up visions of gap-year youngsters lounging on their sleeping bags and munching on crackers. I eyed our small room with its eight bunks. The towels hanging down from thin mattresses to dry, the overflowing bin, the electric sockets crowded with charging phones and the rumpus of backpacks cluttering the floor.

My heart didn't sink though and I came to love these hostels across Siberia. They turned out to be the haunt of smart and savvy people from all over the world, fluent in many languages who told wonderful stories, and were friendly and generous.

With accommodation sorted, it was time for us to see Irkutsk. This city of 600,000 people set in rolling hills rising above the dense taiga. It lies on the Angara, a tributary of the Yenisei, although the River Irkut, giving Irkutsk its name, is itself a tributary of the Angara. The setting alone doesn't account for the city's beauty. That is down to the melange of artists, intellectuals, military officers and aristocrats exiled here for their part in the Decembrist conspiracy against Tsar Nicholas I. No matter how many regulation-grey blocks the Soviet era imposed on the Irkutsk skyline, the delights of its streets remains its lovely timber nineteenth-century houses with their 'gingerbread' carved embellishments still radiating dignity and indomitable spirit of those early dissidents.

It was a drizzly Saturday morning when Boy Racer picked us up. He had no reason, I'm sure, to let his Tourism Department bosses know their important guests were holed up there! He was a friendly man in his late twenties who dressed well, in fact he impressed on us more than once, that he had made a trip to London recently just to buy suits from Marks and Spencers and he wanted to go back. He also loved fast cars, and we were soon to find out quite how much he did love them.

No doubt that's why he favoured 'the Paris of Siberia's' new dull carriageways, as he whizzed us over the River Angara's bridges and down Irkutsk's busy, intricate streets. There was just enough time to marvel at the huge Kazinsky Church, described by Lonely Planet as as 'a theme-park-esque confection of salmon pink walls and flower turquoise domes topped with gold baubles crosses', and the Bogoyavlensky Cathedral, 'a fairy-tale ensemble of mini onion domes atop restored salmon, white and green towers which first appeared on the Irkutsk skyline in 1718 but during the Soviet decades served as a dormitory and a bakery'. There was no Father Victor here to invite the two of us to climb aloft and ring the bells; but our driver was careful, as we drove among the Angara Embankment, to pause at the fine statue of Alexander III, of all the Tsars the only one actually to set modern foot in his Siberian domains. The one place it would have been a treat to stop at and explore was the delicate pastel blue and white mansion of the Decembrist Count Sergei Volkonsky, set in a large stable yard with barn. The life of his countess, Maria Volkonskaya is richly described in Christine Sutherland's 'The Princess of Siberia'. Renovated in the 1980s, the house is a museum telling of the family's exile in Irkutsk. I would have given anything for a peep inside, to get a hint of the magnificent lifestyle of political exile in the 1850s, with its balls, parties and soirees.

Those Decembrist women romantically followed their husbands, and lovers, into exile. Countess Maria had access to money to commission sleighs infinitely more comfortable than the carts carrying female prisoners that Kate had witnessed; and it's reasonable to assume she would have had neither knowledge of, nor contact with, such poor felons.

At the same time she represents a stratum of memorable strong Russian patrician women for whom absolute selflessness was a watchword. Their self-sacrifice was as legendary as it was rare. And it may well be that Kate's own tenacity owes something, picked up in Moscow drawing-rooms, to the example of that generation of women.

Lake Baikal

It was Sunday, and Alex drove us the seventy miles out to the attractive village of Listvyanka on Lake Baikal. This was in part touristic, partly reconnaissance for our next stage north to Vilyuisk but what should have been a pleasant saunter through an edifying landscape turned, despite my remonstrations, into a devil's ride which left him crowing at his racing prowess, and his two passengers pale and shaking; in front of one of Russia's legendary and indisputably grandest vistas.

The world's most ancient (25 million years) and deepest freshwater lake, Baikal curves some 400 miles, backed by the Primorsky range to the West, from near the Mongolian border through South-easter Siberia and contains 20% of the world's unfrozen freshwater reserves. A UNESCO World Heritage Site, its unique fauna make this 'Galapagos of Russia', of exceptional value to evolutionary science.

In an echo of Kate Marsden's intervention 120 years before at Tjumen, Greenpeace and WWF thwarted the re-commissioning of a lakeside pulp and paper mill with a petition containing 125,000 signatures.

Given that its wonders are up to a mile down, Lake Baikal didn't disappoint. Its choppy blue waters glittered in late summer sunshine. Everybody seemed to be out to enjoy it before September turned to October, picnickers, children splashing about, a Sunday market, speedboats lacing the surface with their wakes. All too soon the view would be changed, the lake crusted with two metres of ice, not white all over, but with prism-like shards of clear ice giving a turquoise radiance unique to Lake Baikal. Alex couldn't tell us whether this impressed the Russian military engineers who, in the catastrophic Russo-Japanese war of 1904-5, laid a railway across to supply and provision their Eastern Front.

We enjoyed an ice-cream and watched Russian children splash the lake's foamy fringe on the narrow stretch of pebble beach where families unpacked lunch onto plastic picnic tables and passed the time of day on wobbly chairs set up on pebbles in the late summer sunshine of the 'Siberian Riviera'.

It was mid-afternoon. The prospect of the return drive hit me with an unquestionable statistic: most deaths in the world we know come from road traffic accidents.

I thought of my own two near shaves, the first on a crowded bus in the mountains of northern Ecuador, when we at the front realised that the driver was having to control his footbrake with a string, kept in place by a kneeling boy.

Then there was a horrible near-miss in Cameroon, again on public transport, this time a minibus crammed to the racks with local ladies and with two hefty sows lashed to the roof, when we were nearly overwhelmed by an out-of-control artic, with its tyres shredding, overtaking us on a long descent.

I wasn't having that fate for us, and glanced hopefully at our young driver, as I strapped myself into a back seat. "Can we drive back a bit slower, please?"

"Sure we will, no problem, no problem at all."

It wasn't long before, once again his foot was rammed onto the accelerator, thrusting me against my seat back. As we drove, he talked:

"Did I tell you, I am going to England soon to see Jeremy Clarkson?* Jeremy Clarkson, is a great man."

He had this amazing idea:

"I am going to tell that he should come and race on Lake Baikal when it is frozen with many feet of ice!"

I wondered to myself if the programme producers hadn't already thought of this, they have researchers considering all sorts of faraway places in various weather conditions.

At last, where the safety of his guests couldn't bring him down, a police car momentarily gave us respite. And, nearing Irkutsk, we were pulled over, and our likeable, generous maniac was given a warning.

As he told us, more than a warning would have cost him his job, and car, his Jeremy Clarkson dream. It was in sheer relief that we were ushered into 'Mommy' restaurant with its enchanting surrealist artefacts. Over tea, I realised that the next leg of our trip was going to be the hardest to plan so as to stay true to Kate's original journey.

Monday morning was hot, Ellie and I took a walkabout in the old city but I felt lethargic; I hadn't slept well in the hostel on the thin mattress with so many people in one room. Alex, back at work, was attempting to find us a way down the Lena River. Kate's official 1871 map is splattered with the riverside communities she passed in her cargo boat. Alex was to try and talk on our behalf to the nearby port of Ust-Kut and see if we could hitch a passage on a Russian cargo ship on the Lena.

When evening came, we met Alex at the authentic Mongolian restaurant called Kochnevik, or 'Nomad', and sat on the cool terrace, to receive Alex's news. It was wholly discouraging. There were no boats, no car ferries, passenger ferries, hovercraft or cruise ships, or apparently, rowing boats, ribs, dug-out canoes, coracles

---

* A well-known British presenter of car programmes.

or rafts travelling down the Lena that we could take. There had been, for a few years for legs of the journey, but not any more.

Nor was there any road Northward alongside the Lena. This illustrates all too clearly the difficulties of trying to replicate the route of a historic traveller. But the point was – as it had been for Kate Marsden – to get to Vilyuisk, where her lepers were concentrated in the taiga. Rather than give up, we must bite the bullet, and take the one terrestrial route that offered itself, Lake Baikal. First, though, we will see how Kate Marsden reached her goal. It's our loss, and a considerable factor in her own downfall, that she left so frustrating and minimal an account of this important leg of her journey.

It's curious to reflect that, however daunting the prospect was for Kate, her travel arrangements at least were easier to make, and assured in their outcome. If she wanted to get to Vilyuisk, this, was how it was done. Governors, clerics, colonels and administrators had all made the journey. They knew all the stages, and could not only supply reliable escorts – like Popoff – but keep tabs on their guests the whole length of her journey. For us, travelling 120 years later and against the clock, that whole network was forever lost.

Chapter 13

A POOR LEPER WOMAN DRAGGING HER FOOD ACROSS THE SNOW.

To face page 144.

"The biggest disease today is not leprosy or tuberculosis, but rather the feeling of being unwanted."

Mother Teresa

Having spent her first two days in Irkutsk getting the sledge-ache out of her bones, Kate Marsden made a call on the Governor-General, who received her enthusiastically. He already knew her business, having been kept informed by his colleague further west.

Meeting Kate triggered his conscience over the Yakutsk lepers.

After talking with her at length he eagerly offered his services to help them. The date was 30th April or 1st May 1891.

One can only imagine the situation she had put him in, because if he hadn't offered his support to this unusual visitor, who was courting 1890s celebrity status, his reputation may have been tarnished as churlish. He had clearly done his homework as he corroborated all she had heard about the state of the Yakutsk lepers and when he suggested the formation of a committee of influential people from Irkutsk to support her venture, Kate was delighted. Of course, his active support (as she had guessed) was crucial to her venture. She was thinking of his contacts among the rich merchants in Irkutsk, but the list the two of them drew up on the spot as potential committee members drew on religious, military and civic dignitaries. It included 'the Governor-General, His Grace the Archbishop of Irkutsk, His Grace the Archbishop of Kirensk, the Cathedral priest Vinogradoff, His Excellency the State Councillor Sievers, the Inspector of Medicine, the aid-de-camp of the commander of troops, Captain Lvoff, the Mayor, and myself' (Kate).

On May 1st 1891, Kate's 32nd birthday, the committee sat for the first time. Kate called it 'one of the happiest days of my life, for my plans were now to receive official recognition and aid . . .', and described the proceedings thus:

'At eleven o'clock the captain came to me and read over the order of proceedings in French. Then we drove to the palace of the Archbishop, and as the carriage stopped at the gates, my heart gave many a flutter of anticipation and hope, as well as of nervous, unaccountable dread. We walked up the steps into the hall, where I put on my cap, and then we went into the large reception hall. In five minutes His Excellency the General Governor, in full uniform, came in, followed by the Mayor, Councillor Sievers, and the Inspector of Medicine. After a brief interval the large doors were thrown open, and His Grace the Archbishop entered in full canonicals and orders. The Governor went up to him first and received his blessing, kissing his cheeks and his mouth. A few minutes after the Archbishop of Kirensk arrived, and we all went into the drawing room, furnished with dark and light yellow draperies, which stood out in striking contrast to the robes of the Archbishop and the dresses of the other members.'

She may be forgiven a little vanity. The great men of Irkutsk were gathered, in the best room of a Siberian palace, because of her, and around her; and she sat there in her plain nurses's uniform receiving the hand, and compliments, of each in turn, and – to her amazement – hearing them accede, with coy glances and blushes, to all the measures she proposed to them through the Governor-General and the Secretary, Capt. Lvoff, the Governor's aide-de-camp.

With their business so satisfactorily concluded, a tea-party followed and then a photographer had them all form up for a group portrait. This, if it could only be found, would be a treasure.

On May 27, 1891 an outline was written by the Secretary, Aide-de-camp to the Governor of actions to be taken.

Kate would ascertain the distribution of the lepers of the Vilyuisk Circuit and get acquainted with their exact numbers and the severity of their symptoms. The committee would decide how much support it should offer once Miss Marsden had presented a report outlining the best ways of alleviating the lepers' situation.

The Archbishop would write to the Bishop of Yakutsk and Vilyuisk, entrusting Miss Marsden to his care.

A telegram would be dispatched to the Medical Department, asking them to forward a copy of Dr Krasnoff's 1865 report on leprosy in the Vilyuisk Circuit.

The delay that these administrative conditions imposed might, earlier on, have been frustrating to Kate, but here in Irkutsk it allowed her to review her needs for the next part of the journey. For the long ride ahead, she commissioned a special pair of trousers; and she watched winter relax its grip over the land.

A document arrived (translated for her by Captain Lvoff), showing the positions of the lepers over the preceding sixty-four years. This Kate reproduced in her book. It began in 1827 with the Vilyuisk doctor's report of an incurable disease called leprosy that had been 'devastating the land for some time past.' There was one 'hospital' a yourta or tented house accommodating five lepers with seven other patients, variously afflicted, sharing the same roof. After inspecting this hovel, Dr. Uklonsky, requested the Committee of Hospitals and Medical Institutions in Siberia that a small hospital be built in Vilyuisk, suggesting as an alternative that they might buy his own house for the purpose costing 500 roubles. This in 1834 they did, but the house was useless as a hospital and it wasn't used. In 1840 the Chief Medical Inspector saw the conditions for himself and insisted on the urgent need to build a hospital for twenty-five patients.

In 1843 the Governor of Yakutsk recommended, in a report to the General-Governor that another house, somewhat dilapidated in Vilyuisk be bought and renovated; the Governor was adamant that a purpose-built hospital was preferable. Kate notes that a hospital for forty lepers was built, and opened in 1860, but closed for lack of support three years later. Presumably the inmates were dispatched into the taiga.

No further funds could be arranged, until in 1865 Vilyuisk got a small hospital of its own – but a general hospital, with no leprosy unit. An eight-bed ward was created in 1881 for syphilitics; but as well as being, by now, too small the hospital was unhygienic, 'the air is polluted, the patients have neither linen, bath, nor kitchen.'

The civil authorities had identified eighty lepers spread out around the 'Vilyuisk Circuit' meaning the vast expanse of surrounding forest.

The problem lay in the popular conception of leprosy. There was no cure, and ignorance led to fright. Sufferers were instantly banished from the community, and never allowed back, even to see their families. Where could they go? The forest. Out of sight, out of mind. Where, in the imaginings of the doctors and administrators, did this curse come from? Kate writes, of 'the immense forests, the endless marshes, the dampness of the air, the unclean habits of the natives, their food of rotten fish, water taken from marshes and lakes, the insufficiency of bread, meat, salt, etc., the famine that often assails the country,' as the causes of this frightful disease.

In September 1890 a meeting of the administrative council once more addressed itself to the medical issues relating to the lepers. Would it help if the marshes were drained? The new

Governor General Goremikin insisted on starting from a position of sound knowledge. Let them first summon a specialist in leprosy to give a seminar, after which they would have a far better idea of how to proceed.

The shilly-shallying revealed in these proceedings, going back to 1827, and resulting in no concerted action being taken on the lepers' behalf, incensed Kate Marsden; but her condemnation of the authorities begins with deceptive leniency:

'A critic of these documents who is inclined to be severe on official red-tapeism and repeated delays must remember the great distance of Yakutsk from St. Petersburg (about 5000 miles), and that the transmission of a letter between the two places and back takes many months, and particularly a long time during the breaking-up season. But, notwithstanding any extenuating circumstances, the fact remains that for sixty-four years the lepers of Yakutsk pleaded in vain for a permanent place of shelter. It is enough to make one's heart bleed to read that a hospital opened in 1860 for forty lepers had to be closed three years later, 'owing to insufficiency of means.' Better had it been for their hopes not to be realised at all than for the boon granted to be snatched away after three short years. So, after their brief respite from awful loneliness and misery, these poor creatures were turned adrift to seek again, in the untrodden depths of the forest, the only home which their fellow-creatures would allot them.'

Kate had acquainted herself with what to expect in Yakutia and its coldest place on earth, and that for eight months each year the mean temperature was -92 Fahrenheit (-68.8 celsius).

'The immense forests are scenes of 'utter desolation' and the heat in summer is so great that myriads of mosquitoes and flies infest the air, torturing both man and beast, and attacking especially the sores of the lepers, who sometimes are too weak to keep them off. When once a man is known to be tainted with leprosy, he is thrust out from his people, and driven away, as if he were some noxious animal, into a lonely spot in the forest, or on the marshes, where he is doomed to a living death. He knows that his disease is incurable, and that return to his friends is impossible. A

A leper hut

father, or a mother, a son or a daughter, full of life and energy, whoever the victim may be, expulsion follows immediately on the discovery of the fatal signs. 'No hope! no hope' is the dread sentence ringing in the victim's ears; and as he leaves his native haunts he knows that never more, perhaps, will a loving face greet him, or kind hands minister to his needs, or the pleasant sound of wife, child, sister, or brother's voice fall upon his ears. He knows he may perhaps have fifteen or twenty years to live — a loathed outcast from mankind. The only shelter he can find is some filthy little yourta, which may have been tenanted by another leper, who now, perhaps, is buried near the threshold. His first duty is to make a cross, which he is bound to place outside, as a warning to anyone who may happen to pass to shun him. And so he begins his outcast leper life — a life so absolutely awful and miserable that none can realise it except a leper outcast like himself.'

Summoned – in her own words – by God, to minister to these poor sick people from Yakutsk, she felt bound to face every obstacle to help them, just as she had thrown herself heart and soul into tending the wounded on the battlefield of Plevna.

Gradually the paperwork was concluded to everyone's satisfaction. If only Kate had recorded her own preparations with the same momentum she bestowed on her London arrangements. Where are the plum puddings, the hire of horses, the spring outfit, and the new trousers? What has happened to the magic herb? All she tells us about are letters of introduction from Irkutsk to the Governor of Yakutsk, and the precious one signed by the Empress; and our limited impression of the 1200 miles to Yakutsk comes, not from her scant notes, but from the map of the settlements along the Lena river which, had there been a berth available on a ship travelling downstream, Ellie and I could have at least imagined, and guessed the conditions under which she travelled.

Chapter 14

'Lake Baikal reflects like an optical instrument and responds to changes in the weather so sensitively that it seems like a part of the sky rather than of the land.'

Ian Frazier, Travels in Siberia

The Lena River valley can be said to have given birth to the legendary gulag system. The great river, rising on the Eastern side of Lake Baikal, could be used to shunt prisoners, political and otherwise, far into the isolation of Siberia. Nowadays it is hardly a popular travel destination and only cargo boats ply its waters. I researched extensively before leaving England and found no passenger timetables for passenger boats, but now I heard the news from a reliable source on the ground.

Jeffrey Tayler acquired a custom-built raft, with outboard motor, to travel the 2,400 miles from Ust-Kut to above the Arctic Circle, in the summer of 2004. He calls the resulting book 'River of Reprieve: Descending Siberia's Waterway of Exile, Death and Destiny'. Freedom to travel in the region in no way diminished the threats he felt all the way – from the climate, water conditions, village drunks, and, even, bears. I envied him, though, and still feel resentment towards Kate for her lack of attention to the terrain, company and local people, and the crew of her cargo boat. Surely there would have been stories, too; and of course, in blanking this whole episode she fed fuel to her detractors,not least the vicious Isabel Hapgood. This skilled journalist knew her Russia well enough to contest, all too convincingly, that Kate had not made the journey to Yakutsk, let alone the trek to Vilyuisk, and that the rest of her account was sheer Gothic fabrication.

Undoubtably it would have been uncomfortable and if she had written anything it would have been full of stories of chain-gangs and prison camps, vast forests and squalid and dirty human habitations. Had she felt vulnerable on her own or molested? Was this the secret reason she refused to put pen to paper over that historic and unique stretch of her long and difficult journey? We know it was rough for her, but who was she travelling with? Her scant comment: '. . . forbears from enumerating the many inconveniences and troubles which had to be borne, and which alone might fill a little volume,' leaves me wanting to read that unwritten volume!

Let us fill in the bare bones. To reach the navigable part of the Lena nearest its source in the Baikal mountains, just four miles west of the lake, but further up than we had got with Alex, she reverted to tarantass for the 155 miles. For Ellie and me, there was no bus to the adjacent towns, and in any case the road thereafter turned to track. My research showed that however many rivers joined the Lena, there was now no river-transport until Ust-Kut, 200 miles to the north-east, which is a proper port. So we were condemned to go our separate ways, Kate missing Lake Baikal and my expedition having to forego her experience of the Lena, which went against all my cherished principles!

We could improvise some kind of conveyance to Ust-Kut, nearly 200 miles further on, but there was no guarantee that we could board a cargo ship when we got there – so it was all looking a bit unsafe as a transportation choice and we only had a four week visa.

We agreed that flying wasn't an option, so on our last night in Irkutsk we agreed on Lake Baikal and briefed our boy-racer. And so, early next morning we were back at Listvyanka, driven calmly and expertly by a born-again Alex, smart in suit and tie, helped by him to buy tickets and delivered to the ferry terminal, our destination the furthermost tip of the lake, the town of Severobaikalsk.

As we boarded, he handed us a carrier bag with two ridiculous toy seals, a keepsake of that cosmic lake in fluffy polyester. I grinned to myself as I stuffed it into my already-bursting red barrel-roller; somehow a strangely fitting gift from a petrol-head. As an equally crazy vote-of-thanks for his help, I offloaded a stack of our purple postcards, to spread amongst his colleagues, and of course we hoped we would see him and Jeremy Clarkson united in London!

The ten hour journey from and to the end of the lake was leisurely and rewarding, old and ridiculously deep, we stared out at its shore line as this pearl of a lake curves gently through south-eastern Siberia from the Mongolian border.

One day, the scientists say, it will become another ocean.

'Good people meet'

Anna

Anna and Sasha from Moscow

Like other Soviet-planned cities, Severobaikalsk is dominated by ugly high-rise buildings. It was founded as recently as 1974 for construction workers on the Baikal-Amur Mainline, (BAM). The suburbs are redeemed by the shacks made from railway cars from its early foundation days as a work camp.

From the moment we disembarked, I could see I was going to have tales to tell here! Alex had kindly called ahead; a smiling moustachioed man met us, the spitting image of my pal Graeme in Bristol and so it was 'Graeme's brother' who led us back to one of the Soviet tower-monstrosities, humanised in this case by a thoroughly rustic-Russian blue-painted picket fence. Here, it turned out, his daughter, Anna ran a backpacker's hostel from her flat. The entrance was grim, with rusting steel double-doors to unlock, they clanged shut after us, sending industrial echoes down concrete corridors. I would hate to live here I thought, and there simply weren't enough grey words I could think of to describe it.

With no road connections to the outside world, Severobaikalsk, a city with its population of 28,000, is not a tourist destination. You won't find much of a list of hotels or guest houses, and Alex had been as good as gold in locating Anna's. In the event it defied all our anxieties, proving to be a miracle of the imagination.

Anna, and her little boy had a clean and homely one bed apartment and in the tiny entrance was a child's bike and a mini climbing frame with highly-polished wooden floors. There was a small kitchen, a table with lace-trimmed tablecloth, a small shower room, a bedroom and a lounge; and at night, this became the hostel.

Anna and her son went to stay with her father to allow bodies in sleeping bags to fill the floors to bursting point. We were lucky: arriving earlier in the evening meant that two of the six single beds in the lounge constituting the 'dorm' were reserved for us. We unrolled our sleeping bags and made ourselves at home, waiting for all the other spaces to fill up, as they soon did. The Lonely Planet guides to Russia and half eaten bags of crisps slowly amassed and I felt happy with my alien-to-a-middle-aged women situation. I sat crossed leg on my child-size bed and wrote in my diary and messaged the man in England from my Kindle.

My diary entry reads: 'This is a laugh! In 'The Dorm' are five women of different ages and nationalities and one bearded Canadian man! He is coping well with women undressing around him. The only plug in the room is positioned over his bed, which we have to sit on to connect our chargers.'

So what accounts for these backpackers and how did they come to be here; drifting in all through the evening? The answer is remoteness and discovery – going that extra mile in our globalised world, to discover something more spectacular, and that's more of a challenge to reach. Besides, there's the rawness: up here at the north end of Lake Baikal it's more likely they'll bump into a straying bear or reindeer-herding Evenki than in the beach resort in the south.

Graeme's Brother was a good friend, offering next day to have another go at contacting the authorities at the port at Ust-Kut. We were not too far east to get there, should a friendly captain agree to take two travellers to Yakutsk. With a little time on our hands, Ellie and I took a mini-bus to thermal springs a few miles outside the town for the day.

To the people of Severobaikalsk, living in ex-Soviet buildings, getting away in their free time is important. Nature provides lavishly here, and there is plenty for them to do among the mountains and lakes. In the summer they love to fish in Lake Baikal and to travel by sailboat to destinations down the lake. When the six-to-eight-month winter arrives, the hot springs round the city become the real places of pilgrimage, combining the joys of hot water and snow. Downhill skiing ends exhilarating in a plunge into a thermal pool. Here, near the Arctic, rail has priority over road – more reliably all-weather – and so our minibus lurched and rocked along the bumpy track sending rocks and dust flying.

'Ell and the Canadian are now drinking beer in the kitchen, I am flirting with a mosquito . . .' I wrote to my man in England that night, sitting on the bed. Someone played a guitar in Anna's bedroom, and a girl was trying to sing, with no grasp of the words. A satisfactory reply came right back.

Anna's Dad had tried to ring the authorities in Ust-Kut but hadn't got through so Anna was going to try for us again the next day, this was a good excuse to go trekking; along the shore of Lake Baikal.

We walked through pine forests beside the lake, stopped to eat on beaches, trod over wild lavender and thyme, clambered up rocks to reach beautiful viewpoints over the vast lake, looked after all day by a lovely couple called Anna and Sascha from Moscow who smiled all the time. Straight out of a Chekov play, they made tea with wild blackcurrant leaves and skinny dipped in the lake.

Anna had known enough English to tell us that 'good people meet' while Sasha asked 'Wash and Go'?

We arrived back late afternoon to find the makeshift hostel already full. There were men all over the place, with huge rucksacks and more wet washing and a party was going on around the kitchen table, sharing food and eating and laughter. Ellie and I shared a bottle of wine, Geoff the Canadian sat around in his shorts, and a pair of Amazonian German girls sat around in their bras.

The definitive answer from Ust-Kut was that there was no passenger boat, and the cargo boat captains refused to take two 'beautiful women', as Anna had called us. Bar just turning up at the port, which would involve an eight hour train journey in the wrong direction and the likelihood of finding no backpacker's hostel, we had done all we could to follow Kate down the Lena.

On our last evening at Anna's, round the supper-table, we got talking about Kate Marsden and our own journey and she told us that in the past lepers from Russia were sent to Bayayoya which means beautiful place, close-by on the lake, but the village had been destroyed by the Soviets.

My last act in the Severobaikalsk backpackers' hotel was to sit cross-legged on my bed and itemise my staple foodstuffs for this Siberian trip:

tomatoes
mayonnaise
boiled eggs
very hard dry biscuits
nuts

sunflower seeds
cheese (lacks any flavour)
cucumbers (if I can't avoid them)
honey

The next day, Saturday 17th August 2013, we left on the BAM railway, going east. The station, designed by Leningrad architects, was impressive, a snow-white sail standing out against the sky and the clear blue of Lake Baikal.

It would be a longish journey, almost 2,000 miles, 1,000 more miles than Land's End to John o'Groats.

The next few days wouldn't be monotonous; it never is when you travel through an exciting new land and are open to new scenes and experiences. We were leaving new friends, had a lot to contemplate and I specially wanted time to think about Kate. I wondered if she had had a flinching nostalgia for home; or was her mind permanently set on handing out those Russian New Testaments to the wretched prisoners?

The shabby apartment-blocks of Severobaikalsk shrank into the distance as the train pulled away toward Tynda. The line we were riding on was the Baikal–Amur Main Line; much more recent than the Trans Siberian, it runs parallel to it some 400 miles to the North, serving Eastern Siberia and the Russian Far East. When it was laid the then Soviet premier, Leonid Brezhnev, described it as 'the construction project of the century,' on account of terrain, ground conditions, weather and cost – let alone length, which is just short of 3,000 miles.

The stretch we were now on from Severobaykalsk would take us through five tunnels and through the foggy Severomuysk mountains, where the chief hazard for the engineers was not the rock conditions, but permafrost. It's surprising it was ever completed due to the complexity of its construction.

As ever on these grand Russian trains, the ride was ultra-smooth and soon Ellie and I were nested in our top bunks like a pair of squirrels. Our obliging provinista came by with shrink-wrapped sheets and we scrambled about performing callisthenics making the beds and fitting our belongings into the left-over spaces. I was loving it and looking forward to nearly a thousand miles of cosy living ahead, and, if I craned my neck downwards from the bunk, like a monkey, I could gaze out at never-ending forest. Then there was always the option to try out my extremely basic Russian on our room-mate Olga and her gang of visiting girlfriends, who popped by to inspect us for themselves and we laughed, drank wine and, with their permission, put them on film!

Twice a day the provanista came along with a trolley of brown paper bags containing a runny, meat-based meal on a plastic plate – my reaction was 'nyet spasibo'. Aghast at my rejection of perfectly good protein and unwilling to see a guest of Russia starve in her kupe, the generous Olga thrust the plastic cheese from her paper sack into a white bap and insisted that I take it, right now, before I died! Of course I had my own plastic cheese and white bun to prevent me from starving, not forgetting a rather bland Russian banana yoghurt. Olga became good friends with us, language barriers melted with a mug of wine, while we stopped noticing that one bloodshot eye. I don't know how much she took in about our mission, but she proudly told us about the son she'd just been visiting at University at Tomsk, and pointed to rural scenes from the train window.

Twenty-five hours later and the repertoire of views hadn't changed; tall straight firs, fragile silver-birch, misty plains, broken tree trunks protruding like blackened fangs from even blacker pools. Sometimes the track followed the wide Muyakan or Nyukzha rivers, long smudges of brown rolling their way through unrelenting land-scapes, silent witnesses to a darker past. The towns we passed seems to be grey, uniform, and off-the-peg clumps of cold war high-rises at their grimmest, with seemingly no room for green open spaces, flowers on the station platform, or children's playgrounds. The pre-concrete age instantly drew our eye: there, to one side, demoted from its once prominent place in the former village, would be the one distressed old timber dwelling from before the railway arrived.

My watch said English time, the trains were running on Moscow time and what the hell was local time? I never knew; it didn't seem to matter.

At twenty-seven hours, the grinning provanista brought us oily borscht with chicken, its watery consistency slopped with the motion of the train. I waved it away and retreated to my upper bunk which was an odourless zone and rummaged through my luggage for a cereal bar.

Our cheery Russian room mate Olga was concerned, but not over my diet this time, she had a new worry.

In thirty hours we would reach Tynda, a small junction in the marshy unpopulated depths of Amurskaya Oblast, where we had to change trains and take another one directly north, until the line ended after 500 km at Aldan. Olga insisted, and her friends nodded in confirmation, that this rail line only penetrated pin-deep into the vastness of Sakha Province. I knew from my reading that Sakha was the largest subnational region in the world, bigger than Argentina. They fretted on our behalf: what would we do when we got there? It was a wilderness. Were we to despair on the face of local knowledge, or wish we'd flown – or believe Lonely Planet guidebook, which told us there was a bus to catch? I could see she was anxious for us – she twisted her hands and picked up and put down a well-thumbed, celebrity-gossip magazine.

The locals, whose lives are tuned into the rhythm of the cruel cold of winter, know of course, that no rail or road would be of use for at least eight months of the year; Yakutsk sits on the Western side of the River Lena and there isn't a bridge. In the brief summer months there are ferries and in the depths of winter there is an ice road – in the intervening months Yakutsk becomes inaccessible as the ice is still forming or it's breaking up.

At Tynda, Ellie and I tumbled out with our bags and luggage into the evening sunshine and crossed platforms for the Altan train. In the doorway, Olga perused our platskart tickets – all we could get – with a knowing smile and we walked to our different ends of the train.

Our open-plan carriage with its stubby, uncomfortable beds for up to fifty was a relic of the Soviet era. This mobile dormitory was occupied by passengers from all walks of Russian life slouched on bunks facing each other across a table, keeping up lively chatter, eating homemade pirozhki, pickles and vareniki* and on the other side of the aisle were two tiny bunks for Ellie and me passing our single tub of pot noodles between us.

"It's impossible to sleep," she whispered. "People walk past and knock your feet."

"I can't see where feet can go, the bed's too short! I doubt you could find carriages like this anywhere else but Russia. They were the invention of the proletariat!"

An older Russian man banging my bottom with cup and hand in order to get past nearly caused an international incident and sharply reminded me of dangers that women travellers have always faced but seldom alluded to in their writings. I wonder whether Kate Marsden, mustering her forces in London in 1890, picked up Lilian Campbell Davidson's brand-new 'Hints to Lady Travellers at Home and Abroad', and what expression came to her face on reading –

'Much has been said about the danger to women, especially young women, travelling alone, of annoyance from impertinent or obtrusive attentions from travellers of the other sex. I can only say, that in any such case which has ever come within my personal knowledge or observation, the woman has only herself to blame.' How shocking!

I reclined uncomfortably, as there wasn't room to sit up. The glimpses of forest people picking summer berries gave way to night, but the hubbub didn't diminish, with children taking delight in jumping from bunk to bunk, and all our neighbours crunching their way through mounds of pumpkin seeds. Finally resigning myself, I plugged in to Led Zeppelin on my iPod and lashed my arm to the bunk to prevent rolling out into the gangway. Halfway to Altan, at Neryungi, the train stopped for the rest of the night while we were both snatching some sleep. It must have been somewhere between midnight and two a.m. local time, in near stillness in our carriage and with even the toilet doors locked out

---

* Piroshki, baked or fried bun filled with a variety of fillings and vareniki, a Russian dumpling.

of respect for the station, all the lights came on and an agitated provanista was coming through calling "Quick, quick, where are the English ladies?" Spotting us in our bunks, "You, taxi, Yakutsk, NOW!" we got every word of that. It was then − having shed my trousers − that I instantly regretted my choice of underwear.

To this day, in that quarter of Eastern Siberia, there are probably travellers' tales of that English bottom descending the metal bunk pole in fluorescent pink briefs. Not the first Bridget Jones moment in my life, and probably not the last!

But at least, we said to one another as we clawed down our belongings and unhooked and stowed our clothes, we know that Olga, bless her, is wrong. We're on our way to Yakutsk.

Chapter 15

'The Lena Pillars, famed as the haunts of shamans and Sakha's mythological heroes.'

Jeffrey Tayler 'River of No Reprieve, Descending Siberia's Waterway of Exile, Death and Destiny'

The Lena Pillars

Kate Marsden began her own Lena journey by barge. The produce it carried for more northerly communities downstream was patrolled by rats and mice; vermin 'became part and parcel' of her life. Her mattress, sacks full of cabbages and potatoes, made comfortable rest impossible. When she wasn't swatting monster horseflies, that circled and dive-bombed her she was at the mercy of clouds of bloodthirsty midges that targeted her pale skin and brought on unladylike paroxysms and her arms and neck became swollen. She also felt dirty, really dirty, which she disliked intensely being a nurse who maintained high standards of personal hygiene amongst her nurses and exacting standards in the wards, it troubled her that her grubby nurse's uniform with its blackened collar was now a sartorial disgrace and her lank and greasy brown hair sat in a bird's nest fashion upon her head.

This certainly wasn't the land for a Victorian lady – legend has it that the Yakuts of the Taiga don't wash, on the basis that clogged pores don't attract bugs.

MY HOME IN A CARGO-BOAT FOR THREE WEEKS ON THE RIVER LENA.

The cargo boat that Kate Marsden travelled in

We have no way of knowing her observations of river-bank settlements she made en route, but we do know that her 'heart rose in thankfulness to God, on coming near Yakutsk.'

Kate was too anxious to meet the Governor to dwell on the beautiful Lena Pillars rock formation, on approaching Yakutsk they came close to the shore and the crew shouted greetings to a local man fishing on the bank. They asked him if he had seen the Governor as they had an English lady on board who was anxious to see him, the fisherman shook his head and told them that the Governor had left town. Further dialogue also revealed that he had never heard of any lepers in the local area. Kate wasn't concerned about his mention of no lepers because she knew it wasn't true, but she was very worried that she'd missed the Governor and it was very important that she saw him soon.

Kate writes:

'The only way out of the difficulty was to go ashore, and, by a short cut through the forest, reach another point of the river, where I might hear tidings of the Governor, or perhaps meet with the boat that was taking him away. The master of the barge very promptly offered to escort me. We travelled through miles and miles of dense forest, with only one narrow road cut through, meeting many of the Yakuts in their strange dress, with high sleeves, just like ladies' sleeves at home. We also met strings of carts, drawn by bullocks, with rings through their noses, and only a collar of wood, and two wooden poles to keep them in their places. As we approached the river again I saw an ominous appearance of smoke, as if a steamer were starting. We made our little horses tear away, and on reaching the shore got into the first empty boat we saw. The steamer was now going at full speed, but our man pushed on with all his might. Then, to my intense satisfaction, I saw the paddle reversed, and knew the steamer would stop in answer to our signals. On rowing alongside the steps were lowered; I got on board and saw the Governor, who gave me one of the warmest welcomes it has ever been my good fortune to receive. His account of the lepers was fearful. He begged me to go to them, and said he had made all necessary arrangements for me before his departure. So, after an hour's chat, the steamer speeding on all the time, I scrambled down the side and re-entered that little leaky boat. For two hours we baled and baled, and really that rapid, dangerous Lena seemed eager to draw us into her embrace. It was one o'clock at night, or A. M., according to our ways of reckoning; but it was quite light, and the northern lights, though trying, were beautiful. We landed safely, and, after another little journey, I arrived at last in the town of Yakutsk.'

This is confusing narrative and there is no way we can sort out the discrepancies in it. We get the impression they are on foot, then they have ponies and finally when she sees the northern lights or aurora borealis, one of the most magnificent natural phenomena, quite alien to an English girl, she passes it by with no description at all, in fact it was 'trying'!

The point is that she located the paddle steamer and found a place from which to flag it down. She obtained the undertakings she needed from the Governor, and a perilous additional adventure brought her at last to Yakutsk, to an opportunity to scrub up and recover her dignity, and to the true start of her mission to the lepers in the forest.

> 'The tall, erect, strongly-built physique which seemed made for active and laborious work, the clear cut features, the square and resolute looking chin, all combined to give one, at once, the feeling that this was no ordinary woman, that here was a living example of the steel hand in the velvet glove, of the most inflexible determination of will and of heroic powers of patient endurance, only partially concealed by a most feminine voice and refinement, and most courteous and unusually self-contained manners.'
>
> 'The Nursing Record' 3rd November 1892

Kate Marsden arrived in Yakutsk in June 1891. The white nights would have been at their strongest as the sun does not go under the horizon in the summer and there is small difference in light between daytime and night. But does she talk about having strange feelings, not being able to sleep, when in the deep of night there is sun in the windows and she is trying to figure out whether it is night or day? Unfortunately no. It passes without a mention as she focuses her attention on the citizens of the town.

Kate was looked after there by an Orthodox cleric: 'the Bishop looked after me lovingly and tenderly, as if I had been his own daughter.' Her stay in Yakutsk was very different to mine a century later and she wrote that it 'is not a pretty place, and has a dreary, dead appearance. At eight o'clock the houses are shut up, and there are no amusements or recreations.' She could only imagine what it must be like in midwinter. 'Sometimes the cold is so frightful that strong people cannot go out of their houses for days together. It is not light till ten or half-past, and is dark about two; and this state of things continues for nearly eight months of the year.'

Bishop Meletie

Kate also mentioned that all the ladies smoked cigarettes and thirty years earlier it would have been pipes and for six hours a day, everybody played cards. On arrival at any house, she would first be offered a cigarette and a cup of tea second, and a chair third. While smoking, tea drinking, card-playing and talking were going on around them the men present walked up and down the room which she found bewildering. Etiquette dictated that: 'the gentleman must be the first to give his hand to the visitor, who must take off in the hall his cloak, or shouba, and fur boots. On no account must the visitor enter the room in his outdoor costume, and if he declines the proffered tea he is guilty almost of a crime.' Yakutsk was a dead-end place, bound rigid by its conventions.

Only the houses of the well-to-do had glazed windows. In winter the poorer people used sheets of ice instead of glass and Kate was baffled as to how they kept themselves warm. Whatever people needed to buy came in by water once a year, which entailed stocking up for the months ahead.

Kate's visit to the Bishop was made soon after her arrival, being driven there in a dolgashka, a flatbed of darkly painted boards on four wheels with a central back-to-back seat that accommodated six to eight, all facing outwards behind the horse. This beat the bullocks'-back device that other Yakuts drove. When sitting on this, side-on in 'their tall hats, long, high-shouldered cloaks, high top-boots, and singularly plain faces they looked altogether comical.'

The Bishop received his guest kindly, and in the French that they shared broached the possibility of forming a committee in Yakutsk to facilitate Kate's forthcoming journey to visit the lepers of Yakutia. He undertook: 'to use every exertion to bring the leading people together, and to help the lepers, not only by relieving their material wants, but also by giving them an opportunity of receiving the consolations of religion. He gave me one of the rare copies of the complete New Testament in the Yakutsk tongue.'

Also, most excitingly for her, he confirmed the existence of that mysterious plant with supposed curative powers against leprosy.

'On my referring to the herb he said, much to my surprise and delight, that he had a few specimens, and before I left he placed some in my hands. He could give no definite information as to its curative or alleviating properties. It was, however, a source of some satisfaction that the reports I had heard were not altogether groundless'.

And so, with the help of the Bishop, Kate immersed herself in preparations for her journey to visit the lepers on the Vilyuisk Circuit. In the nineteenth century the province of Yakutia was split into circuits, or districts, for administrative purposes and Kate describes the 'Vilyuisk' Circuit as extending to 883,000 square

**The sample of Wolf's Grass or katshukta that
the author collected in Sakha Province**

versts or 559,000 square miles. She had been told that the land-scape would be one of forests, marshes and lakes along whose shores the local farmers reared cattle.

It's in passages like the following that her colonialising mind comes to the fore: 'The natives, even now, are only in a semi-barbarous state, having but recently been brought under the influence of civilization.'

Knowing their modern successors in their twenty-first century villages, I can't believe she is describing the same people. She writes that 'although considered Christians, they are addicted to many heathen practices,' and that the reason they live so far apart from each other is because they are apt to quarrel with one another.

Most of the inhabitants of the Vilyuisk Circuit were very poor, and how some of them continued to exist was little short of a mystery to her. The fur trade offered a fluctuating source of liveli-hood; and many of the people made odds and ends, such as baskets, vessels for food, drinking vessels, ornaments, and cradles out of the bark of trees. 'Some of these baskets are very pretty, being interlaced with fish scales, which radiate with all kinds of colours. The people live in yourtas, of simple construction, for the most part extremely dirty, and devoid of the ordinary comforts of home life. The yourta for winter habitation is usually made of light beams, well plastered externally with thick layers of clay and cow-dung.'

She made a tentative connection between poverty and leprosy, noting that the most depressed district, the 'Sredni Vilyuisk oulousse', had the greatest incidents of new infection.

At the Bishop's invitation, the senior Yakutsk doctor filled her in on the lives of the lepers. The lepers subsisted, cast out into the forest, and he advised her to take them supplies of tea and tobacco: these were the kinds of luxury that had no place in their present existence. Concerned by the shortness of the season, Kate worried at the time it took to convene the committee, because she needed to start on her uncomfortable and arduous journey.

At last it met. Present were:

Meletie, Bishop of Yakutsk and Vilyuisk

Mons. Ostashkin, the medical inspector

Mons. Smirnoff, the doctor of the district

Mons. Tschevinsky, the doctor of the Yakutsk Hospital

Mons. Nesmeloff, the assistant of the Vilyuisk police

The tchinovnick,* of the Governor

The Cossack, Jean Procopieff

Kate Marsden.

The Medical Inspector told them of his own recent visit – not as extensive as what Kate proposed – and described the conditions and suffering she would witness. Most helpful were the local members' suggestions of the best routes to reach them by. The chief outcome of the meeting was a sketch map of the distribution of lepers, the routes linking them, and the hazards to be encountered, which it was agreed would be particularly serious for her as a woman, and a commitment to providing a party of local horseman to ensure her safety.

---

* An office-holder or bureaucrat serving in the Tsarist Russian government, sometimes spelt tchinovnik.

But this eagerness for her well-being in a man's role seemed to Kate to come with an undercurrent; was it suspicion? It's worth bearing in mind that this was a meeting of men unused to dealing with women on an equal footing especially so dangerous an undertaking. It's as if they were asking, who was she to do this, to take on such a perilous journey? Some members quizzed her on her credentials; Kate wondered if they were nursing the thought she was nothing better than a political spy. There was, after all, always another person in the room taking notes, Kate suspected, in case they needed evidence against her at a future time. Kate had noticed the prevalence of notebook carrying among officials, and their readiness to jot down anything noteworthy.

But, whatever lingering doubts remained among committee members, they had fired the starting pistol and Kate set about making preparations. 'I cannot enumerate everything, but only just a few to give an idea of what we thought it necessary to take. Dried bread (almost as hard as a stone, and which had to be soaked in tea before being eaten) packed in fish skins and boxes, covered with fish skin, and, for this reason, smelling and tasting forever after of bad fish — tea, sugar, tobacco, tinned meats and fruits, biscuits, and an assortment of drugs and an en route basket from Drew & Sons, Piccadilly.'

Kate had to abandon early on the notion that she would be travelling by tarantass; it would have 'got wedged fatally or would have sunk in some treacherous morass before a single mile had been covered in the forest'. She would have to ride, and in terrain like this it wouldn't be side saddle. From now on she was going to have to act, eat, sleep, ride and dress like a man.

Had she been too hasty in her gifts to the prisoners on the road and run out of the money given to her by, among others, the Imperial family? Cossack, Jean Procopieff, was a good man and he guessed Kate had very few roubles left for emergencies and caring deeply about the sufferings of the lepers, offered, to lend her the horses required for the journey and offered his services both as leader of the cavalcade and to help her sign up men to provide security and lead the baggage-horses. Arms would have to be carried, in case of attack by bears. It wasn't particularly likely, but the Taiga was full of them.

When this curious party was ready to leave a photograph was taken of the fifteen men and thirty horses. Kate wasn't proud of the photograph, she knew it would raise comment on her seat and her mode of dress, because she was, of course, having to wear the trousers she'd had made. Interestingly, she was coy about describing this scene in her book, probably already aware that she had enemies out there who would pick over her every word critically and declare how shocking it was that a lady who had mixed in exalted circles – would now dress so unbecomingly and ride as a man.

Kate leaving Yakutsk 22nd June 1891

'I wore a jacket, with very long sleeves, and had the badge of the red cross on my left arm. Then I had to wear full trousers to the knees. The hat was an ordinary deer-stalker, which I had bought in London. I carried a revolver, a whip, and a little traveling bag, slung over the shoulder. I was obliged to ride as a man for several reasons — first, because the Yakutsk horses were so wild that it was impossible to ride safely sideways; second, because no woman could ride on a lady's saddle for 3000 versts, third, because, in the absence of roads, the horse has a nasty propensity of stumbling on the stones and among the roots of trees, which in these virgin forests make a perfect network, thus precipitating the unfortunate rider on to the ground; and, fourth, because the horse frequently sinks into the mud up to the rider's feet, and then, recovering its footing, rushes madly along among the shrubs and the branches of trees, utterly regardless of the fact that the lady rider's dress (if she wore one) was being torn into fragments. For these reasons I think no one will blame me for adopting man's mode of riding, and for making adequate provisions by means of the thick leather boots against the probability of bruises, contusions, etc.'

This is good justification, but it would take a generation and the campaigning of Ethel Tweedie ('Society is a hard task-master, yet for comfort and safety, I say ride like a man') to make trousers and riding astride fashionably acceptable for women.

Probably on the day before leaving – a shop ledger in the Yakutsk archives will confirm this – Kate bought a stock of practical gifts, from thread and mittens to tobacco and good tea, up to seventy three of some particular articles, and had them packed for the ride to Vilyuisk.

Finally, before leaving Yakutsk, Kate's party were invited to the Bishop's house. He held a special service praying for God's blessing and protection for their work. Here, as at the committee meeting, Kate reports feeling out of place – a lone woman among men. And then, since their endeavour was such a serious one, to avoid fuss and time wasting they slipped away from Yakutsk almost unnoticed. It was June 22nd 1891.

Chapter 16

'Yakutia is one of the few places on the planet that still retains the pristine beauty of nature and incredible variety of flora and fauna. Today the world's science community acknowledges the nature of Yakutia as the humanity's unique heritage and a promising reserve of the planet's biosphere, since 90% of the Yakut territories are still untouched ecosystems where nature processes occur unhindered.'

Yakutia Modern Guidebook

A puncture on the road to Yakutsk

If our ungainly mad-dash out of the train in the middle of the night had allowed us to see something of this border town of Neryungri, we would have seen why, more than once, it has been awarded the prize as the most beautiful town in Russia. Set against a mountainous background on the slopes of the right bank of the Chulman River, it was founded by the Neryungri geo-exploratory group during their exploration of the coal fields in the 1950s. First there were tents, then wooden two-storey houses constructed and in the eighties nine-storied blocks were built, although these suited the conventional standards of the USSR, stark individuality emerged which gave the town its unique feel, by facades on the buildings being brightly coloured with balconies, loggias and architectural shapes. A town grew that had a special feel and colour.

In 2007, the 375th anniversary of Yakutia's incorporation into the Russian empire, they celebrated with a fifty-one foot banner carrying a love poem that was registered in the Russian Guinness Book of Records; in 2012 they they followed this up even more publicly with a collective stencilling of lines from Lermontov, onto Neryungi's streets and pavements:

'A single sail is bleaching brightly
Upon the waves caressing bland,
What seeks it in a stranger country?'
Mikhail Yuryevich Lermontov

But now, in the half light, and without a banana or a bun to share, Ellie and I were out of the town and off on the longest road journey of our lives.

Olga's words were still following me; there are no roads, as such, outside the towns and cities of Sakha republic. It comprised a fifth of Russia's area, 40% above the Arctic Circle. Its ten ethnic groups, with their seven distinct languages, number almost a million; and despite its potential mineral wealth, the highways are earth tracks. This one, measuring 500 miles to Yakutsk, may have been initially laid by gulag labour.

There were a diverse collection of seven men with us in the minibus, with a great deal of luggage. A kindly Chinese man leaned over early in the journey and placed a pile of kumquats in our hands. Gestures like this along the way were typical, and lit up a monotony of uninhabitable landscape more extreme than anything we'd seen before on our journey.

We thought of Olga again as we sped through her home town of Aldan. Its fortune was based on gold prospecting, and an airfield was built after Russia's break with Germany in World War II to refuel American Lend-Lease aircraft heading for the Eastern Front.

It was after midnight when the driver pulled in at a truck-stop cafe adorned by blue painted tyres filled with scraggy geraniums and weeds. We trailed in tiredly and tucked into local snacks; knowing this would be our last chance to eat for many hours to come. What was there here for me, in this fluorescent-lit, plastic cave? Crisps, and a dull Russian staple that I was on the point of tiring of and unlikely to cause ripples in the Great British Bake-Off: The Cabbage Doughnut. A group of local youths languished in a corner drinking vodka, they giggled tipsily between themselves, trying out a few words of English on Ellie to gain her attention. Then there were, by the way, the last loos worth their name for the next twenty hours.

There were enforced delays to change tyres; (one was hilarious as the spare tyre escaped the driver's clutches as he pulled it down from the roof and it bounced off into the forest with him in hot pursuit). There were more sojourns in remote Siberian road-side cafes but I quickly realised that it is preferable to engage with nature behind a tree, than to brave those toilet arrangements heralded by a scary walk along a raised plank, where it helps to be able to hold your breath for some time.

We were in good hands with our Siberian driver. Tireless and robust, it was as if he had the memory of those thousands of miles of long straight tracks etched on to his hardened middle-age brow. He kept himself going by joining in with loud Russian pop music pumped out from the radio under a horsehair good-luck charm that swung to the rhythm of the ageing minibus bumping across the miles.

The following afternoon we pulled up 100 km south of Yakutsk at Buluus situated amid the trees, he lit a cigarette, bought a cup of tea and ushered us off to see an amazing phenomenon – the never melting glacier.

This glacier has an independent and defiant nature by existing by its own set of rules; already appreciating its rebellious spirit I studied the valley of ice: it was late afternoon on a hot August day but it was frozen solid – if I had stood there in winter though I would have seen a hot spring running through it. I stared out across it, enthralled by the power of nature and the sheer magnificence of being in such a distant and unknown land, the ice shimmered in its valley sling within the hot taiga, no matter how scorching the sun or how relentless the cold, its temperature stays at +4°C all year round.

The first appearance of the great River Lena took us all by surprise. For a few moments I felt like crying; here was the great historical watercourse, curling its way, without any bridge anywhere, towards the north, ever deeper into the Arctic on its mythical journey. Impassable for so much of the year with loose ice, now it was busy with large ships that haul the bulk of all Northern Siberian deliveries into the busy harbour at Yakutsk. We rolled down the riverbank, in full view of our distant destination and the western bank of the Lena.

We mooched about for two hours at the river's edge under a pink late-afternoon sun, waiting for one of the rusting ferries to take us across. We all needed the breather, my heart was still pumping blood to the rhythm of the minibus: slow down, speed up, drive round a pot hole, crash through another one; and that omits being shaken to bits by the hundreds of miles of corrugations lying across the dusty roads. At last we shuffled back to our seats in the spicy heat of the bus, which, meanwhile, the driver had washed, with the bucket behind his seat filled from the Lena; such stamina deserves a medal. As it happens, we still had many frustrating hours to go.

A red twilight bathed wide landscapes as we drove towards Yakutsk; soon it was midnight, and our kind driver was delivering each passenger safely to his destination. When it came to our turn, he dropped us at a nondescript block of flats where a little note on the wall indicated the hostel we had booked into. Despite having been driving for over twenty-one hours, he unhitched our heavy bags from the roof-rack and deposited them up the steps with a smile. I thanked him, in English, profusely, and he was gone.

We had arrived in Yakutsk, the City of Superlatives, founded as a fortress in 1632 and expanded into a city during the Soviet era, fuelled by the local reserves of gold and diamonds. Famously, it is the coldest city on earth, and the largest to be supported on permafrost and that is why there are three very conspicuous features that I found quite fascinating. First, all the buildings from apartment blocks and houses to factories, university and hospital are all constructed on a frame of stilt-like piles, most made of wood rising about a metre off the ground; second all the essential services, water, sewerage and cabling, arranged underground worldwide, are here lagged and carried overground; and third, and last, the roads are perpetually under repair, as they get washed out in the thaw of the extreme winters.

Kate Marsden's Yakutsk had a population of 7,000, against the whole of Yakutia's 250,000 inhabitants in all. On our arrival Yakutsk had a thriving population of over 295,000 people that of Yakutia had grown fourfold.

The composition of ethnicities compares closely with Kate's list of 1892 – predominantly Yakuts, followed by Evenks, Tatras, Buryat, Dolmans, Yukaghir and Chukchi but the proportions have now changed, and railways and other modern forms of transport have brought in two significant tribes to stay, namely Russians and Ukraininas.

The hostel itself was Chinese-run. Though it was, of course, midnight,it was initially disconcerting to find so many large rooms empty – we'd been expecting something more like the genial confusion of Anna's flat in Severobaikalsk. But even if it revolved around a single shared sink, compared to our poor tired old minibus, and the facilities of the journey, it was spotless, and we soon got our heads down. What we didn't realise at the time was that it would only be for one night.

Next morning I could scarcely open my eyes; I knew how Kate must have felt after sledge and tarantass. Ellie was eager to get out and see Yakutsk while I emerged from the single bed like a sloth crawling down his tree with the temptation of an internet cafe, where Lonely Planet hinted I could collect days of mail and drink coffee and eat pancakes with syrup and brown toast.

Jonathan's Coffee Shop and emails from home helped restore my energy, passion and purpose and soon I was back up to speed as ambassador for Kate Marsden. But she was about to take a back seat for a rather extraordinary reason – there was another welcome waiting for us here in Yakutsk and this was all down to one very interesting man a Professor from the Arctic State Institute of Culture and Art, and the Yakutsk North-East Federal University. I heard about the Professor through the St Francis Leprosy Guild in London, which was founded by Kate Marsden and they said he was keen to correspond with anyone with a special interest in her. That was the start of a year's fascinating exchange of letters in which the professor painstakingly answered all my questions, responded to my ideas and always in long detailed letters that eventually I placed in a file and called it my Prof. file. It was the professor who established the contacts for me in Yakutia which made the journey so much more rewarding.

Lunch had been arranged with a lady called Marta in a restaurant in The Old City which is reconstructed in the architectural style of the nineteenth century and located at the very centre of Yakutsk. We walked through pretty streets that are off limits to traffic and paved with wooden billets (hardwood blocks), past the restored Preobrazhenskaya Church, the Astro Tower, the founder's monument, the memorial to fallen soldiers, a stone column dedicated to the 375th anniversary of Yakutia joining the Russian Empire, and the M.K. Ammosov museum (Ammosov was a prominent Yakut political activist who led an active role in bringing Soviet power to Siberia).

I was looking forward to meeting Marta as she had expressed interest in me becoming involved in a Yakutsk film conference that coincided with our short stay in the city. Filming this trip had always been a very important goal for me and I had left the UK with ambitious hopes that maybe I could make this some sort of collaborative effort with Siberian film makers. The film I shot en route was the gathering of stories, evidence of art, culture, costume, tradition, people, travelling, music and architecture and I was keen to make a documentary that would portray the side of Siberia that is not all snowy wasteland and sub zero temperatures. So I presumed my participation would be giving some sort of workshop or doing some teaching on adventure film making.

I had no idea, until Marta began explaining, what a huge event for us this was going to be.

"Yakutia is one of the few places where much attention is paid to the development of the cinema"

Egor Borisov, President of the Republic of Sakha

Not in my wildest dreams could I have imagined what would happen next on my Siberian journey.

Ellie and I were shown to our table in the Yakutsk restaurant. Marta swept in, cool and brusque with fluent English, an expensive hair cut and a job to die for: bringing together the top players in Russian cinema for a spectacular event. Her opening words knocked us sideways:

"You are very welcome as delegates at the first Yakutsk International Film Festival." Before we had time to gasp, she continued:

"Here are your tickets for the important opening and closing ceremonies." She handed us each an envelope, within it were rectangular tickets, each a beautifully produced work of art, inscribed with our names.

I tried to remain cool – I mean, I was now part of the film world!

"Jacki, we are so pleased that you are representing Great Britain at the film festival and Ellie, you are South African aren't you?"

"Yes", came the sheepish reply, "though I live in England now."

"Oh, that doesn't matter, we are very pleased that you are here and will be representing South Africa at our film festival. What is your role in Jacki's film?"

"Assistant director." I cut in.

"Great, we're so glad you made it here in time. There are many excellent Siberian film makers here you will enjoy connecting up with, and maybe they can help you with your project."

"Thank you," I murmured, although inside I was shouting, 'that's bloody fantastic!'

"Oh, one other thing," Marta continued, "you can move into the Choreographic College Hostel this afternoon, (I later found out this was the Yakutian School of Ballet's digs), and there's a driver located to you and a translator. Relax now, enjoy Yakutsk, move to your accommodation and I will see you at our first event tomorrow."

She handed me a programme that itemised everything going on, to the minute, for the next three days and listed all the delegates and when they were arriving.

Now though she had to leave, swishing out of the restaurant in red pencil skirt and high heels, leaving us bowled over by the turn of events.

I flicked through the pages, and alarm at the inadequate contents of my luggage welled up in me.

"Ellie, it seems that tomorrow morning's an important debate about cinema, and tomorrow night – hey, this is worrying, "Gala Opening Ceremony, depart by limo for Red Carpet at 18.30, oh, and listen to this, depart to Gala Dinner at 21.30."

We looked at each other incredulously, and added, "Tomorrow!"

"What the hell are we going to wear?"

"And what does an Assistant Director do?" prodded Ellie.

"Don't worry, just improvise – or tell people you carry the camera bag!"

We both grinned at the unique situation and then shrieked in unison, "But what the hell are we supposed to wear?!"

As delegates, we would be looking pretty stupid walking a red carpet in trekking trousers. Undoubtably the cameras would be out in force.

"Fedex! How long to get my Karen Millen from Bristol to Yakutsk, do you think Ellie? That would be perfect for this occasion."

"Don't be daft, Jacki – we are in deepest Siberia, and we have to walk the red carpet tomorrow afternoon. Anyway who would pack it up and send it for you?" True I thought, son was in London, new man was in Glastonbury and dress was in Bristol.

What was there we could call on? Not much. Minimum make-up, no jewellery, no heels, no tights, no hair dryer, no hair straighteners, no nail varnish, no perfume, no iron, no fancy clutch bag and certainly no fake tan.

I just had that cotton black and white knee-length dress I had rung the bells of Tomsk in, that had a safety pin now replacing its top button that had pinged off in Irkutsk. Oh, a short black £10 Mango dress from last year. Ellie's wardrobe was no fuller.

"What frightens me is how Russians love to dress up; they are going to be in off-the-shoulder, sparkly, plunging neckline, full-length glorious dresses and we're going to be representing Great Britain and South Africa looking like a pair of tramps."

No way! We were going to, unfortunately, have to flex the plastic and then try a little pick-and-mix deception.

"How long have we got to go shopping?"

"Two hours max," Ellie replied, "once we've got our stuff to the ballet dancers' accommodation." So we did that, with some relief, and after laying out all that we <u>did</u> have on our beds and taken careful note, we set off to go shopping for glam.

The problem is, that Yakutsk, in winter, as Henry Lansdell, the British traveller who stopped off here on his way across Siberia in the late nineteenth century* tells us, 'has the credit of being the coldest place upon the face of the earth,' and the coldest place on earth doesn't show off its beautiful dresses behind plate glass that would let precious heat out.

Yes, there are shopping arcades, but not containing posh outfitters or fancy shoe-shops. These were buried deep inside buildings that to the untrained eye could have been apartment buildings, but for small signs in Russian, outside. These meant nothing to us, and

---

* http://www.independent.co.uk/travel/europe/yakutsk-journey-to-the-coldest-city-on-earth-771503.html

with no interpreter we were lucky to find the shops that would have been useful to us.

The miserable outcome of this mad dash shopping trip for me was:

A pair of black tights (that came out of the cellophane bag with a hole at the toe).

Wedge-heeled sandals with a bit of a sparkle.

A pot of cranberry-crush nail varnish, and a punitively expensive, very eye-catching, turquoise necklace made in Moscow to steal attention away from my misshapen dress from Mango.

For Ellie, the outcome was similar except that she splashed out on a fabulous pair of peach high-heels. I mightn't be in the hi-glam stakes tonight, but at least the South African delegation wasn't letting the side down!

I thought I could get away with the straining black and white frock for the first event, but I was very aware of my lack of sartorial elegance the moment the car collected us to drive us to the Inaugural Function at Government House. We were led into the grand Oval Hall resplendently set up in conference mode with ear pieces for translations, flags, cameras and cut glass tumblers for spring water. Many of the delegates from the film world were already seated, and we were ushered to our named places by a beautiful creature in full Yakutian costume. The Minister of Culture of the Russian Federation smiled across at us, and so did the Chairman of the Russian Filmmakers' Union and the provincial Culture Minister.

The two-and-a-half hours of the event were intensely political, majoring on the globalisation of film and the part Yakutia should play. To host its own film festival was a way to spread their language and reach out to the world. The fact that in 2011 alone forty seven locally based or set films were made, and the building of cinemas, should change the population's attitude to film and film-going. There was urgency in the presentations, and great satisfaction when the girls in costume presented bouquets to the chief delegates.

Then we all trailed out of Government House to converse and swap cards in the city square, where Yakutans milled about among flag poles, ponies and even an ice-cream van lit by the late afternoon sun.

In the hour before being collected for the gala opening ceremony, Ellie and I nipped back to the dancers' digs and morphed from road weary, grubby ducklings into glamorous glittering swans.

It was laughable, I had used that Mango dress as a nightdress on the BAM railway. It was black, it was shapeless, and I just hoped the necklace, sitting resplendently around my neck would draw all eyes away from the dress and the rather naff sandals with the toe showing through my tights.

The stretched limo was already full of Russian talent when it reached us. Of course we could have walked to the Lena Cinema, but why forgo a ride like this? Among the glamorous faces, was

Solbon Lygdenov, in a hoody and jeans. No dressing up for the man who would soon be declared overall winner for his film 'Bulag, The Sacred Spring'.

I heard my name announced after 'representing Great Britain' and then I walked in through a shower of flash bulbs, walked up the red carpet which was lined with a huge crowd of clapping Yakutians, tv cameras, ministers' hands to shake to a TV interview at the other end and Ellie was behind me and soon joined in.

Through a mist of dry ice a plethora of Yakutian talent entertained us that night. They wore extraordinary leather and fur costumes with long silver filigree embellishments, or tuxedos and sparkling gowns and danced to traditional Siberian music.

The Minister of Culture for Sakha Province, sought me out at dinner afterwards. We sat and exchanged vodka shots while he outlined his own interest in Kate Marsden. In the midst of all this razzle-dazzle, a moment of quiet epiphany brought by an unlikely hand, Andrei Borisov's. It occurred to me that I had reached a point in my long journey where people knew about Kate and could relate to what I was doing. There was a love for her here that I began to sense through the Minister's words. We were in a metaphoric port at last; we were anchored.

After a day of film screenings, we embarked at the real River Port on the cruise-ship Demyan Bednyi for a two day cruise up the River Lena.

Forget the ferry crossing. This was the real thing. We were about to experience Kate Marsden's river for ourselves. "It's crazy, Ellie," I said, "we tried so damn hard to get on any old cargo ship, under any conditions, and couldn't; and now we are going the other way in luxury!"

And so we two, and a glorious gang of Russian and international film-makers and stars, and Minister Boris himself, found ourselves, on the morning of the second day, facing the spectacle of the Lena Pillars, all, surely for the first time. I was seeing places that few people in the world would ever see – and for this experience, above all others, I had Kate Marsden to thank.

Both in Yakutsk and on the Demyan Bednyi, I felt a kind of Kate Marsden fever emanate from the local people who knew about her. On the first night aboard, I was asked if I'd give a talk on her. It attracted a large audience, and afterwards people clustered round me with questions and gifts, such was their interest in – and, indeed passion for, the British nurse who had risked her life and suffered hardship and opprobrium for the forest lepers, and whose fund-raising had finally led to the founding of Sosnovka leprosarium outside Vilyuisk.

Back past the Pillars World Heritage site and into port, a last memorable gala in the Pushkin Theatre was followed by dinner at the Muus Khaia Restaurant where microphones were passed round the tables for eulogies to the First Yakutsk Film Festival and cries for vodka toasts. This was a very Russian experience, though amid all the delicacies on offer – I passed on the horse-meat.

We woke up the next day in the Ballet Dancers' hostel eager to prepare for what we had come for, to follow Kate Marsden's exact steps through the forest, to Vilyuisk and Sosnovka and back. No need to stray from her known route, a 567 km (352 mile) forest track which has been there since first colonisation. It steers away from the west-east arterial M56 Kolyma Highway, the road to the coast at Magadan, which in my dreams of a Landrover or Toyota overland expedition we would have made use of. That road, constructed from 1932 to 1953 by gulag inmates under Stalin, is known as the Road of Bones and revered as a memorial because the bones of the people who died while constructing it were laid beneath or around the road.

For our own less haunted road, we boarded a minibus with soft seats, harem-style tasselled and scalloped curtains, bags of nuts, boiled sweets, plenty of bottled water and a bar of chocolate given to me by the Russian film critic Sergei to celebrate when we'd reached the half-way mark of our long journey!

What had Kate got about her person when she set out that morning from Yakutsk? History doesn't relate what use she thought she was going to make of the unfamiliar revolver: the three things she would have been clinging to, as a guarantee of survival, were -along with her precious medal – her whip, her little travelling bag and sack of basic forest rations.

Chapter 17

December 1892

451 Oxford Street, London, the site of The Dorothy Restaurant

I was hugely excited to be meeting Kate Marsden in London again, this time at The Dorothy Restaurant in Oxford Street. It was a drizzly day late in 1892; I walked towards it, taking advantage of the continuous canopy of coloured shop-awnings, well out of range of the horse-drawn hackney cabs rushing past. Though I was an alien, I had swapped my jeans for a costume Victorian outfit, but it looked pretty shoddy against the real thing. The ladies who brushed past me in full skirts and smart feathered hats made me feel a poor shadow of my well-dressed feminine forebears.

Dorothy's was a bold innovation in its day, a restaurant for women only,* serving all classes of ladies throughout the day. I was proud to step into an establishment where the early debates on aestheticism, liberalism and feminist sympathies had taken place and I instantly took to its decor. I was reminded of the Biba shop in Kensington High Street in the 1970s, the windows were hung with richly coloured Indian curtains and dyed peacock feathers; and there were little nooks and ante-rooms painted in deep red with luxurious couches, potted palms and tables dotted around. Kate was waiting for me in one of the luncheon rooms at a table with a white starched tablecloth and a vase of fresh, bright irises.

Fashionable ladies of the 1890s, as portrayed in 'The Girl's Own Paper'

"Now, did you buy your eightpenny dining ticket at the door?" She demanded before I had even had time to sit down.

"Yes, Miss Marsden; as soon as I'd read the notice on the wall saying 'Dorothy Restaurants admit no men'', (Actually I'd been more impressed by the discreet arrow to the lavatories downstairs, which meant that for the first time women didn't have to scuttle back home in discomfort from shopping trips, or avoid that second cup of tea.) I continued, "And I bought yours too." Kate gratefully took the ticket I slid across the table to her.

---

* See in appendices: 'Diana at Dinner' a send up by Punch in 1890 that suggests that the women requested that men be allowed to dine there in the evenings.

"So," I asked, "What do they serve for the eightpence?"

She gave me a look. "A good plate of meat and two veg with bread."

"Right, thank you, but Miss Marsden, you do remember I am a modern journalist and things have changed for women, so don't be shocked when I don't touch the meat bit."

I fully expected a bossy rebuke. Kate Marsden's training at the Deaconesses' Institute had drummed into her that the best way to treat the sick was to feed them up and that there is nothing better than meat. But she let it go; I wondered if it was allowable etiquette for me to deposit my meat onto her plate when it arrived. She would surely mop it up; what justification was there for waste?

She had agreed to meet me again and explain what her journey on horseback through the forest had been like.

I removed my grandmother's hat, it was midnight-blue, soft velvet with a floppy bow, but it just wasn't cutting it. Its shape of things to come look was receiving strange looks from the women smoking and laughing at the tables round us, all with stiff bonnets and tight buns. Once again, I was hating the strong smell of their cigarettes; but I took out my notebook and concentrated on Kate.

She was looking happier than on my first encounter: her eyes were bright and alive and she was holding a brown parcel tied loosely with string for me to observe.

"Look, I have the first draft of my manuscript – I am taking it to my publisher's office this afternoon."

"Bravo, Miss Marsden!" Funny, that; I already had a copy of her book in my bag!

"How many copies is your publisher hoping to print?"

"Well, 500 for the first edition, and the same number in America." Perhaps her life will be easier after it's published I thought, I pressed on.

"That ride through the forest, dear Miss Marsden," I asked, "where shall we start?"

"The Yakut Cossack, Jean Procopieff led the way. He was very kind: he knew I had scarcely ridden since a child, so we set off slowly, sending a detachment ahead with tents. This worried me a little because I was afraid we might lose them in the forest. There was no path, you know."

"There's an unmade road now, but it isn't very solid."

"Well, a post-road from Yakutsk is marked on the map, but only exists in the imagination of its map engraver. The post service, not a daily, but a monthly affair in these regions, is carried on under much the same difficulties which we encountered, along a half-obliterated track, or else through forests and over marshes, with no sign of a path, in the best way suggesting itself at the moment."

Setting out from Yakutsk

"It is such a long way, I'm surprised there is post!" I interrupted, but at this point our food arrived and she tucked in, not waiting for me, stopping only to wave her fork:

"Now, if you don't believe that I rode so far, please look at a map because during the whole of the journey to the extreme points north, east, and west, we were perpetually traveling zigzag fashion, or 'tacking about'. This tedious aspect of the journey was made necessary partly by the rough and pathless nature of the country through which we had to ride, and partly from the lepers being scattered about, remote from each other, and quite away from any direct or straightforward course that we would have preferred taking."

"I see, so you were always plunging back into the forest?"

"Exactly, and right from the beginning the worst of it began. We had not gone far when the horses sank up to their haunches in a bog, and began plunging desperately. I had to hold on to mine with all my might, while the men yelled at the animals to exert themselves. We rode in single file, and when the Cossack's horse in front partly disappeared we knew it was boggy there and must pick another way. As a rule, it was quite impossible to be sure where one was going. On the borders of the forest we camped for the night. Fires were lit, tents pitched, tea handed round, horses unloaded and tethered; then we retired. At the side of each member of the cavalcade lucky enough to possess a revolver or gun, that weapon lay ready, in case of bears."

Camp in the forest

"Good heavens, there really were bears then."

"My dear, the forest was full of them, we could hear them crashing through the undergrowth. Some men were placed as sentries, and also to keep up the fires. In the morning we started early, and our torments from mosquitoes began. They literally swarmed around us, and, in spite of gloves and a special veil-like thing for the head and shoulders, my hands, wrists, and face became swollen to alarming dimensions. These pests seemed to besiege every crevice where they could contrive to squeeze in."

"My poor dear Miss Marsden, your description, of your face becoming swollen to alarming dimensions – that's exactly what happened to my face in Sosnovka. I became unrecognisable as my face was so puffed up and my eyes became little slits. It was horrible, I felt they were crawling beneath my skin. I won't ever, ever let anyone doubt you made that journey."

After being bitten by Siberian insects

Kate stared at me, she had no idea what I was alluding to – those future book reviews that would damn her and accuse her of fabricating the whole journey.

"Did you also find it impossible to drive the insects off?"

"That's right; you see I dared not let go of the reins, which, by the way, were very primitive of their kind and very hard — made with horses' tails. D'you know, before long they wore out my gloves and blistered my hands. Now, all my riding gear, including that quaint Yakut saddle, made of wood — so uncomfortable, far too wide – all wood, and the bridle and reins, and my riding attire, all that I have brought home with me as a curiosity, along with other momentous of sledging and riding. I just have to look at them to be reminded of the difficulties under which our journey was accomplished."

"You brought your saddle back to England with you?" I was surprised by this revelation.

"Oh, goodness yes."

"So, are you going to add a photograph of these curiosities in your book?"

"Oh no, why ever would I do that?" Pity, that would be interesting I thought, there is no record of these artefacts that exists today. She carried on with her story:

"That first day we rode for seventeen miles and reached a point where, the horses and riders being thoroughly done up from struggling in marshes and scrambling through forests, we came to a halt in evening sunlight. Much laborious searching followed to choose a camping ground. The men found a deserted graveyard, and choosing what they thought was a specially cosy spot for me, they put up my tent at the foot of an old grave; I couldn't object; I mean, it would have to do. With the bites and damp ground, there was little chance of peaceful sleep. The cuckoo gave us a welcome, and the Siberian nightingale — very unlike the English — entertained us for hours; but the neighing of the poor horses, tormented by those huge horse-flies, rather sadly drowned the musical greeting. All around, a mist was rising from the soil; and, when I closed my eyes, there sprang up visions of the clean, soft beds and snug rooms of home, only to be replaced by a vision of outcast lepers, starving, and dying in misery."

"That was very tough for you, Miss Marsden, I'm not sure if I could have put up with that."

"Well I daresay; and of course I had to sleep in my travelling clothes, not even taking off the boots. The nightmare eventually passed me by, and I awoke and had breakfast."

"What was that?"

"Oh, tea, of course, and that hard bread which we stood in a bowl of tea to soften it."

The thought silenced her momentarily and, while I picked the boiled cabbage and carrots, I never eat boiled cabbage normally, it may be nutritious, but its just so dull, I glanced at the way she mopped up her leftover gravy with the slices of white bread.

"I'm ordering a coffee I'm sure you'll join me, Miss Marsden. Do you think they have any cake?"

"Not at lunchtime, my dear; but don't forget, our eight penny lunch comes with a hot pudding."

"Oh excellent," I replied and ordered steamed jam pudding and custard.

" Did it rain a lot on your ride, Miss Marsden? My own experience was that if it rained even for a little while, the track to Vilyuisk became an impassable quagmire."

"Oh, my goodness it did; and quite early on I experienced my first forest thunderstorm. It came from nowhere and it seemed to me that the sheer volume of the lightning was the dear Lord's way of compensating for the brevity of the Siberian summer! The flashes were all round us, the rain came down in a deluge, we soon got soaked for our waterproofs were ahead with the baggage. And then, just as suddenly, it stopped and the sun came on hot and dried us off, and no-one took cold. And then we had another diversion, birds of all kinds, flying in all directions, with shrill warning cries and plaintive wails. The Cossack raised his hand and pointed, and there was a horse lying dead. The tchinovnick, you know, the soldier, whispered, as he came up, 'Eagle!' "

"Goodness, how exciting; so what did you all do?"

"Well, our Yakuts stealthily dismounted and crept into the forest; but the eagle was too sharp for them. After proudly surveying us inferior mortals, and making a few graceful movements, he flew away, with what must have been a wood-pigeon in his talons, and dropping something as he soared, which one of the men pounced on as it fell. It was a sizeable fresh rabbit leg, and he delightedly waved it aloft, saying, "I can't refuse such a luxury, hunted and caught for me by the King of Birds."

"Did you ever find a roof to spend the night under, or was it always out in the open?" I was thinking, ruefully, of the Siberian insects.

"Well, my dear, there was one post-house. It was round about midday, and the sun beat down with almost tropical heat. A couple of hours' rest wouldn't come amiss – but, oh, that station house! It just reeked, and the old man and woman – their garments were stiff with filth, and their hands were black; they can't ever have come in contact with soap and water. We peered in through thick hearth-smoke and saw two calves; but we overcame our pride, and laid out the provisions we'd brought, tea, dry bread, and a tin of tongue, and I fell fast asleep on one of the post-house benches."

She paused.

"Yuk." I said, "you're tough".

"Next day, with more bogs and marshes to negotiate I grew so sleepy and sick that I begged for rest, even though the whole area was wringing wet, even under the summer sun. They obligingly stopped for me, and I was asleep in five minutes, lying there with only a fan to shelter my face from the sun. After a few miles more, I felt the same exhaustion seeping through me, only it was all I could do to hold on to the horse, and I nearly took several tumbles in the effort. The cramp in my lower limbs was indescribable, and I had to prise off the cushion under me, because it just wouldn't dry out. That left me on the bare wood of the saddle. Oh the relief when Jean Procopieff signalled a halt for the day, and the tents went up and the sticks were lit for tea. But even when I slept through to morning, I would awake to find the mosquitoes had been hard at work, even with veil and gloves, leaving great itching lumps, that made me sick.

At least those horseflies let us be at night. Once we saw two calves that had died from exhaustion from the bites of the brutes; and wherever our horses' coats were white, they were dotted with blood from the stings."

"Oh, poor things . . . But when did you make contact with any lepers?" I was nervous she would finish her pudding and coffee and get up and leave before we got to the heart of her story."

"Those lepers — they were suffering far more than I suffered. That was the one thought, added to the strength which The Almighty supplied, that kept me from collapsing entirely; but my dear, let me tell you about the bear and then I'll get on to them, I promise."

"Okay, great, and you'll be the only lady I've ever known to encounter a bear."

"Well, you see, the evening after that storm we had set up camp and were drinking tea when I noticed the men talking eagerly together and gesticulating. I asked the tchinovnick what it was all about, and he said that a large bear was in the area. There was a general priming of firearms, except in my case, for I did not know how to use my revolver, so thought I had better pass it on to someone else, lest I might shoot a man in mistake for a bear."

"My goodness, what an adventure!"

"And then, crash, crash, crash among the trees! The horses reared, and I slid off mine, preferring to meet the bear head-on to being dragged off on a mad horse and dashed against the trees. He must have been close, the bear, because one of the baggage horses had fled into the thick of the forest, and had got jammed between two trees. And then another of the baggage horses took fright, and this was worse because its tail was tied to the bridle of the one behind and the pair of them careered round and round a glade with the baggage bumping against their hind legs. Then all the other horses were thoroughly alarmed and we set to calming them — otherwise they too *would have torn away into the forest. These untamed Siberian horses often proved a source of unwitting danger to our limbs and lives."*

"And did you see the bear?"

"No."

"But were you given any advice as to what to do if you saw one Kate?" I glanced at the next table and noticed the women were shamelessly ear-wigging, transfixed by Kate's story.

"Oh yes, we had a few simple devices for scaring them away the men used to sing and shout their hardest; bells were placed on some of the horses, and we had tin boxes half filled with stones in one hand, which we continually shook, thus making a great, clattering noise."

I smiled to myself – that's not far off what it recommends in the SAS Survival Handbook. I could see she had polished off her pudding, and just to be sure I kept her at the table long enough to get on to the lepers, or even the curative herb, I made a show of scraping at the last of the custard in my bowl. But Kate Marsden was in her stride; her whole demeanour was upbeat, alert and positive.

I had one last way I could keep her – a donation to her funds. I was ready in case she asked me, but determined to get in first. From all I had read, once back in England fund-raising was her raison d'être, and she was supremely good at it. I also understood that of necessity she dipped into the general funds for personal needs, and that would, in due course, contribute to her disgrace.

"Before I forget, here's ten pounds towards the leper colony in Vilyuisk, which was built, and will be built and it will serve the community for nearly sixty years and I know that because I've seen the remains. And they love you there Kate, this year they are celebrating 125 years since you arrived there on horseback in the very journey you are describing to me right now. What remains of your foundation out in the Taigahas become a National Monument.

In your very darkest days Kate, remember, they love you for all that you went through on the lepers' behalf.

Kate let a slight smile play on her lips. She meticulously folded the bank note into a near cube, before squeezing it into the tweed purse and then she did an extraordinary thing – she handed me a small folded piece of paper.

"This is for you, a poor destitute leper that I drew, keep it to yourself."

I unfolded it, and there was a little drawing of a leper, simply, in Kate's own hand. I felt truly humbled, it was a historical gesture.

"Miss Marsden, thank you."

"Do people . . . do they think I am a good person? That I did something for the benefit of mankind?"

"Yes, Kate; you may be forgotten for many years among your compatriots, but never, never in Sosnovka."

With a thankful wave she slipped away from me. I made my way to Oxford Circus Tube and was grateful suddenly to be back in jeans.

I had already read the part of the story she hadn't told me. After the near encounter with the bear, they stopped at a yourta whose occupants were able to provide a grand dinner, (by Siberian Taiga standards,) of black meal, pancakes, sour cream, tea and milk, and a dish of fish that had been caught in the summer and kept frozen in an ice-pit. Accustoming herself to the suffocating smoke from the fire of cow dung, she slept soundly, knowing that it would keep the biting insects away.

On these travelling evenings, before sleep, she took out her notebook and jotted down ideas for the leper colony. It fought off the depressing thought, often present as they travelled, that the whole thing might, like the good intentions of the previous years, come to nothing.

Things continued to get very nasty on this first part of the journey to Vilyuisk. They pushed their way through forests, plunged into bogs, slept in more disgustingly filthy yourtas, which swarmed with vermin of many kinds and more than once she was too tired to dismount.

But at last they rode into the civilisation of Viyuisk, and it was here that her kindly guide Jean Procopieff, the retired Cossack of the Yakutsk Town Regiment had to say farewell. In a gesture reserved for visiting grandees, he presented her with a written address towards her and her project. In it he assured her of his good wishes, which one day would come to her rescue when her detractors got their teeth into her book and put it about that she had summoned the whole arduous journey out of thin air.

He wrote the letter from Vilyuisk on July 3, 1891, and confirmed that Kate was the 'friend of the suffering poor who he had visited this distant land, far away from the civilised world, with the aim of helping the unfortunate lepers'. He wanted to convince the population that our 'Mother of all Russians, our most gracious Empress', had approved Kate for so great a work, as the best example of self-denial on behalf of others as these lepers are more in need of help than any other subjects of her Imperial Majesty.

Procopieff wrote that there can be no doubt about Kate's purposes being noble and holy, when she was protected in her work by our most Gracious Sovereign, Mother of the poor, needy, and suffering and he finished by saying:

'My prayer to the Almighty Creator is that he may grant you the possibility of carrying out your good intentions to the end, and thus better the methods of alleviating the disease of the lepers.'

Chapter 18

'You shall not eat or drink in the company of other people but with lepers alone, and you shall know that when you shall have died you will not be buried in the church.'

— Anonymous
Mediaeval Leprosy Edict issued in Treves, France.

A leper hut in the forest

Kate records that Vilyuisk was one of the quietest places she had ever visited. The people seemed extremely easy-going and the few rough roads were overgrown with grass where cows and horses grazed.

She was met there by Father John Vinokouroff, a devoted Pastor to the lepers who often visited them in the forest. Later she met several of the townspeople to discuss building plans and prospects for the lepers. They agreed on an immediate site visit to the location proposed for the much needed, and longed for, hospital, leaving that very evening after the intense heat of the day had died down.

This short trip was a pleasant adventure for Kate and would remain a fond memory. In the party were Father John, Q. Feldsher, the doctor's assistant, Vassily, a merchant, and two Cossacks and they rode for twenty miles through the forest in the cool afterglow till they arrived at the spot that had been allocated.

Kate wasn't happy with the proposed site for the hospital and they must have accepted her reasoning; though knowing that Kate had only about twenty words of Russian, I can't be sure what common language was used. They sat inside a tent and talked over a lively midnight feast, on a scale beyond anything Kate had seen for some time. A roast goose was cut up and put on a large plate which they picked at. The chat and laughter broke the ice before Father John's soft voice led them back to the serious business of building a leper hospital.

'Those poor lepers are looked down upon as the very dregs of the community so that even those wishing to befriend them fall into the way of thinking that the worst is good enough for them.'

Vassily the merchant had his concerns too, 'I can provide the tools, but do we have workmen suitably skilled for constructing such a building?'

'Oh, we must find the best materials and workmen.' Kate insisted, 'We will have the money to pay for the best, but I so want these poor sufferers to understand that it is our Lord who was sending help to them, and, therefore, he can only send them the best.'

The men nodded and grunted their approval, and to the gentle sound of horses cropping nearby the small party wrapped their coats tightly around them and found places in the tent to curl up for the night.

In the morning they visited the site of the earlier hospital which had closed for lack of running funds. There was nothing left except a few stumps in the sand to mark where it had stood – but even after years of abandonment Kate noted that her party wouldn't

Camping out at midnight in the forest

venture close to it. Now she could see for herself how haunted the local people, even people of standing, were of being infected.

Along with one hospital, much of the forest had been hacked down and Kate noted that 'this site was also unsuitable for the new hospital, the forest having been cut away, and there being no shelter or pasture ground for the cattle.'

Nearing the areas the lepers were, to be expected, she was beginning to hear stories about them from the men she was with.

'I learned that some people suffering from other diseases were often exiled with the lepers, and compelled to remain with them as such, owing to the mistakes made by the natives when defining leprosy. I was also told of instances of inhuman brutality being practiced in the name of leprosy, in order to obtain some small fortune from a relative. When once someone becomes a leper all right to property passes away from them.'

Kate learnt a great deal that night from the locals, this wasn't hearsay any more – but straight form the horse's mouth. And the stories of gross injustice added a new shock dimension, because the event had happened close to hand, and could be proved.

The worst was of an uncle who did away with the orphaned niece and nephew given into his care in order to get possession of the cows they had inherited. The death of the little girl could be put down to accident, but to get rid of the boy he hatched a horrid plan: he would tell the community the boy had leprosy, for that, the uncle was entitled to push him out into the forest to fend for himself; and the cows became his. Simple!

Unfortunately his cruel plot succeeded, as Kate reported –

'The only inhabitants were bears and the uncle had formed a kind of kennel in which the child was to pass the rest of his days. It was made simply of a few sticks thrust into the ground, lightly covered with cow-dung and snow; and there the child was left to starve, or to be frozen to death. What his sufferings were can scarcely be conceived. It would be impossible for him to find his way back, through this trackless forest, to his uncle's place. Without food, without warmth, with only five hours' daylight out of twenty-four, frightened by the sounds of wild creatures, shaking with cold, and startled by the fierce winds howling in the forest, driven to the verge of madness, this poor child passed at last into God's keeping.'

The police officer spoke, who was an eye witness.

'I found the bones of the boy,' he lamented in the flickering fire-light, 'the shelter wasn't large enough for a dog. On the floor there was a little straw, the outside was covered with cow-dung, snow, and earth. Just a few yards in front I noticed a place in the ground freshly moved, and, on scraping away some snow, I found the dead body of the child, not placed in a coffin, but just covered over with earth; I opened his stomach and found only a little clay which he had eaten ; the body was perfectly healthy otherwise; there was no disease, and no sign of leprosy.'

Kate went quiet and stared into the fire. She thought about her brothers and sisters, and of her games with them in the garden of the lovely house in Edmonton, where there was always enough to eat. She recalled the laughter, and then the pain as one by one they sickened and died. She murmured into the fire:

'Whatever nationality you are, we are all the same. Oh all you gentle mothers, who would rather die a thousand painful deaths than a little one of yours should be subject to such cruelty, that it's up to us to prevent such cruelty. By our unflagging interest, our sympathy, help, and prayers, let's prevent the occurrence of a similar instance of wrong-doing anywhere in the world.'

The man responsible for the boy's death was arrested and imprisoned, but what justice was that for the children, or the leper community? Such an act was hard to erase from Kate's mind, and she thought more and more about how she could help and make a difference in this lonely, bleak part of the world.

Kate listened to them talking in the failing light, all agreed how utterly demoralising it was for the men, women, and children herded together in the same filthy yourtas. 'They live like animals, and with animals, for even the cows dwell in the same hovel' one local man said, and looking up, continued, 'We are Yakuts, we are good people, so why are we allowing our fellow man to send only the worst of their cast-off clothing to the lepers; it's a crime, these garments are fur skins, that are not given away until they can be worn no longer by the owners and they are filled with vermin, filthy beyond description, and often nothing but a mass of rags, I hate this, why can't we do better?'

The party nodded in agreement till another police officer spoke up, 'Where the lepers herd together, they themselves bury their dead, and the priest goes once a year to read the prayers over those who have died during the year. It's disgusting, and having Miss Marsden here, well it's made me realise, see, that we should do better, it's damn awful.'

They rode back into Vilyuisk through tall larch and silver birch trees trembling and swaying against the dawn light of a Siberian summer. Kate felt invigorated: this slog had turned into an adventure, and these men, colleagues and companions, accepted her for what she was and what she offered. Even though she mightn't understand all their Russian, she was following it and getting most of it translated. Look how far she had come; a speck in an ocean of trees, far from anything that was recognisable as part of her world and upbringing. At last she could feel her efforts were paying off: what she was finding out on the spot made for an attainable outcome.

The next morning a slightly reinforced party of eleven set off from Vilyuisk for Mastach, to show their visitor an actual leper settlement – her first. They travelled the first ten miles by boat, before riding into the Taiga. Kate noted that they travelled through forest that seemed ominously devoid of life and movement. Each crack of a twig under their ponies' hooves was amplified and intrusive and this became more apparent when the outline of a yourta, and its plume of smoke, showed between the tree trunks. As she stood within the fire-smoke to get momentary relief from the biting insects, she heard a slight rustle as a youngish woman appeared through the bushes. Her rags barely covered her. A boy of fourteen, perhaps, shyly followed. As Kate wrote:

'Her tale of woe was soon told. Her son was supposed to be a leper. The head of a neighbouring tribe, having decided that he was infected, condemned him to be separated from his mother, and to live alone in the depths of the forest, ten miles away from any other hut or human being.

THE WAY IN WHICH THE LEPERS ARE HERDED TOGETHER.

Lepers herded together

218

After being in the forest some time, he became so maddened by the torture and misery of his solitary life, that he begged his mother to allow him to come at night and sleep near her. She consented, and made a small room at the back of her hut, into which he crept every night. But the fear that his shelter should be discovered and the indulgence stopped, kept him in a constant state of alarm. I arranged with the chief that the child and his mother should be protected, and the boy permitted to remain with her. I can never forget the terrified appearance of that boy as I went near to touch him; he at first flinched, expecting that I meant to hurt him. Even after being at the place for some time, he still shrank when I went up to him. He was made to think himself shunned and dreaded by everyone, and was bound to retire and keep as far away as possible at anyone's approach. The shrinking of that child would have touched the most callous heart; it spoke such volumes.'

And so another tale of harsh injustice brought Kate face to face with the world of leprosy.

All their outward way the eleven men, many from the forest itself, used boy-scout like skills to mark out their way back, bill-hooking the worst undergrowth and planting poles in the swampy bits. But some rode forward supporting the way for Kate and the main party. The Yakut members presented a colourful picture in their strange native costume with high shoulder pieces, colourful handkerchiefs covering their heads and hanging down their backs. While the wild, un-groomed and unkempt horses added to the drama of the scene.

On and on they went, Kate's riding skills being constantly challenged by the stumps and roots of trees which the horses frequently tripped on. Now and then her horse sank, but into concealed holes, well hidden among the roots, and their hooves became entangled in such a way that only a Siberian horse could extricate itself; this terrain went on for miles and miles.

Coming to a lake, they spotted two yourtas and pointed.

'After all those months of traveling I had found, thank God! the poor creatures whom I had come to help.' But was she ready for the reality of the horrendous sight that awaited her? She writes:

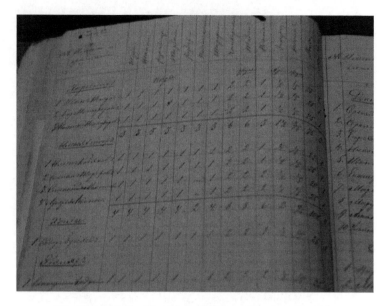

**The Yakutsk Archives have ledgers showing the gifts
donated to the lepers by Kate and her party.**

'A little crowd of people. Some of the people came limping, and
some leaning on sticks, to catch the first glimpse of us, their faces and
limbs distorted by the dreadful ravages of the disease. One poor creature could only crawl by the help of a stool, and all had the same indescribably hopeless expression of the eyes which indicates the disease. I
scrambled off the horse, and went quickly among the little crowd of
the lame, the halt, and the blind. Some were standing, some were
kneeling, and some crouching on the ground, and all with eager faces
turned toward me. They told me afterward that they believed God had
sent me; and, my friends, if you could all have been there, you would
no longer wonder at my having devoted body and soul to this work.'

Kate had gifts with her to give to the lepers and as she passed
them about their poor distorted faces beamed with delight and
their fear of this strange foreign woman, not here in some way to
punish them, began to fade. Rather she was an angel appearing out
of the harsh forest, a vision sent by God to bring mercy and

kindness. The gifts were of real practical or psychological use, and her distribution of them passed into legend, so that Kate Marsden is still an angel in Yakutia today.

Ledgers in the Yakutsk archives show a careful record of the gifts bought there by Kate before she left.

In the photograph above, the column down the left specifies the leper settlements and the people there, and across the top the items that Kate would hand out to them: coats, hats, mittens, shirts, scarves, tobacco and headscarves. In a separate list fur coats, tea, thread and fabric are itemised. The page shows seventy three hats, seventy three pairs of mittens, seventy three scarves and seventy three winter coats made of sheepskin. There is also mention of 'good' tea.

Kate also took with her the services of a very useful man from the staff of the Governor of Yakutsk, with enough French and Yakut to act as her translator. He was Sergei Mihailovitch Petroff, and his signatures on two short reports in French by Kate Marsden in the Yakutsk archives, are substantial proof that she did all she said she did.*

A scene from leper life

---

* Although a review of Kate's book, presumably by Hapgood, called 'Her story is false, has no foundation in fact, says she saw but one sick person and drew on her imagination throughout. ' Petroff is quoted as the man verifying her falsehoods, Hapgood's lying shows the lengths she went to undermine Kate Marsden.

As they rode on through the forests of Yakutia seeking out the lepers, Kate sensed that each settlement had been forewarned by some kind of bush telegraph. As they appeared from their hovels to greet her they held out fingerless hands and lifted their faces contorted with pain and hopeless misery; their disfigured smiles made Kate shudder.

The condition of the yourtas that they lived in shocked the medical inspector, Dr. Smirnoff, who was of the party, and sending two official documents to the regional government about them. What he says, foreshadow what Kate writes in her book:

'One is struck at the sight of the smallness of these nomad huts in which they dwell. Light hardly penetrates, and the atmosphere is so infected by the conglomeration of the lepers and the exhalations of rotten fish that one is quite suffocated on entering them. These unfortunates have neither beds nor linen; their clothing consists only of sheep and cow skins, all in rags, and it is under these conditions, without any change, that they are obliged to live tens of years, till at last death releases them from their sufferings. Not far from these huts one perceives graves with crosses on them, indicating the places where the lepers bury each other. The door is so small that one is obliged to bend to be able to enter. The hut is very low, and hardly any light enters, and the atmosphere is so foul that even the fire which is continually burning in the fireplace cannot purify it. The filth of this hovel is disgusting; the dirty table and the few benches covered with filthy skins, in lieu of beds, comprise everything in the place. I found six men and three women huddled together in this infected hovel. It is inexplicable how so many people get to be lodged in so small and low a hut. The clothes of these lepers consisted of skins (of cows) all in rags and holes.'

Kate further comments:

'The tchinovnick for special services, Mr. Shachourdine, in his report, contained in Protocol No. 3, states that the interior of these yourtas is not known to me, as, however much I wanted to get acquainted with the interior of the said huts, I could not get into them, on account of the fearful stench, similar to that coming from a dead body; which was due not only to the lepers themselves, but also to the food that they ate, consisting chiefly of rotten fish.'

But clearly she had poked her head inside, holding her breath for as long as it took:

'The yourtas, swarming with vermin of many kinds, were made out of the trunks of trees, fastened with wooden nails, and covered with cow-dung, of which the floor also consisted, mixed with earth. The windows were only one foot square, and were covered with calico.

The lepers have no beds. Round the inside of the yourtas were placed trunks of trees, upon which were fixed pieces or planks of wood. On these the lepers slept, closely packed as near to each other as possible, the feet of one to the head of the next, men, women, and children were all mixed together; calves were also kept there in the summer, and cows during the winter. There was no kind of sanitary arrangements; and, sometimes, in the depth of the winter, none of the inmates venture outside for days together. In this place the lepers eat, cook, sleep, live, and die. If one of them dies, the body is kept in the hovel for three days. The smoke fills the place — stifling both the lepers and the cattle. Not long ago they had smallpox among them, and four of their number died and the dead bodies were kept in the same yourta for three days. The dead are buried only a few yards from the dreadful abode, so that the lepers cannot pass their threshold without being reminded of the end daily drawing nearer.'

But there is also the story of a wrong righted, which Kate is proud to recount as due in large part to her presence in the survey party.

They came to a yourta and among the lepers a young girl was pushed forward, showing no signs of the disease. She had been born after her mother had been confirmed with leprosy and sent away from her village. The child had lived all her eighteen years there, and the mother, perhaps instinctively drawn to the foreign lady with the gifts, appealed to the visitors for their compassion, and to take the girl out of this lonely hell-hole into the real world. Kate's party talked together and agreed that it was a sad and tragic situation; and the ispravnick*, surprisingly and honourably, agreed to take the girl into his own home as a servant, since he was 'resolved to break the spell of terror that ruled among the Yakuts'. Kate, overjoyed, wrote:

'All who try to appreciate the full significance and after-effects of the brave chief's decision will not hesitate to class him among those whose hearts have the true ring of heroism, and of that charity which is the essence of the Christian religion.'

Already the presence of Kate amongst the group of men was creating a change in public attitudes, and a glimmer of hope was apparent in the lives of the sorrowful Yakut lepers.

A DOG'S SAGACITY IN SAVING LEPERS FROM BEARS.

This picture from Kate's book reads 'A Dog's Sagacity in Saving Lepers from Bears'

* In Imperial Russia an ispravnick was a local administrator who was charged with leadership of local law enforcement.

It was during the next leg of her journey around the Vilyuisk circuit that Kate Marsden and her party encountered that bear. It was Kate's horse that first picked up its presence, becoming restless, pricking up his ears and standing still. The other horses behaved in the same way, until first one, then two more, attempted to bolt. When the animals had been soothed, the tchinovnick rode forward through the silent forest and spied the bear 'crouching in an ominous manner'. Doubtless, on a signal, all hands set to, rattling their tin boxes, and all throats roared, sang and yelled. It was undoubtably a worrying time for Kate, as for the horses; but probably most unpleasant for the bear!

The day's drama didn't stop there. Back on the river, they were supposed to row about 'twenty versts' (thirteen miles) up a stream, but made slow headway against the swollen current. Soon a terrific storm set in; violent gusts tore across the water, forcing the boat against overhanging trees or the bank itself, the men in a crazed panic yelling their heads off. The ispravnick stumbled ashore and Kate gamely leapt for it, but the ensuing ten mile forest hike back to Vilyuisk on an empty stomach was almost too much for her. She owed her safe return to the kind soldiers, and once back she went straight to bed and slept for twenty-four hours. It was as well: later they would set off to a different compass point on a circuit of 1,000 versts, or over 600 miles.

On the evening of 27th July they left again into the huge forest. Although she felt rested, Kate knew this was going to be very tough indeed; after all, what other woman of her day, who wasn't even a trained horsewoman, had ever undertaken such an expedition?

Bu there was a moment of great comfort for her, among the little crowd seeing them off was the face of the girl 'lifted' from the leper yourta, scrubbed and healthy, with a great smile as she waved to Kate.

Once again, their first few miles were by boat. All went well, and they reached their mooring at midnight where a group of men were seated around a log fire. Kate immediately enquired why another fire was burning a few yards away; they lowered their voices to explain that a solitary leper was there, hoping to see Kate.

She wasted no time in going across to the poor man – even though no one else would, except Father John, who acted as interpreter between them. Kate's angel status had gone before her, and the man, in his filthy rags, wept, touching the ground with his forehead before looking up and slowly telling her his pitiful story. He had lived totally alone in raw nature for many years, shunned by all humanity. Kate wrote of 'the flickering fire giving him a weird appearance, while the branches of the trees in the background formed a slight shelter.'

Kate gave him what would be useful to him, but she went further, comforting him with the prospect of a colony being built where lepers like himself would be taken care of properly and humanely.

Leaving him with this spark of hope, Kate, as she walked back couldn't help hoping, for his sake, it would be soon; but she noted that her men, warming themselves round their fire, flinched as she approached. Prejudices against lepers ran all too deep.

Back aboard and rested, they rowed on for thirty miles and stopping at an unnamed place that Father John and Kate considered would be suitable for the new leper colony; before carrying on up the river where their ponies were grazing. Kate mentions her shock when the priest fell on his knees and cried at his gratitude for what she was doing to help the lepers. 'He implored me to use every effort so as to bring my plans to a speedy result, promising to pray for blessing for each step of my way, for, truly, I had come to help the most miserable of human beings.'

This pattern of travelling deep into the night meant they could shelter and rest in the torrid part of the day. It brought back the pleasure of adventure to Kate. It was at this landfall that they rested, recouped and talked.

'Under a very picturesque shelter made of branches of trees stuck into the ground, and which had been prepared for us by the Yakuts, we discussed the plans for the hospital and the needs of the lepers. Then we mounted and rode off, twenty-five men and myself, with thirty horses, some of them carrying baggage.'

But the horror of a leper's life returned to haunt her at Hatignach, there she saw twelve men, women and children, 'scantily and filthily clothed,' huddled together in two small yourtas, covered with vermin.

'The stench was dreadful; one man was dying, two men had lost their toes and half of their feet; they had tied boards from their knees to the ground, so that by this help they could contrive to drag themselves along. One man had no fingers; and the poor stumps, raised to make the sign of the cross x were enough to bring tears to the eyes of the most callous. On my approaching them they all crouched on the ground, as if almost terror-struck at the very idea of anyone coming near to help them.' No miracles here; but some relief. And the plight of a dozen human beings set of record.

The party travelled through the night to reach the next settlement 150 miles away. The days were by now too hot to ride in, but brought a curious advantage: the horse-flies were far less interested in the beasts and their riders.

During the next night's ride Kate learnt of the woman who had been put in a yourta with a madman.

'For four years this poor woman had to live with a madman in the depth of the forest, away from every human being, never sure from one hour to another of her life. Just picture the constant dread she must have lived in — at night, hardly daring to close her eyes to sleep; during the day, ever on the watch for each movement the man made, knowing well that, should he attack her, there was no hand to protect her, no ear to attend to her cries for help — for miles and miles around nothing but the dense forest to echo back her voice. As, bit by bit, this information was translated to me, a tremor went through my whole being; while, deep in my heart, I thanked God for sending me here to help these helpless, forsaken ones.'

Usually the forest was a deadly hush, with just a shiver in the branches of the tall birch and pine. It wasn't just the scent of bear that spooked the ponies; it could be a shadow, or a branch in the forest canopy whipped by a sudden gust, or a sudden shower of pine needles. Kate was always on the look out for hidden stumps or logs to avoid, and cavities in the forest floor – so her eyes were forever downwards. She couldn't for the life of her work out how the experienced riders always knew where they were going, and could steer a correct course through the sea of trunks.

After many hours' ride, as night turned into day, they came on the hidden hovel of nine more lepers, whose lives were worse than anything Kate had yet seen. Two women timidly stepped out of the shadows, followed by a man of about forty; but what struck Kate was the two children, completely unclothed. On enquiring, she learnt that in the depths of winter they only kept warm with a layer of hay, secured to them with any available rags.

Kate sat despondently among them, flicking away the flies that landed on their wounds. Now she could feel the terrible pain these outcasts had to endure; they writhed, wept and whimpered, staring through vacant eyes at this foreign woman pulling unimaginable gifts of comfort out of her pack.

Speechless at the sight in her experience of their torment, Kate wrestled with her faith. How could God test a human being in such a terrible way?

Kate wondered why wouldn't some of them in desperation, throw themselves in the path of the bears to end their miseries?

Restless to be gone from this scene, and holding well back from it, the Yakuts set off at speed as soon as Kate remounted; to them the contagion hung in the air ready for them to catch. Now she understood the villagers' superstition which she hadn't picked up on that first hideout from Vilyuisk with Father John and the two cossacks. At least she had with her, on this expedition, Smirnoff to talk sense and head off any possible insurrection. And so for a while she rode in the slipstream of the others in silence, her thoughts disturbed only by an owl's call and the large rat that darted close to her pony's hooves, causing him to shy. Her dejection at what she had seen was compounded by an infinite weariness that made it difficult to stay in the saddle.

It remained a constant source of surprise, the number of children she found enduring this wretched isolation. These at least could benefit from the new leprosarium, and even live to see a cure. The very next day a tiny burrow of a yourta revealed a man, two women, and a child. Kate writes in her book:

'One of the women had been afflicted with leprosy in all its worst aspects for years; she was almost naked, having only a dirty strip of leather over her. By her side was her husband, who, although free from leprosy, nobly determined to share his wife's exile. Her child, too, preferred to accompany her mother rather than remain with the village. Neither husband nor child will ever be allowed to enter the community again. Close by was a woman who had just been confined. And there were also two children here, born of lepers, born to live among lepers, and doomed most likely to become lepers, either from contagion or hereditary taint.'

It was fortunate that Dr Smirnoff the Medical Inspector was with them. He was there on the ground, and would be – or at least his reports would be – when the leprosarium came to be built.

Whatever thoughts each of the party was carrying, strung out now in single file, were swept aside by the big Siberian adventure that happened next.

It was as if specially laid on for this English visitor, and Kate's prose takes on the sparkle of the best travel writing.

She began to notice that the tread of the ponies' hooves had a different ring, as if riding over a shallow-roofed tunnel. Her tchinovnick explained at once: he'd come across it before. The peaty subsoil was in a state of slow combustion, often over a wide area of taiga, all but invisibly because there was vent for the smoke to rise: 'The burnt earth creates great hollows, and there is always danger of a horse breaking the crust and sinking into the fire.'

Kate remained content to follow where the others led; she was probably too tired, anyway, to be frightened. But as darkness came on, the evidence became more alarming.

Through the gloom she could make out distant lights which, as they became brighter, seemed to make the horses restless. Tired as she was, she found it almost impossible to control hers. When they emerged through the tree line into an open area an extraordinary sight presented itself.

'The whole earth, not the forest, for miles around seemed full of little flickers of fire; flames of many colours — red, gold, blue, and purple — darted up on every hand, some forked and jagged, some straight as a javelin, rising here and there above the earth, and, in places, seeming to lick the dust, and then, having gained fresh energy, springing as high as the others.'

This adventuress was witness to something that the Royal Geographical Society would later acknowledge as rarely seen, this extensive natural underground fire was even more phenomenal – (and we would say, counterintuitive) because the soil below was permafrosted. There is no way she could have made it up and a note to Isabel Hapgood and her other subsequent detractors: the men travelling with her testified to seeing this extraordinary experience. But she alone could find the words for what she saw, the flames 'endowed with life', and the 'lurid spectacle' resembling 'a high carnival of curious creatures, let loose for a time from their prison house, careering about in fantastic shapes'.

There was no way but across. The party therefore had to ride through the fire, Kate looked across the burning fields and wondered how it was possible to cross it alive. With great caution they filed across, on ponies that were edgy, hesitant and shivering. All eyes – human and equine – were smarting; and so they continued to near the far edge of the smouldering plain.

'All went well for about three miles. Suddenly we heard an ominous, crashing noise behind and then a loud cry, which was instantly taken up by the whole cavalcade. We stopped our horses and waited for the worst to happen. In a few minutes there came, dashing at full speed into the midst of us, a poor frightened baggage horse, which, stepping into a hole, had taken fright and darted away, the baggage boxes getting loose and thumping against its hind legs as it tore along. It made straight for us, and, in another moment, would have thrown me and my horse to the ground had not the tchinovnick deftly turned the mad creature aside. Then the poor thing bounded on and went far ahead, and we heard the boxes crashing against half-burnt trunks of trees. All our horses were straining at the rein, and seemed bent on starting off wildly after the one that had disappeared; but we gradually soothed them, and then pushed on. The smoke was still blinding us; and, not being able to see in the least where I was going, I loosened the reins and just let the horse go where he liked.'

Brave lady, great team, tough ponies, Kate was tired to the bone by the time, on safe ground at last, they camped that night; a bear could have ambled into her tent and she wouldn't have noticed.

Within days, Kate's exhaustion would cause her health to break down; but in the meantime, talking with Smirnoff and others over the encampments they had visited, about the near-nakedness of almost all the sick people, she heard one story that would stay with her – that of a leper woman who really did live naked, her clothing having been confiscated and burnt to stop her repeatedly raiding a particular village for food. No wonder that one winter her body was found under a tree.

All around the leprosy-free areas of the Vilyuisk Circuit, Kate could have heard the name 'leper' used as a swearword because the local folklore had it that measles, scarlet fever and smallpox were handed out by God, but leprosy was the work of the Devil. Her soldier escorts might be biting their tongues, but they were carriers of these attitudes. Even with the leprosarium built, it would take time for people to feel more kindly towards them.

Doubtless she had been nursing her pain for sometime, one day she had to be lifted down from the saddle, and laid on a blanket on the ground. She put it down to 'suffering acute pain from an interior access', but Dr Smirnoff medical officer and the isprvnick feared she might be dying; but Kate awoke and bravely remounted her horse, and was able to carry on for twenty miles.

Their forest camp site that night was an area that had been destroyed in a wild fire. The wind whistling through the trees, caused the branches to crack and crash down around them and kept her awake; so the next day was a struggle for her.

The party came on a leper couple whose feet were so eroded they could only crawl. Here too there was a child. With some difficulty, one of the soldiers got Kate down and helped her to remount once she had given them chosen gifts and whispered words of comfort to them. Later on, a solitary woman, so disturbed at hearing human voices that she flinched, confessed she was too weak to collect the scraps of food left for her at a safe distance. It was becoming increasingly obvious that these poor creatures were dispatched to 'dead' areas no one else would want to go to, as far as possible from any settlements. She also learned the system, and content, of the food donations. There were agreed places where it was deposited a couple of times a week. It consisted of meat, pickled or rotting fish, milk and tea – which no self-respecting bear would bother with.

When she came to write her book about the journey, half expecting there would be those who would read her exploits as those of a female Don Quixote, Kate adds a forty-six page appendix. The bulk of which consists of letters from Father John Vinokouroff, who had accompanied her on both fact-finding expeditions from Vilyuisk, and in whose confidence she remained throughout her visit. These, of course, were written after her departure from the town, some no doubt reaching her back in England. But there is one, full of deep gratitude, from Gregory Eremieff, the Golova or chief of the tribe of the Sredni Vilyuisk District who had accompanied her on the last and longest expedition, written before she reached Moscow. He thanks her for her brave undertaking in going into the worst areas of his land to visit his poor lepers: 'If I may express my earnest desire framed in this request, I beg that, if possible, you will lay at the feet of Her Imperial Majesty the Empress the expression of our loyal and devoted love and gratitude for Her Imperial Majesty's immediate protection of our unfortunate lepers.'

In addition she includes letters from Mr Paramonoff, the doctor's assistant or feldsher who had gone with them, who writes:

'As a citizen and Christian, I am bound to express my sincere gratitude for the hearty interest and self-sacrifice, which it is not possible to describe, but which, as your constant fellow-traveller, I saw in every step of your difficult and dangerous journey, full of every possible privation.'

Most touching of all are letters from the lepers themselves, dictated and translated by a Yakut-speaking Government clerk, Vasilliy Nikolaefi Novine:

'Loving Patroness Miss Marsden,

We thank you very much for the great gifts you have sent us, which we have only just received. We will always pray to God for you. We are still living in the same way as when you visited us. The frightful disease is torturing us in our miserable little huts; and we are suffering from cold and, in addition, from hunger. Only God alone knows and sees our wretched life. Last summer the crops failed; so that now the community cannot even give us one pound of flour, and we have not even a proper kettle to boil our tea in. Lord, protect our benefactress, Miss Marsden, like the apple of Thine eye.'

A second one says:

'This day we have had the happiness to receive your holy gifts, and also your letter, for which we have given a receipt. We thank you from the depths of our hearts. The Lord Jesus Christ will grant you heavenly and earthly happiness. We have to inform you that we live in a sad condition, suffering from cold and hunger in addition to our terrible disease. You yourself has witnessed our unfortunate existence. Our hope is in God, and in you for charitable help. We are constantly praying to God for your health and long life. May the Lord God bless you. After your visit one of our number died.

Signed by:

The Lepers of Loutchinsky and Togouisky

Nassleg of the Sredni Vilyuisk Oulousse.

Monday, February 24th, 1892.'

She concludes with four reports, the last two her own but witnessed and countersigned in Yakutsk. The first, of the meeting of the Yakutsk provincial Committee for public health concerning the preventive measures to be taken for leprosy. This shows they were discussing implementations of the conclusions drawn, on her exhaustive ride, by Kate Marsden. That, at least, boded well for future change. It reads, in part, 'The aim of this commission will be to study the documents already existing in the provincial administration concerning leprosy; to make known the former measures which have been taken to check this disease; to explain reasons why these measures have not been carried out or continued; and to gather present information about the condition of the disease, and the best way of combating this disease now, that when the question may be fully decided by the Provincial Council measures may be adopted in due form.'

The next document is a long and detailed report by Dr M Smirnoff, the Medical Inspector who accompanied Kate throughout. He goes to great lengths to describe leprosy, its symptoms and their treatment in society. He outlined what his region had done in the past to contain and ultimately, isolate leprosy, and number and document the lepers that he and Kate visited and named all the places: Yanhonshy, Toguisky, Loutchinsk, Tebinsk, Kakouisk, Kobiansk and Mukutchinsk. There is great compassion in Smirnoff's description of the ways in which leper families tried to stay together.

Kate adds two summaries (written by herself, originally in French) of the difficulties of the journey; the originals were signed off by Sergei Michailovitch Petroff, the tchinovnick for special service to the Yakutsk Governor, who had been assigned to her for the two expeditions to the lepers.

On the return journey to Yakutsk Kate's party rode about seventy miles a day. By now there was little food left, and shortage of sleep was catching up with her. The feldsher shot wild duck which they cooked and ate with the remaining dried black bread, which by now was two months old. They refilled their containers with dark brown water from stagnant wayside ponds. The going was no easier, their horses tired easily, and bears were never far away. Her inner resources already depleted, Kate sat through further thunderstorms and struggled their way through dense forest and floundered over the bogs and marshes which their tired horses sunk into. Many times Kate was soaked to the skin and had to stand by a fire to get dry.

Twenty miles from Yakutsk and a cart was hired into which a layer of straw was strewn and Kate was placed on it – she re-entered

Yakutsk 'like a wounded soldier after battle'. It was 31st July 1891; and this part of her journey had taken thirty nine days.

I am not sure if Kate's journey by horseback really did amount to 2,000 miles, but I shall give her the benefit of the doubt and applaud her for such an endeavour and for paying such huge respects to her escorts when she finally parted with them. As a young Victorian woman she had placed herself at the mercy of a group of strange man and they had acted with the deepest respects towards her for two months. She calls them all 'chivalrous and devoted, without exception' and adds that 'never for one instant did they betray the confidence reposed in them' and 'may God ever bless them for all the help they gave me!'

The kindly police ispravnick, who had travelled the whole way with them, handed her a letter. Kate's book gives it in full, as it is, deservedly, reproduced here:

'Having come to the limit of the circuit in my government, and having thus finished the special and extraordinary commission of my chief to accompany you and protect you through your journey to the different places where the leper dwellings are to be found, I deeply regret to be obliged, by the duties of my service, to bid you farewell and to return to Vilyuisk. But, before expressing to you, Miss Marsden, my sincere and quite special respect and heart-felt esteem, I beg of you to allow me to say a few words about the importance of your visit to the Vilyuisk Circuit, but especially to the Sredni Vilyuisk oulousse.* Her Imperial Majesty the Empress, who is always thinking about the good of her people, having informed you about the intimations that had reached Her Imperial Majesty concerning the sad condition of the unfortunate lepers of the Vilyuisk Circuit, and getting to know your desire to inspect them, has graciously deigned to allow you to personally witness their sad condition and truly unbearable and deplorable position, and to get acquainted with the local means of treatment of leprosy, if such exist, and also to determine the best way in which a hospital

---

* The Vilyuisk Circuit was one of the five Circuits of the Yakut District that time and consisted of four oulousses including the Sredni Vilyuisk ouloss.

could be constructed for them. How far it is necessary to build a hospital you have now been able to judge for yourself. You have yourself seen sixty-six lepers in twelve different places, that is, almost all the lepers officially known as such in the circuit. What can I add to your own personal impression? The purport of these words is only to direct your attention to how terrible a scourge leprosy is for the whole of the population, but especially for the Sredni Vilyuisk oulousse, where it seems to have its nest.'

Kate's terrible ordeal through the harsh Siberian forest was already having an effect – local dignitaries were talking about the lepers and the necessity of a hospital for Vilyuisk was inscribing itself in official documents.

Kate could not have made up the extraordinary events of her equestrian journey. The gratitude that the sad lepers heaped upon her was so genuine; her detractors were too ruthless, too quick to scorn her, because the love and good will she was spreading created an impression that far outlived their lives. That is why they still call her The Angel in the province today.

Chapter 19

The Road to Vilyuisk

The road from Yakutsk to Vilyuisk today is 400 miles of rough track which even a shower can turn into a quagmire of squelching ruts.

Earth-moving machinery is kept at various points, working round the clock to smooth out the road and make it passable – most of the time they are fighting a losing battle, like a child running its finger through the chocolate topping on a cake while its mother attempts to ice it.

It rained heavily for us.

It was never going to be a low-key departure, the last passenger saw to that. After an interminable wait outside a scruffy apartment block, a final passenger, a gruff character in his forties, in baseball cap and denims, clambered on board and slumped into the rear corner. A minute out, he began shouting. We all exchanged glances, this was an inauspicious start to a very long journey.

"Blimey, what's with him then?" I whispered to Ellie, the Russian speakers yelled at him to shut up.

"Vodka." She surmised.

We'd only being going for five minutes when the driver pulled over; the raised voices were causing him concern and he instructed the man causing the scene to get off.

Defiantly, he waved his chinking plastic bag aloft and clambered over our legs and thighs in his clumsy haste. I'm surprised he didn't get punched by one of the men.

Then, helping himself to the driving seat, he took off shoes and socks, while the driver untied his holdall from the roof. We could have been hijacked! Ejected, we drove off – leaving the man standing barefoot in the mud.

Our cramped little mini bus was less Queen of the Desert than Queen of the Mud. Gold pom-poms and tassels dangled across the windows; a padded interior and cream leatherette roof with black studs; it all went well enough with the Russian pop streaming from the driver's console. Content to view the passing landscape, we prepared for the long hours ahead. They might be ten, they might be twenty.

Ellie read the road sign leaving Yakutsk, "565 kilometres."

"What snacks have you got?"

"Well, I think I've probably eaten most of them in the two and a half hours we've been waiting to leave!"

"Oh, so we'll back to cabbage donuts at the rest stops, then!"

In the forest, autumn colours were emerging; already you feel the chill. Our driver drove expertly through liquid chocolate, expertly gauging the deeper ruts and pools. The ice of winter is so much better for driving we were told; it becomes uniformly impacted and you don't need to slow down.

We had a new friend with us, Zinaida, a striking, dark-haired Yakut sent from Vilyuisk to escort us to her home town. If I could have anticipated what was in store for us there, I might have guessed why she was dispatched to meet us. But I hadn't a clue and loved having her company with her near-perfect English and quiet demeanour; while she kept the welcome prepared for us a complete secret behind that quiet smile.

The bus stopped after a few hours and we wearily piled out.

"This is the border between Yakutsk and Gorniy Region." Zinaida told us. "I am going to make a ceremony." Ellie and I followed her across to a tree made unrecognisable with bits of rags tied onto its spindly sticks of branches, so many that they were killing the tree. "This is the wishing tree," she said, "I'm going to give the tree some yoghurt pancakes."

Damn, I thought – I am fond of Russian pancakes! Hers joined others in various states of decomposition round the roots along with cigarette butts and a clutch of zippo lighters. We made a wish with orange ribbons which Zinaida handed us, while noisy lorries shot past us; and I wished for a journey that didn't see us trapped in syrupy Siberian mud, or spirited off by bears or yetis.

I was such a small pin prick in this ocean of forest at that moment that I also wished we could get back on that bus and drive away from here. I was picturing a parallel universe in which the bus stayed put and the endless forest filed past – forever . . .

Ellie was interested in the eclectic assortment of items tied to the tree, she pointed out a toy penguin, cigarette packs, roubles, and a spoon; diamonds, in this region of prodigious diamonds, were conspicuously missing. The tree, reflecting squalor, grew ever creepier as late afternoon shadow temporarily engulfed it.

Our driver was on the roof of our minibus securing the luggage as we posed for photographs in front of the dirty tree. We re-boarded the minibus, sitting with the detritus of a long journey around our feet. Our fellow passengers were still picking their way along a boardwalk to the public toilet; a hole in the ground where a fog of black insects greeted them.

Clouds gathered above the tree line, dark and ominous, I didn't dare think of rain – if we slid off the road who would pull us out when it got dark? We were now five hours in and articulated lorries struggled in mud up to their wheel arches.

"Worst bit of the road, Ellie."

"I was just thinking, if you're a young person in Vilyuisk, that's a twenty hour bus journey if you want to go out to a concert or night club."

Ellie grinned, "Zinaida just said there are two cafes but no restaurants as such in Vilyuisk – but there is a town canteen."

Now our driver was tacking his way down the track, using whatever tyre groove that proved the firmest. We bumped and jostled and rocked past a gigantic tractor manoeuvring a culvert-pipe into liquid mud. Lights were coming on. Our music console blared out movement and good cheer and the tassles jiggled. The old pair behind us sat impassively, she tiny, with wispy hair combed across, he with his white moustache and eyes so sad I thought he was about to start crying; he looked down at his knees throughout the whole journey.

"Ellie," I wondered aloud, pointing to the Taiga beyond the mud-splashed window "do you think Kate Marsden ever thought about packing it in and going home when she was out there?" We passed a dejected man standing with feet apart and hands rammed deep in his pockets, his small once-white lorry mud-berthed at an alarming angle off the side of the built-up track, two wheels buried up to the hilt. But Ellie was absorbed with her iPod and didn't hear me.

I thought inwardly, she really was mad wandering out there; in that world of silver birch and pine growing from pools of still, dark green water, landscapes without feature or landmark, wet earth and never-ending green horizons.

Ten hours in; we spotted our first Yakut ponies, the rare native breed from this area that can adapt to the extreme cold of Yakutia, they can locate, and graze on, vegetation through deep snow-cover and survive without shelter in temperatures that reach −70 °C.

We were being jostled and banged about worse than ever when the driver put on a Russian film on the overhead screen. Ah! That's what the plush decor was about. No more minibus, but a travelling Gaumont or Waldorf Astoria! But Ellie was staring out of the window, more intent on spotting the 280 km sign, the signal that we were actually half-way.

Before we'd left Yakutsk, the young Moscow film critic called Sergei had knocked on our door and handed us a bar of special Russian chocolate for just that moment.

"Now!" said Ellie. There it goes. And in a mood of celebration we cracked it open, and shared it among the three of us while a fight scene in a room with a bed, a sofa and a refrigerator played out on the overhead screen.

The golden glow of a September sunset was filling the end of the long straight road. Spires of bedraggled tree-tops stood out crisply against the gold and mauve backdrop, and a lemon hue hugged the skyline, creating an extraordinary light in the forest. The battered minibus drove towards it, while the sunset exploded into a ball of red burning light, turning the sky yellow, and chased by an angry mob of black storm clouds.

We wouldn't have seen such a spectacle a few months earlier. Then this region had white nights, continuous daylight. Autumn was on its way now with its rain, a portent to the hardy locals of eight months of deep snow and ice, setting them battening down the hatches in preparation for the winter nights when temperatures plummet.

We stopped to refuel at a rather fifties garage; it was dark now and we all got off to mark another border crossing. Zinaida spirited more pancakes from her bag and made her offering to the resident wishing tree, to which we too tied our ribbons in the glow of the bus headlights.

I dreamed of sleep. I curled myself up into the smallest ball possible, but the lights and music turned right up, making sleep fitful at best hindered by the bounce, bang, accelerate, roar and shake of the seat.

At last, twenty-one hours, and as shaken up as a Martini later, we arrived in Vilyuisk. By now it was late morning, and we couldn't wait for a shower and a snack. There aren't any hotels and Zinaida directed us to a house with a vegetable garden around it used for overnight salesmen and lorry drivers. Here we could drop our bags and spruce up, but as quick as we could be – you see, a driver was waiting outside to take us to meet the Mayor.

Indeed, the Mayor of Vilyuisk, Alexander Shipkov and Sergey Nicolaevich Vinokurov, the Head of the Municipality of the Vilyuisk District welcomed us into the Town Hall, shaking us warmly by the hand. Behind him, a whole roomful of dignitaries had been patiently seated round the mayoral table counting the hours and, who knows, betting on our arrival. Vilyuisk takes this in its stride; to me, being so late was an embarrassment.

I took in the large boardroom with its array of trophies and collection of decorated three-legged ceramic pots. At that moment I knew nothing – why had they been waiting so long, beautifully turned out in their best suits? Why those two t.v. cameras in the corners of the room? Look at me: wearing the same pair of skinny jeans for over twenty four hours, with my hair tangled into a blonde firework look; I felt like Kate Marsden complaining that her bonnet was dirty on being presented to the Egyptian Khedive.

Kind words from Mr Nicolaevich flowed into our ears in Ulyana's English and gifts from the principality were handed to us. I opened up my 1871 map from the Royal Geographical Society. The historian and the Museum Director stood open-mouthed and wished they could make a copy but the town had no way of reproducing it. Slowly, with help from the translators, I briefed the great and good of Vilyuisk about our journey, and who it was in honour of.

And then I twigged . . . Why hadn't I seen it? It was Kate – the Angel, Kate the first woman and first English person to visit Vilyuisk, Kate their heroine whose inspiration built the leper hospital, Kate who brought the small sub-arctic then into the eyes of history, Kate the subject of the town's museum. And now here I was, with Ellie the first people intentionally following overland in her footsteps and they were so proud that I had done it in her name. They were celebrating Kate and they were celebrating me and Ellie, as Kate's twenty first century embodiment.

I'd had no idea that they revered her this much. I sensed their love as we posed for the many photographs, they lined up behind the table for the final iconic shot; Kleopatra held up the pudding; the Mayor the copy of the letter from Balmoral Castle endorsed by Queen Victoria; the Head of the Municipality, the box of tea I had given him; the historian his beloved map and each of the others brandished one of our purple postcards.

I tried to pass my Christmas pudding on to Kleopatra, but they all said no, no, wait, we have big celebrations still to come. I wondered if there was a chance to escape and brush my messy hair.

No, there wasn't. It was time to go, the car had arrived. Kate, listen, what happened next is because of you! Off we went, not having a clue of the magnitude of events that would unfold before us.

Chapter 20

Leprosy and Love

**The remains of trees in Sosnovka representing
Kere Katrine and Moloosoy Uyban**

Kitchik Muterey styled himself as the Prince of the Vilyuisk
settlement, called Kulyatsky 2. Ruthless and cold, his wealth came
through backhanders, mostly involving horses and land reclaimed
from the neighbouring forest. He built himself a fine wooden
house where he lived with his wife and daughter, the substantial
fence that surrounded the property was testimony to his concern
about prying neighbours and a warning to any local boys who
might take an interest in his daughter.

One particularly harsh winter a local couple died suddenly
within weeks of one another, leaving their young son, Moloosoy
Uyban, an orphan. It was greed rather than altruism that led
Kitchik to propose to the head of the municipality that he take the
boy in and give him a home: he knew that the fourteen-year old
had inherited his father's dozen cows and a horse with its foal.

And so Moloosoy lived in Kitchik's house, but more as a slave than guest; and within months since he was a tall and strong young man he was carrying out back-breaking work for him. Needless to say, unpaid. What kept him there wasn't so much the high walls; these he could easily have scaled, it was his feelings for Kitchik's daughter, Kere (Beautiful) Katrine.

The couple fell in love, but kept it quiet from Katrine's parents. She knew her father, in particular, would go ballistic if he knew.

Four years went by, and Moloosoy was still enslaved by Kitchik – even though he had undertaken to the authorities he would take him in until his eighteenth birthday. He was loathe, of course, to part with the boy's livestock: they were valuable to him.

Katrine also turned eighteen and her father suggested to her that she marry a rich man from Sredne-Vilyuisk region; indeed he had it all arranged behind her back. Kere Katrine was incensed, and refused point blank. She was Juliet to Moloosoy's Romeo. Her father was a dominant figure one not to be crossed, and she would stand up to him – but this story has a very different ending.

Unwisely, Katrine told her mother, in confidence, that she was in love with Moloosoy; her mother, of course, told her father. He was so incensed that he instantly tried to think of a way of getting the boy out from under his roof, but he was reluctant to part with the boy's cattle and horses, losing the free labour of the boy was bad enough.

What he came up with was indescribably cruel.

Kitchik Miiterey called on his local doctor, Pavlovsky. He invited him fishing, putting in the boat a great hamper, filled with grilled fish and vodka, and poured him shots liberally. As the afternoon wore on and Pavlovsky became more and more inebriated, his manipulative friend mentioned to him that he suspected the young man he had fostered was showing signs of leprosy. He was extremely convincing, describing the symptoms so accurately, that Pavlovsky was taken in, and consented to signing a paper there and then stating that Moloosoy Uyban is suspected of being infected with leprosy and must immediately be sent to the leprosarium.

The boy's fate thus sealed, without any explanation he found himself being escorted by Cossacks from Vilyuisk to the leprosarium in Sosnovka. Once there he was forced to stay the night alongside patients who had the disease, and in the morning he was given a medical examination.

The leprosarium doctor found nothing at all wrong with the young man, but he couldn't be set free having been in contact overnight with infected patients, which condemned him to staying there for ever. It was a one-way journey; once you had been with lepers you could never return to live among healthy people again.

Moloosoy resigned himself to the bitter fate of having to work among the sufferers there for the rest of his life, chopping wood to heat the houses, cleaning the yard, and, in the summer, making hay in the fields. As for his inheritance, well, that was lost and gone.

Naturally Kitchik Miiterey was very happy with the outcome; he had everything the way he wanted it, including the income from the cattle and he was pretty sure his daughter would now marry the fellow he wanted her to. What he hadn't anticipated was the depth of the girl's love for Moloosey who, had so inexplicably vanished.

Kere Katrine may have been the daughter of a thoroughly ruthless man, but she was a sweet girl who befriended the poor labourers who worked for her father. One of them, who was treated no better than a slave, was called Bedeke. Now, he knew what Kitchik had done, and the exact fate of poor Moloosoy Uyban. Bedeke agreed to visit the leprosarium under cover of darkness to try and see Moloosoy for himself.

Next day he came back and told Katrine everything he had seen in the leprosarium. He had spoken to Moloosoy, and he was perfectly well. Kere Katrine was overcome with disgust that her father could behave in such a way, and decided to do something that would change all of their lives forever.

It took a strong person to do what she did, cutting herself off from family and friends, from future prospects and from freedom itself; but she was adamant.

Kere Katrine ran away. She went to the leprosarium, met up with her beloved Moloosoy and married him. By doing so she had condemned herself to life within its confines.

When the news reached Kitchik Miiterey of his daughter's action, he was incandescent with rage, and died soon afterwards. She had sought justice but not revenge: she had never expected, nor wanted her father to die. She sustained herself with the thought that she had married the man she loved.

The couple lived a long and happy life within the confines of the leper colony, and were allowed to build themselves a small dwelling a short way from the other buildings. As a sign of their love they each planted a tree at the entrance of the drive to the leprosarium, one a birch, the other a larch. These trees stood for years after the couple died, and the locals noticed that when the birch died, the larch which had till then been perfectly healthy, cracked from top to bottom.

Since then the local residents like to plant trees in pairs: a larch here, and birch there.

Chapter 21

'Travelling. It leaves you speechless, then turns you into a storyteller'

Ibn Battuta

The Mayor of Vilyuisk Mr Nicolaevich with the Plum Pudding we carried across Siberia in Kate's honour

Vilyuisk is one of the oldest towns in Siberia, with a population of over 10,000 people. It's uncertain when it was founded, but it certainly goes back to the 17th century, when Cossack pioneers set up winter huts near the River Vilyuy. For a town nestling in the Siberian taiga, so far from any city, with poor communication systems and transport, and with a sub-arctic climate, it positively bustles with life. There is a sports stadium, a local history and khomus (Yakutian harp) museum and many monuments to a mottled past, whose major component is having served as a penitentiary for almost two hundred years. Many participants in uprisings were sent out from Moscow and St Petersburg, including Heinrich von Fick who served an eleven year sentence there. Also, Count Franz de Santi was held here. He was a specialist in heraldry, and later designed the emblems of most of the Russian cities. He was thought so much of a danger that he was kept in shackles and had nine guards. In January 1828 Decembrist Muravy-ov-Apostol was here; for just a year. The seed potatoes he brought with him cropped before he left, and, who knows, their distant offspring may still be in the garden of the house where we dropped our bags.

The town has another claim to fame! The minor planet 2890 Vilyujsk, discovered in 1978 by female Soviet astronomer Lyudmila Zhuravlyova, is named after her.

Observed from 30,000 feet, the lakes scattered throughout the Lena-Vilyuisk Taiga have been likened to the stars of the Milky Way, being arranged in chain formation, connected by depressions into which melt water flows in Spring. To quote the Yakutia Modern Guidebook: 'These chains are turned into 'ot-uryakhs' or grass rivers, which are completely devoid of water in summer and turn into a watercourse when it rains. Ot-uryakhs become overgrown with thick grass which make good hayfields which are a characteristic detail of the Taigalandscapes.' We have the equivalents, winterbournes in chalk land geography, and swales in modern urban planning.

From my short time in Yakutia I was beginning to see why it was called one of the world's unique places; so much of the province's three million square kilometres remains untouched. According to an ancient legend, when God was flying over Yakutia, his hands froze and he dropped most of his treasure, and the gold and diamonds landed on the Siberian Taiga.

If we'd have carried on, past Vilyuisk, on that bumpy quagmire of a road, for another 600 kilometres through the Taigawe would have reached a real town of treasure – Mirny, the source of a sixth of the world's diamonds. This is the home of the Kimberlite Pipe, a geological formation, in which at the end of the nineteenth century the first and largest diamond deposit was found. The 'pipe' is a trace of the plug of an ancient volcano which erupted between 70 and 130 million years ago; and the hole is where the lava forced its way to the earth's surface. The pipe is still the shape of a giant carrot, whose toe is purportedly filled with hundreds of tons of diamonds; in 1980 the largest diamond in Russia was found here and named '26th Congress of the CPSU'. The mine is no longer operational, but the giant cavity, which no pilot will fly over for fear of getting sucked in, has become, like other giant quarries, a tourist attraction.

I was becoming ever more aware of the province's roots and its ancient traditions. The stage shows at the opening and closing ceremonies of the International Film Festival had introduced me to a feast of national dances and harp playing; now I was keen to see and hear more. I couldn't remember travelling in a country where the preservation of its customs and identity was so strongly endorsed, by all members of the community.

Sadly, though, I would never be the person to write with authority on its polar or multinational cuisine. Yakutia's culinary traditions are based on the basic and honourable premise that food is to make the eater feel warm. Calories are crucial, and the backbone of their cuisine is fat meat and fish, preferably deer, foal, beef and elk. The fish they consider best for cooking are sturgeon, broad whitefish, ovule, muksun and sheefish. Traditional dishes are almost devoid of vegetables, partly due to the difficulties of growing them in permafrost soil, with a growing season of four months; although I would come to appreciate the ubiquitous cloudberries growing on the forest floor.

In cooking meat in Siberia, there is very little wastage when in preparing a slaughtered beast, the stomach, kidneys and liver are saved, along with the blood. All the entrails are cooked and eaten in various forms; marinated, pickled or made into sausage. The main national dish of the Yakuts is stroganina, which is thinly sliced slices of fresh-frozen fish or meat (deer or foal) flavoured with salt and pepper and eaten raw. Other national dishes are: khaan, a blood-sausage made from the blood of various animals, though the most favoured is foal; prerem, deer sausage which is used for snacking during travel; oygos, horse ribs which are grilled or stewed and covered with dough; indigirka salad, fresh-frozen fish cubed, seasoned, and served cold; and raw deer meat.

A vegetarian in Siberia is a strange breed; and most inhabitants of Vilyuisk would argue against the likelihood of a non-meat eater surviving in such a climate. I fully appreciate that.

I am not a vegan, and I don't fall into the category of vegetarians who lecture to their friends on the benefits of eating vegetables to 'Save the Planet'. I am content to be left alone and not eat animals, a view that manifested itself in me as a small child, when I questioned my mother as to why we eat baby animals. That was forty odd years ago, and though it has been more challenging to me when travelling than at home, it has never been impossible.

India is my spiritual home for its wonderful vegetarian food; Africa could be very tricky indeed, particularly when, crossing the Sahara Desert I was invited to share cous cous laced with lamb by Tuaregs; living in Turkey was a joy because of its prodigious varieties of fresh fruit and vegetables, but not so good when I ate in its restaurants; France was impossible for years, (they just didn't get it), but things have changed for the vegetarian there now; America has no concept of dining out without a mega-burger or slab of steak; while Spain and Malta feel sorry for you and gave you meat on your plate as a gift because they think you can't afford it. On longer expeditions, through mountains or rivers, thank God for creating freeze-dried expedition food!

Siberia was going to be the hardest of the lot, particularly since I am a great lover of living horses and hate to see them served up on plates!

None of these concerns, fortunately, bother Ellie, who eats meat. At the town canteen, grabbing a quick lunch, (we were ravenous), before 'departure to Sosnovka', as it stated on our programme, she could choose from a basic but hearty menu while I ordered a cabbage salad, and a tomato and cucumber salad. It was served through a hatch by ladies wearing pale blue baseball caps, and I took it to a table covered with a wipe-clean flowery cloth. It was fine, I was happy, and because I was Kate Marsden for the day, I got no funny looks.

At the end of our long and eventful overland journey, we were witnessing for ourselves the unconditional love for the enigmatic English nurse, Kate Marsden, expressed by the people of this small wooden town buried deep in the Siberian taiga. Vilyuisk's civic reverence for Kate, as demonstrated in that council chamber had made my own journey worthwhile, and I was appreciating Kate in a way I hadn't done before.

The Municipality car sped us away through the forest. I didn't quite know where we were going. As we bumped along, I thought about their winter days here which are short, possibly sombre, certainly chillingly cold; and how cherished short, summer pleasures like this must be!

After half an hour the car, and the ones following, turned off the unmade road and stopped on a grassy track that led off into the distance. The delegation poured out, and were joined by other suited men and women in summer finery.

I looked out across the landscape; pastureland, interspersed by clumps of forest lay under a clear blue sky dotted with cream-puff clouds. A light breeze gently shook the trees along the lane; it was a fine day in Yakutia.

The eyes of the delegation were on me; they were waiting for my reaction to a small fenced enclosure that the translator walked me towards, and which we entered through a picket gate.

The splintered remains of two old trees stood within the enclosure; one seemed to be a larch and the other a birch. An angelic young couple in traditional clothing stood holding hands between the broken trees. He was dressed in a long, slim-cut, beige coat, fringed at the shoulder, and with gold trim sewn down the front. The girl was wearing a voluminous white dress with long cuffs, puffy sleeves, a matching white headscarf and the outfit was resplendently finished off with the long silver filigree jewellery, hanging to beneath her waist that I was to become so familiar with.

"May I present Kere Katrine and Moloosey Uyban. They fell in love with each other, and despite many difficulties they joined together."

I just stared at the wonderful scenario devised for my visit, while the couple smiled at me and unconcernedly flicked insects from their faces.

"The boy planted the larch and the girl the birch."

I really wanted to stay with this lovely tableau, but we were summoned back to the car, along the bumpy green lane, the actual way to Sosnovka; powerful memories were being created.

"Do you see the people waiting for you?" I looked out in front of me, there they were, many colourful figures lining the lane at intervals. A mood of deep humility was creeping over me . . .

We got out and walked, I could hear tiny bells tinkling, and saw an elderly lady coming towards me – almost running. Her long white costume included a long-backed hood of white fur and a horse's tail tied to her waist. In her hand she waved a stick with the bells and more horse's hair and her costume shone with beautiful strands of white satin ribbon that sparkled in the sunshine. She circled the stick around my head.

"She learns that you have been in many places." The wind picked up, and she held on to her hooded hat. Her eyes were earnest; all her energy was going into to this encounter, because of its significance for her.

I looked up the track which widened at this point, bordered by spindly trees. Now there were the ridges of recent car tracks, and there were people waiting – right into the distance.

"This is help from the mosquitoes," Ulyana our translator explained, swishing herself with what looked like an entire horse's mane tied colourfully to a stick "Kate Marsden used such things also, and the bells are all part of the ceremony."

We walked slowly towards the next waiting figure, once more in the long white local costume festooned with silver filigree, "She wishes you a good trip" explained Ulyana, and the bells and the horsehair hummed round my head. The white car we had been in trailed us.

Long shadows along the dusty earth preceded us, the sun was low in the sky, the insects flew round our faces like hyper-manic-biting machines, and dive bombed the camera lens; but at that particular moment I was too humbled to care, and too pre-occu-pied to wave them away. The people waiting along the road began to smile and sing as I stopped to meet, and shake hands with, each one.

A man in a white padded and embroidered tabard worn over a lime- green tunic came next; he was holding a sword, and wore an impressive helmet with a point sprouting horsehair, and suede boots that ended above the knee, with triangular panelling round around their tops.

"These are characters from Olonkho, a heroic epic tale of the Yakut people," our translator explained. That belted costume looked so authentic on him,and was so lovingly constructed. I thought to myself.

"The insects are flying into my eyes," Ellie complained, waving her arms.

"I think they are midges, they bite like buggery, and I bet their bites are going to come up in welts later." I said with dread.

"Sadly," Zinaida cut in, "insect repellent doesn't work or I would have given you some."

I hadn't thought about it before, and didn't now. There hadn't been time then, and there was far too much to see now. But, I knew they would enjoy my tasty white skin. I'd done my research, and knew that they drive up out of the permafrost in summer, and eat off any living creature; I had been expecting them.

The receiving line of mostly white, but also green and red, costumes showed no signs of ending and we passed the lovely couple impersonating Katrine and Moloosey once again. "Hello, the love birds!" Ellie called, waving.

Kleopatra, the red-suited doctor in charge of the psychiatric hospital that now stands on the footprint of the leprosarium, walked with us and Ulyana translated her words, "Kate Marsden was met by the people in this way; not quite like this, but everybody greeted her". A wolf-like dog ran past us barking – "you see, even the dogs are pleased to see you!"

Next in the line was a stout man with arms outstretched in a welcome. He was wearing a grass green coat bordered in gold and burgundy, and the cap type hood I'd noticed before that hung partly down the back, trimmed with fur. Then came two children, who must have been about eight, beautifully attired, the little girl in a bright yellow tunic and ornately embroidered head-dress, the boy in a belted brown tunic with fur sleeves and fur hat. The little girl began to recite for me as I came up close, followed by the boy who chanted in a meltingly true treble, verses of what I now know were traditional Siberian songs. Both performed with great seriousness, their arms straight by their sides. We clapped and praised the children.

"Those are pieces from Olonkho, the heroic epic tale I told you about," whispered Ulyana in my ear.

"This is amazing," I replied, "look at this lady coming next."

"Truly amazing."

She was once more dressed in that vivid lime-green, this time with a floral collar and cuffs, topped off with a little navy blue straw hat. She waved her switch around her head and smacked it at her cheeks, the flies were remorseless. Many more costumed men, women and children were lined up in the lane, and I felt for them, having to wait for us, while swarms of the almost invisible terrorists ate them alive.

"Ellie, what's particularly humbling is that all these people are standing amidst all these horrible midges; they're biting them, they're biting us, they're in my hair, up my arm, they're whizzing around the camera, and these people are standing waiting for us in all this."

"Yes, and they're getting worse and worse, you know."

"They're down my blouse now." I said, resisting the urge to itch.

"I know, I'm swatting them every few seconds, they hurt as well; but thank heavens they can't get into our jeans!"

I turned to my lovely Yakut translators, "My goodness, there are still so many people waiting for us, I feel so honoured that you have done this for us. Kate Marsden would have been so happy for us."

We shook hands with many beautiful Yakutian ladies, with their distinctive, oval faces and narrow eyes, decked out in silver jewellery, embroidered hats and dresses. One lady in a pink embroidered costume was introduced by Kleopatra:

"This is Valentina, she is the leader of our women's movement." Valentina bowed and waved her switch; we had to keep moving.

Steering us into a small spinney of birch and larch, Kleopatra took us to where a middle-aged lady in horsehair hat and green cloak with red and gold sleeves was exchanging the baby granddaughter in her arms for the Yakutian harp, or khomus. There, in the dappled sunlight, she played this small metal instrument, considered to be one of the oldest musical instruments in the world, for us, by placing the flexible reed between her parted teeth and plucking with the finger to produce a note. This ancient sound vibrated through the swaying tree trunks – I was familiar with the Jew's harp played in British folk music – but this was different – it's haunting tone was the backdrop to a film that I was living.

A young lad in a leather jerkin and a large medal on a head band shot a sharpened stick into the air with his home-made bow, a cross on a tree caught my eye and a lady in a mustard dress trimmed with sequins stepped forward to shake my hand.

"We have to go over there," our guide pointed across a large grassy flat area towards distant timber buildings, two storied with zinc roofs. We had amassed an entourage, all moving in their direction. These were among the first houses to be built at Sosnovka. So this was it! This was the settlement, Kate Marsden's place, and the goal of all my planning and travelling.

Another colourful group of ladies stepped forward to meet us – "eighty years old," exclaimed the translator.

"You look so beautiful," I told the first lady, dressed in red, her white cloche hat adorned with a fan of feathers trembled in the breeze.

"Eighty-two years," said the next one in English, waving her whisk. "my name is Maria!"

Ulyana said, "You know, she has been learning that line all morning!" And all the elderly ladies burst into giggles.

Almost at the settlement now, we met an older couple in national costume. Each had a speech to make, and Zinaida whispered her neat translation. "He's telling you that it was his relatives who helped build the first houses for the people that built Kate Marsden's hospital."

We moved on, our pace quickening towards the largest of the large wooden plank structures, now, as Ulyana explained, carefully preserved and containing the doctors' offices.

"This man," she continued, "wants you to know that his mother worked in the leprosaurium." I shook hands with him, his lapels weighted with medals and hat resembled a small stetson. He stood with his little wife in a white raincoat, an expression of sheer pride remained fixed on his face throughout.

Director Kleopatra led us round the side and pointed out the part of the building, with blue-painted windows, housing the tiny museum dedicated to Kate Marsden, the date 1895 stood out prominent on the wall.

We were aware of music intensifying nearby, and bells ringing out; I had wondered where they all were, that great crowd of villagers that had accompanied us up the grass lane. With Kleopatra in her red suit, we were only five or six left.

Now, round a corner, there they all were, in their hundreds, lining the field's perimeter, and I realised my reactions were being filmed for t.v.

What I was about to witness was monumental in relation to every experience in my life up to that point; more ambassadress and adventuress, less school-teacher and middle-aged mother.

The song that went up – everyone sang – was for me, as Kate's representative, the air was full of laughter and happiness. What should I do, in my jeans, with the biting midges behind my sunglasses and in my hairline and – for heaven's sake – pointing my camera-lens in all directions? The least I could do was hand it to someone else. You'll do I thought, turning to the suited man next to me, part of the official delegation, and asked him in gestures, if he'd mind carrying on filming for me. No, he nodded, that's fine. Both our translators burst out laughing: this was Dmitriy Makharov, a well-known figure locally, the ex-mayor of the Vilyuisk region, a very important man!

Sosnovka, September 2013: an impromptu summer holiday set amongst the remains of a wooden leper hospital, to remember the Sakha regional heroine; Kate Marsden, and to welcome me, a contemporary Englishwoman who had travelled across Siberia in her footsteps.[*]

---

[*] See appendix on notes on the Sakha traditional costumes

Chapter 22

The house in Cooden Drive today

I took the train to Bexhill on Sea and soon found 15 Cooden Drive, 'Silver Willows' as it was then called. It was a sweet detached house with freshly painted sash windows with a small willow tree in the front garden. I knocked hesitantly; I had sent a postcard the day before, but I wasn't sure Kate had received it in time, or, indeed, was even in Bexhill. The slight elderly lady who answered, not Kate, didn't bat an eyelid at my loose hair and orange t-shirt but led me through to where Kate was sitting. It was the same Kate, but changed. Now sixty-one, her bent shoulders and the older person's veined hands clutching the sides of the green armchair were a shock to me; a sign that her energy had gone and with it her extraordinary drive – that had fired her passion.

"Miss Marsden, I do hope I have found you well." She looked up at me, looked me over, a little perplexed but a half-smile, that I knew so well,

appeared on her lips. My visits made her feel acknowledged and gave her
hope for a future that this dreadful War had all but obscured.

I presented my gift, a large tin of excellent shortbread: "This is for you
and the sisters to enjoy." She took it and her fingers stroked the cellophane
wrapping and studied the coloured stag in his tartan sash atop a Highland
crag.

"Well, that's a very fine gift, thank you my dear."

"You know, Miss Marsden, I promised to tell you about my journey to
Vilyuisk in your footsteps. I've brought you this," – and I held out a
colour photograph; the spark returned to her eyes as she examined it.

"I have been wanting to tell you . . ."

"All in colour, too," she murmured, smoothing its tatty corners.

"Well, you see, I walked into a field in Sosnovka and there were
hundreds of people waiting for me; apparently they'd been planning it for
months. I'm so sorry I always well up when I talk about it . . . sorry."

I looked away for a moment, to the view, a lawn, a picket fence and
then an uninterrupted view of the English Channel.

"The celebration, it was for you really, you never managed to get back to see what you'd achieved, so they saved it up, and 125 years later – they put it on for me."

"I am amazed," Kate fiddled with the photograph and the biscuit tin; *"I am so glad they did that, but do tell me, what it was like for you?"*

"I have never, ever, experienced such warmth of humanity, such public love for an individual – such effort to provide a pageant of such immaculate detail. Sakha folk-music greeted us on arrival, then a khomus, you know their harp thing, took over and filled the field with those haunting sounds – and the people all lined up for me to reach them and shook my hand and smiled at me, and photographs were taken and every villager from Sosnovka and many from Vilyuisk was there was there, throwing themselves into it. Those costumes though! They were exquisite, all hand stitched, and worn with such pride!"

Kate stared at me, her face, pale and lined, now strangely expressionless.

"Many had dressed as people you will surely have met, the merchant in leather jacket and wide, flat-brimmed hat and his family, the group of Cossacks with their commander, with shining medals and red-banded blue caps, the priest and his wife, with his black stovepipe hat and silver cross, a group of nurses all dressed just as you prescribed, with long skirts, snow-white aprons and caps bearing a red cross and then, you won't believe it, they introduced me to you!"

"Me?" Kate gasped.

"Yes, they'd dressed up a lady who works in the new hospital's canteen to look just like you, in a dove-grey suit over a white shirt and a little hat pulled over a tight bun, she wasn't as tall as you though – and she didn't smile either." Kate raised her eyebrows.

"There were more bearded cossacks, and townswomen in big floral dresses. You should have seen, and heard, the singing consort of female doctors, all in snowy-white matching outfits with huge amounts of ornate silver jewellery around their necks, around their heads, around their waists and hanging down as huge pendants – all this topped off with fur-lined hoods with fan-shaped crowns on top. I couldn't take it all in, I felt such respect for them – and I mustn't leave out Katerina! This beautiful lady with wonderful Nenet features, round faced with narrow eyes stepped forward and hugged me, well, you really; it was she who

had helped to organise it all . . . and your name rang in the air the entire time."

Kate sat, transfixed.

"When we came to the end of the semi-circle of people in the receiving line, there was very loud bird song – or it could have been the khomus, I couldn't tell. They motioned me onto the porch steps and the costumed villagers closed in around me. A lady in a scarlet embroidered hat with a cascade of chiffon flowing from its crown stepped forward with, oh, you must have had this, a tray with a loaf and bowl of salt. I pulled out a lump and dipped my bread in the salt. Smoke curled skywards from a wooden cup, and then the white-bearded Cossack Chief spoke words of greeting – in Russian – into a microphone and a lady with an extraordinary voice sang into it, I have never heard singing like it before, it was truly staggering. All for you, and for your great gift to Vilyuisk and Sosnovka."

"Well, well, well. So they haven't forgotten me."

"Forgotten? You are a saint there, Miss Marsden. Well, that ancient ceremony continued, with the three ladies in white again. They stepped towards me with a ceramic bowl on three-legs. I remembered from Tomsk that it was fermented mare's milk or kymys . . . I took a sip, it was fizzy and warm.

We all linked arms in a circle and danced and sang, sliding across the dusty grass, two steps one way, two steps the other and as the music speeded up, I lost myself in a colourful blur. The music and laughter got louder and less inhibited. My hands were clutched tightly by strangers, and my feet somehow knew what to do."

Kate sighed. I knew what she was thinking.

There were more group photographs; then I gave a little speech into the microphone, right from the bottom of my heart, acknowledging the day's display of warmth and kindness and all who had made it happen: they all clapped me with crazy enthusiasm.

"If Kate Marsden could have been here today," I said, "she would have loved today's event."

"So, Miss Marsden, holding the brown box aloft, I carried on. 'This is the Kate Marsden Plum Pudding. She distributed 9,000 New Testaments, which are represented by these postcards; she carried a great deal of tea, so I've brought some too and given that to the Mayor. As for this pudding, it

has been taken out and photographed all across Siberia. Now this is a very special pudding and, it has to be steamed, so, (with my eyes firmly on Kleopatra) save it for a special occasion and, if you want to be very English, serve it with custard or rum butter! And I hope you enjoy it very much.'

Everybody clapped. She took the brown cardboard box and everyone clapped some more, and cheered as she opened the lid. With all eyes upon her, she took out the Plum Pudding, wrapped in gold paper which glinted in the Siberian sunshine, thousands of miles from the English Lake District where it had been lovingly prepared and stirred.

The dignified Cossack now took over the microphone testifying that Kate Marsden donated all the money she had brought with her to Yakutsk, spending none of it on the way, and that money was used to build the hospital and the church, although unfortunately fifty years ago the latter burnt down and because of the politics of the day was never rebuilt.* He then passed it to Kleopatra, who thanked us profusely for coming and presented Ellie and I with gifts, including a horsehair rug and a ceramic bowl, like the one we had sipped kymys from."

Just then the other Miss Norris came in and stood there listening, with an enamel tray, two cups, teapot with quilted cosy, silver strainer and milk jug. She looked at Kate's nervous fingers struggling with the unfamiliar cellophane, and gently lowered it to the table beside my chair and poured the tea.

I gently eased a finger under the cellophane wrapper of the tin and helped Kate choose a shortbread. As I did so I stared into the face of that dauntless, resolute woman, and found that she was crying.

* I had read that in 1932 the Communists wanted to burn down the church, but patients from the hospital encircled it to protect it.

Chapter 23

THE PROPOSED LEPER COLONY.

It is hard to say how much input Kate Marsden had in the building of the Sosnovka Leprosarium, but she certainly was its inspiration, helping choose an advantageous site, and giving precious nursing advice to those who would get it off the ground. Once back in England she had architectural plans drawn up by John Dixon Butler, but it is not known whether these were the ones used.

She was not to be aware of the storm clouds gathering in London and Auckland, that would eventually stifle all her fund-raising efforts for lepers, and stay to dog her for the rest of her life.

Kate returned to Yakutsk ready and able to take her mission forward. When she arrived there on July 31st, her immediate priorities were washing herself for the first time in forty days, a change of clothes and, of course, sleep. But it was not long before the scenes she'd witnessed in the forest took priority over her own needs.

Resolving to leave no stone unturned in making the lives of the lepers more bearable, she met Father Meletei and informed him of what she'd seen during her journey and convinced him of the need for instant action. They discussed plans to raise funds, and she referred him to the officials who had accompanied her in regard to the best location in her estimation for a future colony, namely Sosnovka. There is no further evidence that her mission was still considered suspect in Yakutsk, but as Kate writes in 'The Leper', evidently the transcript of a speech, given in Chicago, "They thought I must have some political object in view, and Yakutsk is the country of political exile."

Kate was able to inspire confidence in people through her magnetism and ability to convey in words the horrors she had witnessed. They also warmed to her persistence, her determination never to give up.

From the material in the Yakutsk archives, already referred to, it would seem that Kate requested that a second party be sent out immediately, before winter made travel impossible, to distribute comfort goods to the lepers in the forest. Among the beautifully written ledgers is a record of winter and summer clothing, for thirty-four men and thirty-four women being purchased. Her own acquisitions, made of course before she had witnessed the extremity of the lepers' conditions for herself, had been gratefully received but insufficient.

It was only after she was satisfied that she had done all she could in Yakutsk that she set off down the Lena River to Irkutsk on the beginning of her return journey.

In Irkutsk the Governor-General of the town summoned a meeting, and invited Kate to report her findings, and pitch an appeal to those attending for money. They listened with a mixture of horror and awe to her assessment of the Yakut lepers'.

'I have seen with my own eyes these poor outcasts who live in the depths of the very densest forests, sometimes alone, sometimes in large numbers herded together in one small hut. The villages in the area meet once a year and discuss residents who look like they may have the disease, they dread it so much that in their language a devil and a leper are synonymous terms! Sometimes a person with a skin disease is turned out into the forest – that is a death sentence, he can never return. They live on the worst imaginable food – like rotting fish and the bark of trees, when they are left food it is at quite a distance to their huts and the lepers have to walk or crawl, according to how their condition is, to get it. When he is too weak to get the food, then he or she dies of starvation. It is such terrible treatment of these dear, honest folk, who merely got sick . . . men, women and children all herded together into one hut . . . and this in a country with such a hot short summer followed by nearly nine months of winter where the thermometer goes down to seventy degrees below zero. Please, help me to help them, I implore you.'

A first donation of 1,500 roubles was collected at the meeting, but that sum would eventually grow to 20,000. Her appeal was a sensation; she had pricked the city's conscience.

Kate left Irkutsk in early October and headed for Tomsk, arriving in November. Here too she began to appeal for funds, and at her meeting with the Mother Superior of the local Orthodox convent, poured out the story of her journey and the heartbreaking sights she had seen. The outcome was, seemingly more than she could have hoped for: the Mother Superior promised to send out nuns to Yakutsk to nurse the lepers, provided that the authorities there approved. They may not have, though, because (according to her Chicago lecture) she immediately appealed – back in Moscow – to her Imperial Majesty, the Empress, in consequence of which five devoted Russian sisters from the hospital of Princess Shahovsky, in Moscow left almost immediately for Yakutsk.

In Moscow, she approached the Church authorities. She must have shown them the Gospel story of the healing of the leper, because she got them to agree to devoting the annual collection on the Sunday when that passage is read to the relief of Russian lepers.

Kate was showing initiative in her fund raising and, at least in Russia receiving acknowledgment for that.

What had happened to the notorious healing 'herb', which had been one of the early objectives of her Russian expedition? It was now no longer being discussed. In Chicago, though, the next year Kate confirmed its existence. She had found it, and tested it, but it didn't provide the basis of a cure; it only alleviated the suffering, or so she thought.

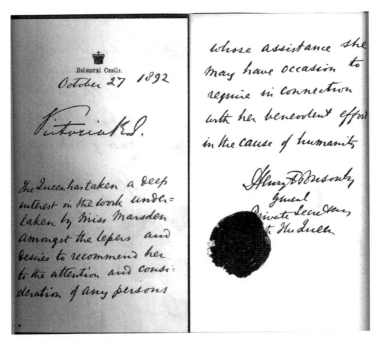

A letter of support written on behalf of Queen Victoria

After Kate Marsden left Yakutsk, things began to happen there. Consciences had been tweaked and attitudes radically changed. In the spring following her visit a basic colony was created at a place called Sosnovka, nine substantial yourtas serving the combined districts of Vilyuisk Oulousse, and Verkhne- Vilyuisk. The cost came to 2700 roubles, presumably drawn from the sum she had left behind. By an order of the Yakut Governor, Dr Ghimmer was appointed as a doctor to the settlement in 1893 and it was he who expedited the building of the hospital to replace the temporary colony. The construction for this began in 1894 and was completed in 1898, with the church constructed in 1897.

In addition to the 20,000 roubles raised in Irkutsk, it is possible to itemise the sums gathered in the wake of Kate Marsden's visit: 1,450 roubles were sent by Kate herself from Irkutsk to the Yakut Governor; the monastery in Tomsk sent 500 roubles; miscellaneous donations from Siberia, over 10,000 roubles; merchants' and tradesmens' donations: Nemchinoff 10,000 roubles, Kolenko 5000 roubles, Kolchuginoff 5,000 roubles; and from London, a further £2,400; all the proceeds of the first edition of the book: 'Puteshestvie'. (Travels of Miss Marsden to the Yakutsk region), published in Russian in Moscow 1892.

The early Russian book about Kate's journey that was published in 1892

Put together, this amounted in 1891-2 to a substantial figure. In an interview with The Woman's Herald on November 5th 1892 she is quoted as saying: 'I collected £4,000 in Russia, which is

Kate's journey from Yakutsk to Moscow was as hard a journey to make as the outward one from Moscow to Yakutsk, but she felt fired up, and that helped her to withstand the hardship. People were really pleased to see her along the way and grateful that she was safe and well and, of course, for the last leg from Zlatoust she was reunited with her old companion and friend Ada Field, now fully restored to health. She conferred with various committees, and large donations began to come in towards her work. Nobody had ever expected she would succeed in her mission and that success was beyond her own wildest expectations. She arrived in Moscow in December 1891, nearly eleven months after setting off, having covered more than 12,000 miles, most of it on tarantass, sledge, river barge and horseback.

Understandably exhausted, she rested for a few days before setting off for St. Petersburg, where she had notions of establishing a scientific society to investigate the condition of lepers and find ways to offer them relief throughout the Russian Empire. She received the support of Professor Peterson, and for the next four months was busy in both St. Petersburg and in Moscow, engaging the support of the Russians, for their lepers. She had another audience with Her Imperial Majesty, who took a great interest in the outcome of her journey. Kate made what would be her last appeal to her for personal help on behalf of the lepers.

'Her Majesty took the most lively and tender interest in the lepers, and promised to exert all her imperial influence to help forward the work. Her Imperial Majesty also headed the list of donors to the fund which was shortly started.'

This moment may be seen as the apogee of Kate's fame, renown and influence. She could do nothing wrong – yet. Her time in Moscow was coming to an end, and she found just one more ally, Countess Tolstoi.* Kate wrote in her book:

'It goes without saying that my ideal of an almost perfect Englishwoman is Miss Florence Nightingale; as the queen of nurses to suffering humanity, she stands forth as the embodiment of what

* Countess Tolstoi, Lady of Honour to the Empress of Russia.

a woman can and should be. Next to Miss Florence Nightingale, the woman I love and reverence the most is the Countess Alexandrine Tolstoi.'

What makes her so useful to Kate's future plans was her mixture of intelligence and discretion; she was held in general regard, but her linguistic gifts made her perhaps the one person in Moscow to whom Kate could explain in fullest detail what she had experienced and the objects of her mission.

It would be interesting to know whether the impetus to write the very abbreviated story of her travels to, and work in, Yakutia was the direct outcome of her meeting with the Countess. In any case, the 'Travels of Miss Marsden to the Yakutsk Region' was translated into Russian and was signed off as authentic by the Russian official who accompanied her and she showed it to His Excellency the Head Procurator of the Synod.

After his approval it was published by his instructions by Torletskaya, advertised in a national weekly paper and the Procurator ordered 40,000 copies to be printed and distributed throughout Russia. The proceeds were to be devoted to the Leper Fund, to which the Procurator had himself already contributed $1500. She noted:

'The newspapers then took up the subject, and discussed it from various standpoints, thus giving further publicity to the wants of the lepers and the measures proposed to relieve them.'

Kate swept through Moscow impressing many and gathering more money and accolades, though one name is conspicuously absent from these last triumphant months, that of Ada Field. There are inactive patches, which point at illness or mental exhaustion but her endeavours still led to beneficial outcomes, and she was fired up with ambitious plans for the future.

When she reached England she received the hearty approval of Queen Victoria in a letter commending her efforts and the work which she had accomplished and wished to accomplish. This was a key to awakening a wider interest in her work throughout England, and numerous contributions came to her from all sides. In the spring of 1892 she began to write the book which finishes:

'In bidding farewell to my readers, I earnestly and humbly ask for their prayers that I may be guided and supported in the work to which, by God's grace, I have been led to dedicate a feeble and faulty life; and the best prayer that I can offer on behalf of you, dear readers, is that Christ may ever dwell in you, and you in him, that you may thus be ever bound up with his life, and bound to the heart of suffering humanity, responsive to every throb of pain, and eager to relieve the children of sorrow.'

It wasn't a flawless masterpiece; it lacked detailed descriptions of the journey which played into malevolent hands, but it succeeded in its main aim of impressing on the reader the harrowing plight of his and her fellow-beings, the Yakut lepers.

Chapter 24

The difference a century makes

'I looked up and she was standing there'

Rounded shoulders, forehead lined from staring into a computer screen, trying to make sense, darkness outside, blinds not drawn, long day struggling to write about a complex lady . . . who was suddenly there.

A gloved hand steadying her tall frame on my chair back, in a royal blue velvet blouse with a lace collar, a long serge skirt and, and no hat; in fact her hair looked very fancy – and she had a ribbon in it. I looked up at her and saw those slightly drooped almond eyes, the sharp nose and the almost haughty expression. She looks quite pretty I thought when she's not dressed as a nurse.

"You have a question for me?" She brushed dust off a sleeve.

"Yes, I do, many actually." I was having to adjust to having her there, I'd been alone all day writing and hadn't talked to anyone, so I jumped

straight in. "Your interest in the prisoners, the Siberian convicts, where did that stem from?"

"Men and women walking thousands of miles – in chains – through snow; wouldn't your heart bleed for them? Such misery, brought about by petty crimes. I bought provisions from the peasants waiting outside the rest houses to distribute to bring them some little comfort. When I was granted leave to enter the jails, well, I found unimaginable horrors . . . profound darkness, dripping water, terrible smells and dying people. I would hand out the Testaments to them, a little square of tea and some sugar, just to make them experience a little meagre comfort."

The irony of that situation wasn't lost on me – the Russian Imperial Family had donated large amounts of money to her to travel to eastern Siberia to either locate a plant that might cure leprosy, or to bring back hard evidence of the plight of Russia's own lepers, only to have it used to bring humanitarian relief to prisoners banished to hard labour camps.

I looked up at her as she stared into a mirror on my wall. "But why? You put yourself in so much danger."

"Ah, but who would have done it if I hadn't?"

English angel. She wanted to elevate herself onto another plane; perhaps a place where she felt adulation. Nobody, apart from Ada, spoke up for her though. Many chose not to believe her.

"Miss Marsden, I know you made that journey and I'm going to be fair to you. Why else would they love you so much in Vilyuisk and Sosnovka, where your hospital is built?"

"My leper colony, have you seen it?" She was smiling and her hand gently gripped my shoulder for a brief moment.

"Yes, Miss Marsden, I told you I have, I am one of the few Western European visitors that has ever visited."

She muttered under her breath, but the moment of joy didn't last and she looked sad.

"Things aren't good, you know."

She looked down at my shapeless knee-length dress and flip-flops, far too casually dressed for her even in my own study! The distance between us was great. But then it was good for her to see the freedom that women had achieved in the future that was bravely fought for by women like her. She was in some important way, a new woman; she had undertaken a brave and heroic expedition, the likes of which few women have experienced since and she was now fighting for recognition of it, recognition that was so desperately owed to her and to women of her time who chose to break free of the fetters of a patriarchal society.

"You're only half-dressed."

This time she sort of smiled as she said it.

"Miss Marsden, there are no self imposed uniforms in my world, no dress codes, no tight corsets or brown woollen stockings, no hats unless it's a wedding, no gloves unless it's cold and no one to tell us off about it. Most people just wear t-shirts and jeans, to tell you the truth." She remained expressionless; she had, of course, been born in the wrong era, whereas a world with freedom to express oneself would have suited her so much better. Myself, I couldn't have borne to dress the way she did.

"Is there something wrong Miss Marsden?"

"Yes, they say in the papers that I am no longer the lepers' friend, I am no longer permitted to raise money for their cause. They say I have been exposed, but why?" She turned to me and looked me in the eye. She needed someone to listen who would understand.

"Go on, Miss Marsden" I said, "I'm listening."

I had plenty of time and was bemused that my great heroine had chosen me to pour out her heart to; a girl from the next century, the hatless bohemian writing her biography.

Out of the funny old handbag came a copy of The Times dated August 17th 1894, folded over to the letters section. She pointed her finger to the headline 'Exposure of Kate Marsden'. The first few lines read: 'The scandals in connection with that sweet woman have at last culminated, I am thankful to say, in the complete exposure of the leper's friend'.

"Why, Miss Marsden, this is so desperately damning!" I was rapidly scanning the page, fearful that at any moment it would turn to dust in my hands. "Your character is being shot to pieces – how could such words be printed in a free world?"

"A free world?" She almost wept with the words, "They say what they want, they trifle with me and damn me. They talk about me on the omnibuses – in front of me, behind their hands, outside my gate. No one believes in me any more since Certain People took against me."

"But, look, Miss Marsden, you fund-raised for a leper colony to be built, and that was a great and noble thing to do."

She looked at me, hard and long, "Yes, but you are the only person to know that, because you alone have seen it."

She was right. I had seen it, it had been achieved. All thanks to her.

I read a chunk of the article aloud: "For some time past, as you know, Truth and the Charity Organisation Society have had Miss Marsden's case in hand, and a considerable time ago the former warned charitable persons against entrusting further moneys to her. It is not, however, till last December, when the 'dear sister' returned to St Petersburg laden with plunder for the Chicago Exhibition, that her friends could be persuaded to take any action with regard to the charges against her."

I turned to her with widening eyes. "That is such dreadful vocabulary to use, it's so sarcastic and downright nasty, why the word 'plunder' for god's sake?"

"Well, now you are taking the Lord's name in vain!"

"True, I beg your pardon," I said, "and friends? Are they friends?"

"Apparently not." She snorted.

" 'The Nation', that it mentions here, is an American journal, isn't it? And what were you supposed to have done? Taken money for the lepers in Chicago, and not handed it over to your charity?"

"Well, you see, I certainly did take out my travel expenses, I am quite poor you know."

I perused her clothes and boots, not new but certainly not those of a pauper. In the society that she mixed with she had to look respectable – so where did that money come from?

"How did you fall out of favour so catastrophically? What did you do?"

She went quiet.

"You must have done something."

I read on, the letter was written by The Secretary of the Committee set up to investigate her – the Rev. Alex Francis, Pastor of the British Church at St Petersburg.*

---

* Kate Marsden forwarded a copy of the committee's report of February 28, 1894 (countersigned by A P H Medhurst, British vice-consul and acting consul in Moscow) to the editor of 'The Times'. This report was published in The Times on August 18, 1894 and found that 'in all essential points' Kate Marsden's accounts, both narrative and financial, had been fairly and honestly discharged. Nevertheless, she could never free herself of its accusations.

'I communicated the result of the inquiry to Miss Marsden's London Committee, whose chairman informs me that he and his Committee recognise that Miss Marsden's leper work is necessarily at an end, and intend immediately to dissolve. His Excellency M. Pobedonostzeff, Ober-Procurator of the most Holy Synod, has authorised me to state that he will be pleased to receive and forward to Siberia, for the relief of lepers there, any moneys contributed for that purpose which may still been the hands of the London Committee.

On the formation of the Investigation Committee, Miss Marsden engaged that, in the event of the enquiry resulting in a decision adverse to herself, she should surrender all the decorations, commendatory letters, etc., bestowed upon her by Imperial and Royal personages – an engagement which it is now my painful duty to call on her to fulfil. An acknowledgement of the truth of the gravest of the charges against her has at last been made by Miss Marsden in writing and communicated to me by her London Committee, and thus I have, at least, the sad satisfaction of knowing that no possible injustice is done to her.' Alex. Francis, Pastor of the St. Petersburg British-American Church and Secretary of the Committee of Investigation. Kingswood, Loats Road, S.W., August 15th 1894'.

"The Reverend Alex and I were always such good friends." I heard her mumble.

"Miss Marsden, my dear lady, just what can you have done? That doesn't sound like a close friend at all, and why oh why were you forced to hand back your medals? After all, you earned those for your work in the Turko-Russian war."

"I'm not going to hand them back, I shall say they are lost!"*

"Good for you!" and we sniggered. "But Reverend Alex?"

"That wretched man was forced to go against me, he needed to preserve his church in Russia."

"It says here that valuable assistance was given to the St Petersburg Committee by, amongst others, the London Charity Organisation Society and Lady Henry Somerset." Kate smarted beside me.

"Injustice! That woman slammed me, shamed me, shunned me, but look at her – just look at her own life."

---

* She certainly didn't! Her medals and gold brooch from the Queen are housed in the RGS

I looked incredulously at Kate, "what are you talking about?"

"Her husband, Lord Henry, preferred men, her marriage was doomed from the off, yet she wouldn't turn a blind eye to his infidelity, and defied social conventions by separating from her husband and suing him for custody of their son. A pride like that was always bound to sniff me out, and hound me, if she could find any scurrilous rumour to stick to me."

"Miss Marsden, what are you telling me? Are you telling me there is something else?"

"She herself was ostracised from society, so she knew what it felt like when she did it to me in turn! And now she runs the Temperance Movement."

"Ah, she thought you were, what, a drinker?" Kate looked at me, without speaking. I was illuminated by naivety.

"And Miss Willard, isn't she a good person?"

"Well, she should be. She's American, and a temperance reformer . . ."

"Oh another anti-drinker then, sorry. I do beg your pardon. Please don't stop."

"Women's suffragist . . ."

"Well, that's a very good thing, isn't it?"

"Yes, but she's another prude, all the good she is supposed to have done, oh, yes, but actually she wanted alcohol banned because she believed the myth that white women were in constant danger of violation by lusty, drunken black males." I took a sharp intake of breath.

"No! So what about Mrs Andrews then, didn't she support you?"

"Well yes, rather more; she rides about London on a bicycle, and I do rather like her. But she was influenced by the other women."

Then there's Dr Kate Bushnell, did you get any support from her?"

"No, she's another American, firmly in the grip of Miss Hapgood." She spat the last words, I could feel the venom.

"Who has never met me, doesn't know me . . . and she absolutely hates me — and she is so influential. She wishes I'd never been born." I watched her hands shake; and although I had read every word, good and bad, written about her, and understood her ambiguity, bossiness, pushiness, her social climbing . . . I actually felt thoroughly sorry for her. Where had it all gone wrong?

But why hadn't I realised it sooner? That Kate Marsden was accused of something very unacceptable in the 1890s. I looked up at her. Did she feel like I was going to be like all the rest?

"Miss Marsden, It makes no difference to me, the biography I am writing is not judgemental – I am writing about your achievements" I handed back the cutting, "this is scurrilous gossip, let time be a healer, Miss Marsden, I believe in you."

And then she was gone. I turned back to my computer and began a search on the biggest rumour-monger of her day – Isobel Florence Hapgood.

Chapter 25

"It is shameful to rake up private personal faults which have nothing whatever to do with charitable work."

Queen Victoria referring to the Kate Marsden scandal.

Scrawling handwriting produced with a spluttery ink pen announces the papers gathered together in a file in The New York Public Library:

'The Kate Marsden Case (which covered Europe, Asia, Austria, N. America and would probably have covered

also, Africa and South America, <u>had I not stopped the woman's career</u>)'.

I.F.H

Kate's monumental fall from grace would never have happened had it not been for The American Isabel Florence Hapgood, a writer and translator, particularly in Russian. She appears initially like Othello's motiveless Iago; but a closer look reveals there were motives: a very deep-seated resentment and jealousy. Kate had strayed onto her patch, Russia, and bolstered by her work there and the pamphlet that had been published, her name had become a household word amongst the educated middle-classes – making Hapgood seethe. In a careless introductory essay to her papers she writes her excuses for comparing Marsden to Milton's Satan:

'In July 1891 I received from my correspondent, Mrs Lucy Alexayeff, a letter from Irkutsk, giving me her experiences of K.M. during a very short meeting, her impressions, and what little information she then possessed – and asking me if I had heard of the woman.

That little convinced me that the woman was an Adventuress, and I said so to Mrs Alexayeff, begging her to send me all the details she could collect. My original motive was to protect from her people who had been very kind to me in St Petersburg, in particular, the Countess Alexandra Andreevna Tolstoy, of the Winter Palace. I inferred that, if K.M. had secured Imperial patronage, Countess T. might become involved. My inference was correct – but belated, as it proved: The Countess was already deeply interested, and had committed herself as a Patroness before I ever heard the woman's name.'

Hapgood's prejudices are obvious, her language and vocabulary ungrammatical and venomous, in her notes scribbled onto the letters in the extensive collection, which amount to reams and reams of gathered gossip. Before Kate's journey to Russia, Isabel had reigned supreme with her pioneering work introducing Russian literature including Tolstoy to English-language readers. In 1895 she published 'Russian Rambles', a lively account of her visit to that country. For twenty two years she was a correspondent, reviewer, and editorial writer for the New York Evening Post and the Nation; unfortunately for Kate Marsden this meant her persecutor had power, and all the right contacts. Her review of 'On Sledge and Horseback to Outcast Siberian Lepers' begins:

'Anything more absolutely devoid of literary merit, grammar, or claim to attention from the intelligent public than this volume, it would be hard to find. The slender story is told twice, in some cases three times, and consists chiefly in the narration of such petty detail of travel as would be likely to impress a dull person unacquainted with even the rudiments of life in the country traversed.'

What is so tragic is that a person was allowed to be so publicly destroyed with the help of the press over a facetious personal vendetta. It was easy to charge people with fraud, deception and immorality in letters and articles that would be reprinted in other countries of the world. What Isabel Hapgood never did, was credit Kate in any shape of form with what she had accomplished earlier in Bulgaria and the money she had raised for the hospital – she seemed to be in denial about anything productive or positive.

Isabel Florence Hapgood

There are about forty five letters from Lucy Alexayeff in the file, they are sprawling, barely legible missives that run to sixteen pages at a time. So now that Hapgood had her Irkutsk song-bird on board, she worked on the rest, 'with the now added incentive of protecting Americans from the fraud as I learned that she was planning a piratical trip to the United States.'

Hapgood badgered Alex Francis, the editors of papers and magazines in New Zealand, America and England, the Charity Organisation Society, the leading lights of the Women's Christian Temperance Union and the organisers of the Chicago World's Fair that Kate was planning to attend with Ada Field; her openly hostile letters invited their recipients to write back with any slurs against Kate Marsden that they may not even have considered of any relevance previously.

She stalked her, among the papers is a list of dates and places that Kate lived in from as far back as 1876 to the 1890s, e.g. – 'Exmouth July 1882, Hastings Feb 1883, Wadhurst June 16 1883, mother left Hastings Sept 10 1883 . . . etc'

Slowly she reined in anyone who admired or befriended Kate, and homed in on those who had a substantial grievance against her. One of these was Ellen Hewett of Wellington, New Zealand. It appeared that in 1889, while in Berlin, she had been found staying in a small hotel with Kate Marsden by Elizabeth Lovering, who was in correspondence with Hapgood. This is part of the letter:

'38 Adams St. Winter Hill, Somerville. Mass.

Sept. 11 1892

Trusting to your promise as to safe return of all important letters, verifying statements concerning Miss Marsden. I enclose the letters of Mrs Hewett, widow of an English officer who lost his life among the Maoris of New Zealand years ago leaving her with several small children in her early womanhood. She had some little property of her own and about the time she was nearing middle life became one of Miss M's dupes through the latter's influence over her religious nature while Miss M. was endeavouring to interest the N.Z. people. Mrs Hewett, a beautiful and almost devotee woman, with affectionate, credulous nature was led by Miss M. to believe that she was converting the latter from Romanism to protestantism. She obtained complete influence over Mrs H. borrowed and borrowed from her small fortune, and finally persuaded her to visit England where she (Miss M.) was going there to interest people high in position in her plans for the lepers. Mrs Hewett paid many of her bills including the dress etc., in which she was presented at court, and such complete possession did Miss M. obtain over her, that Mrs Hewett's best friends became alienated through their knowledge of the constant drain being made on her ever-diminishing finances. If she resisted and tried to assert herself Miss M. either frightened or cajoled her and finally persuaded her to accompany her to the continent where she had designs on the various Courts, using the utmost ability and finesse to gain her ends. In Berlin, where I met her, at the same Pension (Spring of 1890), I was impressed with Miss M's cold, strong personality . . .

I noticed that Miss M. observed our conversation closely, that she kept Mrs H. to herself as much as possible, and that the latter deferred to her on every occasion . . .'

Mrs Lovering writes that Ellen Hewett confided in her that she felt the need to get away from her because 'she had long since lost confidence in Miss M. having seem so much duplicity and violence of temper as well and longed to go free but didn't know how to.'

Later on, Ellen Hewett wrote to Hapgood in person and told her that Marsden had hit her and caused her actual harm that she had not yet recovered from.

As Isabel was pursuing her rigorous hate campaign by letter, Kate was enjoying deserved success in London. She was very good at speaking and in October 1892 addressed an audiences in Harley Street that included the Duchess of Teck and Mr and Mrs Baden-Powell; and in the same month she was invited to Balmoral to be received by the Queen and within a few weeks was elected as one of the first female fellows of the Royal Geographical Society. On the 15th December she spoke to a large audience at the Polytechnic In stitute, after which she received a hearty applause. In February 1893 favourable book reviews and articles about her Siberian trip were being published.

H.R.H. THE DUCHESS OF TECK.
(*Photograph by Russell & Sons.*)

The Duchess of Teck, or Mary Adelaide, a granddaughter of George III and great-grandmother of Elizabeth II. She held the title of Duchess of Teck through marriage and is remembered as the mother of Queen Mary, the wife of King George V. She was one of the first royals to patronise a wide range of charities.

As Kate Marsden was planning her fund-raising lecture tour of America, Isabel Hapgood claimed she took 'entire charge of the case' and was geared-up to prevent it happening. She was incensed by a glowing article printed in the 'English Review of Reviews' in August 1892 by the outstanding columnist William Stead called

'The Quest of the Holy Grail', writing of Kate's leper endeavours in Siberia. She writes:

'I remonstrated very vigorously with Mr Stead (whom I had met in St Petersburg) and he replied with a letter as amazing as his article, to the effect that he had twice refused to notice the woman, but had yielded to emphatic requests from my friend, Countess A.A. Tolstoy. It took six months (or more) of argument, on the part of myself, Miss Willard and Lady Henry Somerset, to make him do his plain duty – even after he was convinced by the evidence – and retract his recommendations.'

Kate had thought that William Stead was a friend to her but Hapgood's letter-writing campaign gathered apace and soon changed that. She wrote to Queen Victoria (who, amazingly, never capitulated to her and in an obscure way continued to carry a flag for Marsden), the Prince and Princess of Wales, the Emperor and Empress of Russia, The Duchess of Saxe-Coburg-Gotha who was a contact of Hapgood's through Countess Tolstoy and to the Queen of Denmark.

'From everyone except Queen Victoria I received replies. I had suggested to the Queen of Denmark that she exert her authority and influence over her daughters, the Princess of Wales and the Empress of Russia, and reduce them from the scrape into which their support of Kate Marsden had got them and I offered to show convincing evidence to any official representative whom she might choose to send. She sent Mr Henri Braem, long Consul-General of Denmark in this city, and I convinced him within ten minutes.

As for Queen Victoria – if she ever was given my letter at all, she gave her the golden Angel of Victory. What the English Royal Family felt immediately afterwards about this – possibly because of my letters to them all, or, at least in part, can be seen, on behalf of herself and Dr Kate Bushnell.'

Slowly she persuaded everyone to withdraw their support for Kate Marsden, making her proposed trip to America almost impossible.

On 6th October 1894 a lengthy article titled 'Exposure of Kate Marsden' was published in the 'New Zealand Evening Post' by 'the Special Correspondent of the Dunedin Star', the tone of which suggests the pen of Isabel Hapgood herself. The bias and lack of professional journalism is evident throughout 'For over eighteen months Miss Marsden travelled about the Continent, enjoying capital times and raising money for 'my lepers'.'

The article comments in detail on the report of the investigation committee, that had been assembled to investigate claims of Kate Marsden's inappropriate behaviour, citing Isabel Hapgood of New York, U.S.A. as a valuable source of information. It states that Hapgood: 'during a period of four years has been endeavouring to accomplish what at last has been achieved – the complete exposure of one of the most clever and daring female imposters of the day'.

A letter, from Kate? to another woman? now lost and not quoted in the article, provided the most damning evidence against Kate. It was, however, impounded by the Russian police and is now lost. What did it say? We don't know. The journalist then jumps around topics but indicates that three questions were asked her by the committee. Firstly, did Kate borrow money against property that she allegedly owned in New Zealand? – Yes. Secondly, did Kate Marsden ever own or inherit any property in New Zealand? – No. Finally, did she ever commit any act of immoral conduct with a woman? Finding – yes, she had immoral relations with several women in different countries. Was that what she was admitting to in the lost letter?

None of these accusations seem to have any basis and in due course she protested and was exonerated – but she never fully shook off the accusations.

Next the committee investigated funds that she is said to have embezzled, and money that she 'robbed' from a 'large number' of people, mostly wealthy women, and a good many of them moved in society. Apparently the Investigation Committee had the names of women and 'letters confessing their guilt'. Nothing resembling that seems to be in any archive today.

There was no lack of people in New Zealand who wanted to assist the committee, they had amassed documents from the managers of two accident insurance companies who attested that

Miss Marsden acted fraudulently and sworn documents from the Registrar-General of New Zealand from two 'well-known medical men' and others suggesting that false statements she had made about her charitable work in New Zealand had led to her being received by the Queen of England and members of the Royal Family.

The article suggested that she had gone to Germany to 'escape the consequences of her misdeeds, or to exploit the German people. But our report will follow her. She has written several letters at different times threatening legal proceedings, but has never followed them up. They were merely bluff.'

It was at this lowest of low moments in her life that I had met her in Pymmes Park, when she was planning to leave for Germany to lie low for a while; but it was obvious now that the scandal followed her there. What could she do when a world-wide mass of accusations were thrown in her face? She attended some of the first meetings of the committee, and she answered questions in writing. 'When confronted with documentary evidence, she left St Petersburg while the committee was in session and returned to England.' She'd walked out on them.

I wondered why; and then it occurred to me – that Oscar Wilde was soon to go on trial in London for homosexual acts, and Joseph Soames, The Times' solicitor, was having her investigated by the 'same private detective who had traced Wildes's male prostitutes.'* How awful it would have been if they had actually interrogated her and forced her to talk about the 'intimacy' with women she was accused of.† Mentally it would probably have been more than she could bear.

She left, never to return to Russia; since she was told, in no uncertain terms, that she was no longer welcome.

Sadly, throughout all the dastardly processes of Kate Marsden's persecution and particularly in the hundreds of papers in the Isabel

---

* Heroine of Russia cast out into the cold by William Millinship. The Times Monday August 15 1994
† Lesbian activity was never against the law.

Hapgood file, there is not a single mention of Kate's brave nursing in Bulgaria, her journey across Siberia and her drive to build a leper colony in Yakutia.

In fact, at the time the committee were summing up and reaching their damning verdict – the hospital in Sosnovka was being constructed, with the money she had raised. Among them all, she was the one with a solid achievement – perhaps of world importance – to show.

Chapter 26

The Kate Marsden Hospital in Sosnovka today

On the footprint of the leper Colony in Sosnovka, is a psycho-neurological clinic named after Kate Marsden, with Kleopatra Koryakina as the Director.

Ellie and I were given a full tour of the cheerful cottage hospital, meeting many patients along the way who seemed thrilled to meet the visitors from England and South Africa and some gave us gifts of cloudberry jam they'd made and stored in plastic coke bottles.

With the doctors from the hospital flanking us we walked away from the small wooden hospital towards the forest, stopping at a series of bent and rotten wooden partition walls with empty blackened window frames and the remains of roofs lurching precariously towards earth. This was what was left of Kate's hospital, amazingly recognisable after decades of harsh Siberian winters.

The Sosnovka Leprosarium

Remains of one of the buildings, these
were dismantled in the 1970s
A store house in the leprosarium, in the foreground is the
entrance to an ice house for storing dairy products

The original bridge as it looked in 1912 with the
family of Telie-Ivanov Semen Victorovich.

The bridge today. The residents of Sosnovka are adamant
that Kate Marsden designed this bridge herself

Victor Victorovich, a medical assistant and nobleman with his wife Augusta Alexandrovna in 1908. After finishing medical school he was sent to work in the leprosarium where he worked from 1910 to 1920.

Victor Victorovich's son Ivanov Semen Victorovich with the author

"Spasibo" I uttered and my eyes searched the remains, a forlorn pile of timbers; but to me and the prestigious delegates from the hospital around me – they were so very much more.

Collective rumination about Kate may have stirred her unhappy spirit to join us. As a speck of dust in the huge forest, in the wind playing upon the silver birches, tossed upon each leaf as a dappled ray of sunlight, how she would have loved to see it, to be here, to feel all that love.

We continued to stare at the ruins in front of us, that were slowly decaying into the damp earth and I broke our reverie:

"It won't be here much longer, why don't you cover it with a large corrugated tin roof and stop anyone walking over it."

They all looked perplexed, "why would we do that?" One of them replied.

"Because it's an ancient monument. What will visitors like me have to see in five or ten years time?" There was a very animated nodding of heads and muttering in Russian. "We agree, nobody thought of that before." I smiled to myself, proud to think that since I began my mad venture to recreate the travels of these early female travellers I may have saved not one, but two significant buildings from the ravages of time and given them archaeological status.*

We visited the tiny Kate Marsden Museum, the museum with, almost, no visitors and I admired the way they had been gathering small items. I stood there, promised to send them all I could, and am proud to say I have been doing so ever since. I have sent them copies of all the prints of Kate Marsden that are in the RGS collection, a copy of the 1871 map, copies of letters in Kate Marsden's handwriting that I gathered for the writing of this book and when I returned in 2015, at their invitation, I presented them with a first edition of Kate Marsden's book which was signed by her and photographs of her newly cleared grave in Hillingdon cemetery. On that visit I was surprised to find out that there had been few, or no, visitors to Sosnovka since Ellie and my visit two years earlier. I was also amused to see the plum pudding that had travelled across Siberia with us in a glass display case. I asked them

---

* The first one being Gergan the monk's house in Hundar, Nubra in Northern Ladakh. My findings are with the Archaeological Survey of India.

what the doctors had done with the custard I had sent over from England to eat with the plum pudding, "We ate it on toast," came the reply, "it was very good!" I have promised to donate them the extensive material I have collected for the writing of this book once it is published. So that Sosnovka becomes a hub for Kate Marsden research.

The next day we were taken on a sightseeing excursion round Vilyuisk, but by then my face was so swollen with the insect bites that I wouldn't come out from under a voluminous scarf! I shrank from the photographers and cursed my milk-white skin which was so appealing to midges. (Ellie, with a little bit darker complexion escaped my misery, and fortunately, did not get the same bad reaction.)

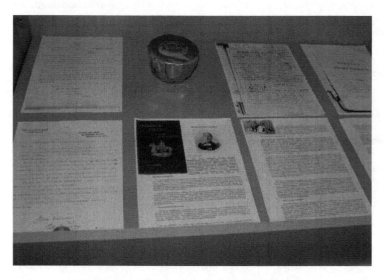

The Plum Pudding that came with us on our journey is now an exhibit in the museum

We had a fascinating day visiting the Local History Museum, the Vilyuisk Teacher Training College and its own museum, the Ethnographic centre and then Balagan – a traditional Yakut house lived in by Efrosinia Petrova – before returning to Sosnovka for a final visit. This time we had tea with Kleopatra in her office – a tea consisting of whipped cream, tinned fruit, slices of fat, home made bread and cucumber salad. We were there to discuss the empty plinth outside her clinic; waiting for a Kate Marsden statue and for which she showed us the designs, and asked our views on them.

Kate Marsden would like to think I received such fabulous hospitality in her memory, but the torments that she suffered did come to haunt me too – later on that day, the little grey biting gnats had bitten me so severely through the scarf and my clothes that my face blew right up, and I had nasty swellings around my back and stomach too. On leaving the village, in the forest after a few days my skin recovered; but she had to endure that discomfort for weeks.

My last visit in Vilyuisk was to meet Nina Protopopova, an eighty-six year old retired journalist who had edited the Republic newspaper for many years and gained a place in the Russian Guinness book of Records for her length of service. She was one of the first writers to publish a book that included Kate Marsden's journey in it. She had flown to Vilyuisk for the 2nd of September Celebrations in which her deceased husband Nicolai Kondakov, a hero of the Soviet Union, was to be celebrated. She agreed to meet me and greeted me warmly wearing a navy blazer so covered in medals that I wondered how so elderly a lady could stand up. With the help of Ulyana the translator we eulogised about Kate Marsden over a cup of tea for an hour and then my busy schedule whisked me away.

The journey back to Yakutsk through the Taiga took fifteen hours instead of the twenty coming. We slipped and slid around again in the chewed-up mud, and watched vehicles being hauled out of it, but the time flew by with so many memories of Vilyuisk and Sosnovka to process.

We flew, this time, out of Yakutsk as the sun was rising, leaving a lustrous glow on the braided strands of the River Lena, while in stark contrast, in the morning half light, the black forest loomed towards the horizon. Dense and chilling, the Siberian Taiga brings no relief to the eye, as it spreads interminably west; now and again a glint denotes a small lake, a white line a train track or a rough road. The sun came full up, pouring its illumination into the forest, but it still remained a relentless dark unforgiving area of secrecy, suffering and remoteness. As each hour passed, nothing changed, it went on and on and on and I found it hard to believe that an English woman had travelled through it on a rough cart in the icy grip of winter. My own journey, by train, bus, boat, taxi and, to be sure, a bit of walking, had been remarkable too because, as I looked out onto that horizon I realised that my own horizons had altered significantly – it had changed me. I had been the recipient of love from a Russian village, such appreciation, for making the long trek out to visit them that I felt energised and motivated. I would return to the UK and among the many challenges ahead of me I would put the record straight – that Kate Marsden should be celebrated and not vilified anymore.

The remains of the leper colony today

Chapter 27

1913

The Dorset Road house in Bexhill-on-Sea today

Shadows played on the glossy anaglypta wallpaper, Kate walked into the front parlour, slowly followed by the Norris sisters. I was visiting her at Dorset Road in Bexhill on Sea, a modest new house with a small front garden, large airy rooms and parquet flooring.

She was fifty three and as sad as when I had seen her the last time. A stoop was evident and her lips were thin and set into an unflattering scowl. Alice and Emily, the Norris sisters, sat on either side of me; the three spinsters stared sweetly at me and my jeans and striped jumper with heeled boots, but were far too polite to comment, I took to them straight away.

"May we sit in, my dear, do you mind?"

"Of course, it's a pleasure." I replied handing over the usual offering, this time a tin of deluxe double chocolate biscuits, I remembered how much Kate had enjoyed those chocolate biscuits at Pymme's Park and I thought that these would be a real treat.

"And are you married my dear?" Miss Alice asked, in her sweet little voice, she reminded me of my late grandmother. "You don't have a ring on."

The gold brooch given to Kate in October 1892 by Queen Victoria

That's interesting, I thought; perhaps she thinks that no husband what tolerate a wife wearing trousers! "No actually, I've been divorced for many years, but I fell in love with another man the week before I left on my journey across Siberia . . ." All three women stopped what they were doing and looked up, "But it didn't work out."

"Oh dear," Miss Emily mumbled, "maybe you'll meet someone else." Just as hard in the twenty first century as the early twentieth, I thought to myself, feeling the gaze of three spinsters upon me.

The chocolate biscuits were passed around and the women positively beamed and once again, Miss Emily scurried off to make the tea.

Kate's lap was deep with papers, I had told her that we'd go through her life, the bits I'd missed, and her withdrawal from leprosy work. "Well, it seems so long ago now . . ." she used her long bumpy fingers to record the events, "In October 1892 I went to Balmoral and the Queen gave me my beautiful gold brooch." She lifted it from a red velvet box on a side table and fingered it, she was reluctant to let me hold it in case it turned to dust. I was surprised she still owned it, I thought she'd had to hand it back after the committee investigation, "and in the same month Princess Christian presented me with the silver medal of the Royal British Nurses Association, and at the end of that wonderful month, I was elected a Fellow of the Royal Geographical Society."

"Well done, that was great, quite an accolade, I was probably about the fifty thousandth!" We laughed, well she almost smiled and I laughed, she wasn't doing humour any more.

"You know my book was published in 1892," I nodded, I knew it well and was glad to see how she still so proud of her writing, "and it was widely reviewed."

"I'm so pleased, how much did it raise for your leper colony?"

" Well, my dear, with my Leper Fund as well, we had collected £2,400 by 30th June 1893 and sent most of it to Father Konstantin Pobedonostzev of the Holy Synod in St Petersburg and work began on the leper hospital in Vilyuisk soon after."

"Most of it?" I enquired.

"Well, you know, we have a few expenses." I didn't react, that was what she was criticised for, but, I thought surely all our High Street charity shops have administrative costs to pay and she'd donated all the profits from her book, she could easily have kept that to live off – but she didn't.

"What happened about the herb? Did you have it tested for its curative qualities?"

"Yes, but the conclusion was that it only gave sufferers temporary relief".

"Oh like drinking whisky for a bad cold?"

"Exactly." She answered with sadness in her voice. What a lot of effort I thought, such hopes that she'd found a cure.

Miss Emily held the door open and Miss Alice brought in the tea tray. The presentation was immaculate; the china tea cups were flower-patterned and the embroidered tray cloth was snowy white and starched.

As Kate spooned white sugar into her tea with a slightly wobbly hand her voice became sombre and flat, the Norris sisters looked on with concern. "I went to America with Miss Field at the end of 1892, it didn't go very well." Her moist eyes stared into her tea cup; all her hopes and dreams were swirling around in its muddy depth, the years, the anguish and the love she'd once felt.

"We had a stand in the Women's Building at the World's Fair, where we exhibited a model of the building that we'd had designed for us by Mr Dixon Butler, he designed police stations you know, there's one of his in Hackney."

"And you sent photographs and drawing of that model to the Queen, didn't you?"

"Yes . . . how did you know?" I didn't tell her I'd seen all the archives that referred to her at Windsor Castle; I wanted to hear everything from her voice, her perspective, hear the emotion crackle. I wondered how far she'd go.

"I wrote a lovely brochure on the lepers to go with my stand, it was so nice to hand it out to people, tell them about my cause and the lepers in the forest, so badly treated and cast out. But then . . ." she paused and the quiet room waited until she was ready, "that Hapgood woman, started to write articles and letters, she criticised my fund-raising methods and wrote things to turn people against me and the people read them and weren't so friendly any more. They came and stared at me."

"So what did you do?"

She considered me for a while, "I wrote letters back to the press, I asked my friend Mr Johnson to write a short biography of me, I made sure everyone knew that all the finances were in the hands of Miss Field and tried as much as I could to keep the moral high ground," She blew her nose, finished her tea and looked down at the papers on her knees, "I know," she spoke softly, "that when things were very bad for me, when I was ill, after my accident in New Zealand, that I got friendly . . . with women, I enjoyed their company, *too much and I met women sometimes – who liked me too." The room went very quiet, the clock ticking on the mantelpiece seemed deafening.*

"But, you see, all I wanted was for them to donate to my leper fund."

Kate was staring hard at my jeans, probably wondering if they were comfortable, she was examining the pockets stitched on the back. "Dear Miss Marsden, like you, when I see a female friend I give them a hug, sometimes a big hug, and we kiss each other on the cheek."

There was a pause, the poor Norris sisters looked worried about what was coming next! "Did you ever do more than that?"

"Not really," she blushed . . . "not very much different." I revelled in my quiet triumph, she was a New Woman, I had never been able to find a scrap of evidence that she acted in a way that would have offended Victorian sensitivities, not that it would matter today. I didn't ask her more, the moment didn't allow for it.

"And Miss Field, what happened to her?"

"Oh my dear, she returned to England and although I still received a letter from time to time, I never saw her again. It had all mentally exhausted her, the rumours and imputations and the gossip and the humiliation."

We all smiled awkwardly and Miss Alice got up, removed the tea cosy from the pot and poured us all another cup of tea.

Bexhill-on-Sea Museum 1914

"Did you know we are starting a museum here in Bexhill?" Miss Emily chirpily announced, anxious to change the subject.

305

"No, how lovely, what gave you the idea?"

"Oh, mostly Miss Marsden's wonderful shell collection, and our bits and pieces too that we have gathered over the years. Our friends in Bexhill are always telling us that they have objects they don't know what to do with, you know, paintings and little statues from Egypt. We have been granted Shelter Hall on Egerton Road, right on the park. It is so exciting."

Miss Alice took over, "It's all Miss Marsden's efforts, she is so good at all that organising, she has submitted a petition to the Corporation for the establishment of a museum, arranged public meetings and it's she that has persuaded local residents to donate their items."

"She is marvellous, and has done all the work so far."

I was so pleased to hear some cheeriness in their voices and in their lives, but I knew that it wouldn't last for long.

I slipped away closing the door gently behind me, leaving them to cogitate my strange visit and as I knew I would never see her again, I wondered if she'd told me all she could. The story is that she had a stroke soon after my other visit in 1918 and rapidly faded – mentally and physically.

I desperately searched my brain for more reasons that Hapgood could have hated her so much, did she cover herself in glory for having skewered the,(in her mind,) villainous Kate Marsden? Possibly, she never herself raised a penny for charity or sponsored any worthy cause while Kate did.

Isobel died a bitter and twisted woman whose so called 'friends' had disappeared like the melting snow when she failed to produce any more juicy gossip. She was the tabloid's side kick, who was dispensable. Kate's promising career had been destroyed for short-term gain for Hapgood.

Who knows how much more Kate may have achieved if she hadn't suffered the wrath of one woman.

Chapter 28

Kate on the sledge

By 1894 Sir Henry Ponsonby was fending off letters purporting to reveal the bad conduct of Kate Marsden to a point where he compared her to an infectious disease and wished he'd never heard her name.

After the letter to The Times by the Rev. Alex Francis, Kate decided to sue him but couldn't raise the money to do so, but she wrote an untidy scrawling note to Queen Victoria pleading with her to believe her innocence of all accusations – the Queen, however, remained silent, perhaps sheltered from such a letter by the conscientious Ponsonby.

In 1895 she wanted to root her life back where she felt she could escape all the battles that were raging, and helped to set up the St Francis Leprosy Guild. It was agreed that she would represent the charity as a speaker, and her expenses would be reimbursed.

In 1896 Truth magazine published an article, probably penned by Isabel Hapgood, in which she was charged with 'immorality, dishonesty and lying' and she was pressurised to give up her association with the St Francis Leprosy Guild.

She moved to Philadelphia but was hounded out by the local press after they reported that she had contracted leprosy and she moved on again, travelling to Hawaii, on the ship 'Warrimoo', but once again trouble had preceded her and she wasn't allowed to disembark at Honolulu by the Board of Health.

By the end of the century Kate had felt forced to withdraw from leprosy work although her hospital in Vilyuisk now had seventy-six patients and was very successful. In 1906 the situation softened and she was presented at court again – this time to Edward VII and ten years later she was nominated a free life fellow of the RGS.

In the intervening years more sadness and humiliation affected all three women when, in 1913, while the Bexhill Museum was still in its planning stages, an anonymous letter, enclosing The Times newspaper article of August 1894, was sent to the Mayor of Bexhill-on-Sea. Kate's entreaties to her innocence were ignored and she was not allowed to work for the committee anymore. In fact she was removed entirely from her own project and made to think that she had brought disgrace and scandal to the seaside town. In one of her many long letters appealing to the Mayor to reconsider she wrote:

'I was the subject of certain scurrilous and lying articles in the papers you mention . . . I was advised by Queen Victoria to refrain from all legal action and simply live it down. It is most strange and true that these lying rumours and malicious reports should be now unearthed after nearly twenty years, at a time when I am trying to do a little for the town in which I live and which I love so dearly.'

To quote from the Bexhill Museum book by John Betts: 'The Mayor obviously had made up his mind and was not going to change his decision, as his reply two days later confirmed:

'I am sorry you should consider that I am judging or condemning you. All I have stated is that in view of the matters referred to in my letter to you, I think that as Chief Magistrate of the Town I ought to disassociate myself from co-operating with you in the undertaking you desire to promote.'

That was the end of it and Kate's small happiness was scotched by a society so quick to judge and believe what the newspapers say.

One does wonder though, whether it was Isabel Hapgood who sent the Mayor and the committee the cutting from The Times and The Nation, but Kate's fall from favour was so complete that after she died the Norris sisters sent the Museum a framed portrait of Kate; it was rejected and returned to the sisters, causing them much distress. It was accepted by the Royal Geographical Society who also own her other small treasures, and look after them with pride.

Kate Marsden carried on living in Bexhill on Sea, with the Norris sisters until at least 1920 and in 1921 she published 'My Mission in Siberia: A Vindication', hoping finally to clear her name. Unfortunately it read like a facsimile of 'By Sledge and Horseback to Outcast Siberian Lepers' and produced little impact.

In 1926 Kate Marsden was living in London again and started a world wide collection for leprosy, but by then nobody knew who she was any more. A year later she had a stroke and was cared for by the kindly Norris sisters before living out her last years in the Surrey County Lunatic Asylum, Springfield House, in Wandsworth, which had opened to serve the pauper population and had, at that time, 1,848 patients. She died on the 26th March 1931 and was buried in an unmarked grave in Hillingdon Cemetery.

On the 26th March 2014 a grave-clearing party convened at the cemetery. Kate Marsden's grave was located, and tended and loved for the first time since her death, by a group of us including Kate Renouf, a firm supporter of Kate Marsden whose patient research had located the spot.

Quite remarkably, an actor from Sakha Theatre in Yakutsk, Kupriyan Mikhailov, had been told in a dream to take his shaman's costume on his planned trip to London with a small party improving their English. Once in the United Kingdom he was invited to the grave-clearing, something he had not known about previously.

It seems very fitting that as we removed over eighty years of neglect, the costumed shaman performed a ritual involving flags, drums, dancing and chanting. As smoke curled from a three-legged pot in his hands we all felt in our bones that we'd brought the love to her that had been lacking during her lifetime.

There is now a plaque on the grave, presented by the people of Vilyuisk and Sosnovka; and an anonymous well-wisher has planted geraniums in neat rows over the grave.

Every day, hundreds of students look out of the windows of Brunel University, across a Victorian cemetery of crooked gravestones, without a clue that an extraordinary nurse, who undertook one of the coldest, longest and hardest journeys ever undertaken by a woman, is buried in a quiet corner.

The Herb

Fragrant Fern
Aiken, S.G., et al.,
Flora of the Canadian Arctic Archipelago

The Yakutians I met were all familiar with the herb that Kate Marsden had been seeking; in fact the Mayor of Vilyuisk gave me a cup of tea made with it. I drank it, but wasn't gasping for a second cup! They know the plant as Wolf's Grass or Katshukya and I asked various people if they were able to obtain samples for me – and was thrilled to receive one from Vilyuisk and one from Yakutsk, the samples were the same and so I knew I had the right plant!

A very opportune dinner party in Clifton led to a positive iden- tification of the plant. I found myself sitting opposite a botanist who listened to my story of the plant and was very keen to have a go at researching what it was.

Ask an expert! Within days I knew all about this magic herb that had created such excitement to Kate and was partly responsible for sending her across Siberia.

The plant is a fern called Fragrant Fern or Woodfern, (Dryopteris fragrans (L.) Schott (Fragrant Fern). My sample was determined by. P. Rooney, and confirmed by F. Rumsey.

It is a deciduous perennial herb from the genus Dryopteris, is mainly distributed in Northeast China, Russia, Japan, Korea and North America. There are two books written in the nineteenth century that would have been very useful to Kate, if she had seen them.

One is 'The native flowers and ferns of the United States in their botanical, horticultural and popular aspects' published in 1878 and the second is 'Beautiful ferns from original water-colour drawings after nature' published in 1882.

In 'Beautiful Ferns' the author writes that the "Yakoots of Siberia" use the plant in place of tea and also that the pleasant odour of the plant is very prominent and can be compared to the fragrance of raspberries.

Does the fern have any curative qualities though? A study by scientists of the Northeast Forestry University in China has made some interesting findings and have suggested that the indigenous plant has a long and rich history of folk medicine and this use has arisen from its versatile use in treatment of various ailments such as psoriasis, acne, erythra and dermatitis and as an effective antibacterial, antioxidant, analgesic, anti-tumour and immunomodulatory agent. Moreover, oral administration of its decoctions is effective for treatment of rheumatoid arthritis.

Sadly for Kate Marsden is this note in 'The Native Flowers and Ferns of the United States in their Botanical, Horticutural and Popular Aspects'. It says that 'It has been under culture in English gardens since 1820, and is still popular with the hardy fern growers there, notwithstanding the influx of new favourites'.

So Kate didn't have to travel to eastern Siberia to find it; it was right here under her nose.

Beautiful ferns from original water-color drawings after nature
Boston :D. Lothrop and Co.,1882, [c1881].

The Chicago World Fair

The Woman's Building, designed by Sophia Hayden

The fair that Kate Marsden had a stand at, was The World's Columbian Exposition also known as The Chicago World's Fair, which was held between May and October 1893 to celebrate the 400th anniversary of Christopher Columbus's arrival in the New World in 1492.

In the centre of the Fair, was a huge man-made lake that was designed to represent the long journey that Columbus took to the New World. Chicago beat New York City, Washington, D.C., and St. Louis for the great honour of building and hosting the fair.

The Exposition was a highly successful social and cultural event which had a lasting influence on architecture and the arts. It was also a great boost to the mood in America at the time and turned world attention to Chicago, showing the world that it had recovered its status as a great city since the terrible fire that destroyed so much of it in 1871.

Kate's exhibit in the Women's Building consisted of photographs and signed letters and a plan of her leper village by Mr J Dixon Butler, architect to the Metropolitan Police.

Sadly there is no record, that can be unearthed at present, of the model of the leper colony or any other drawings by Mr Dixon Butler, but there is a drawing of a leper's home in the 'Woman's Building Catalogue' that was part of her exhibit.

MODEL OF A LEPER'S HOME.

316

The entry says 'Her appeals for help touched the heart of her queen, Victoria, and reached the ears of the Empress of Russia. They are rendering her assistance. In Russia and Siberia she raised money enough to erect temporary habitations for the lepers and she came to America for the purpose of raising more money with which to complete her plans.'

In 'The Book of the Fair', there is another reference to her, still sadly without any illustration, it states: 'Soon after the Russo-Turkish war, Kate Marsden, an English woman and nurse of the Red Cross society, journeyed east to Siberia for the purpose of founding leper missions, and near the Swedish and Norwegian booths is a model of the village which she established in the province of Yakutsk. it consists of two hospitals, a school, a church, houses for lepers, and their attendants, and workshops for those who retain the use of their limbs. Fronting the models, is a miniature of one of the miserable hovels in which she found a number of unfortunates lurking in their forest lair.'

SWEDEN'S EXHIBIT

The Swedish Exhibit was next to Kate's exhibit

Although this period was difficult for Kate, with Isabel Hapgood furious that she was on American soil and exhibiting at the fair, we can only hope that seeing the rest of the Chicago World Fair was an inspiration to her.

The Bexhill-on-Sea Museum

Bexhill Museum opened its doors in 1914, although, as previously mentioned, Kate Marsden was an important part of its inception, she was consequently erased from any credit for it for the rest of her life. The museum was housed in the Egerton park Shelter Hall, built in 1903 and continued to expand to what it is today.

It all seems to have started with Kate's shell collection! In the Bexhill Chronicle on September 28, 1912, there is an article entitled 'Proposed Museum' – A WONDERFUL COLLECTION OF SHELLS – Miss Kate Marsden's Gift to Bexhill'. Which reads: 'There was a pleasant 'At Home' on Thursday evening at the residence of Miss Kate Marsden, F.R.G.S, of 61, Dorset Road, in order to give her many friends the opportunity of inspecting her wonderful collection of shells, which she has gathered from all parts of the world during a long and varied course of travel.'

Inside the museum in 1920, just after the Museum reopened after WW1. Between the pillars are Rev Thompson and a young Henry Sargent who had started work as the director

319

There is no doubt that Kate, Alice and Emily, spend much of their time discussing and enthusing about the project and garnering support from their friends in Bexhill.

Later on in the article it reports that: 'This magnificent collection of shells – land shells, sea shells, and all other kinds of shells – Miss Marsden has offered as a FREE GIFT TO BEXHILL. In the hope that it will form the nucleus not only of a Natural History Museum, but also a museum of a general character.' The Rev.J. C. Thompson was also involved at this early stage in the museum's history and in the article it mentions that he, 'has himself collected many things of interest, local as well as general, and would hand them over to a museum. He believes that there are many others in Bexhill who would do the same.'

There can be no doubt that Kate was the main driving force – perhaps she felt she had finally found another project to put her energy into.

The Bexhill Observer comments at great length in an article entitled: 'MUSEUM FOR BEXHILL, Miss Marsden Explains her Scheme, Possible Opening at Easter'. It seems she gave a fundraising speech that she gave to Members of the Bexhill Commercial Association, 'With an enthusiasm which does her infinite credit.' What is interesting though is the high esteem she was held in and the way she engaged the audience.

'Dealing with the question of securing accommodation for the exhibits, Miss Marsden said it was difficult to get certain members of the Council to understand what was wanted. Some thought that she wanted a place as large as from Bexhill to London. (Laughter.) She explained to them that she wanted three feet space in which to place articles to explain about each of the Colonies, and similar spaces for other things. They wanted the people who could not travel to learn a little about the world. They wanted people to live a freer life than they did, (Hear, hear.) . . . Much amusement was caused by Miss Marsden's explanation of how she obtained the promise of exhibits from the great manufacturing, shipping, and railway companies. They got everything, she said, for nothing.'

BEAUTIFUL SHELLS FOR BEXHILL MUSEUM.

THESE SPECIMENS WERE EXHIBITED AT MISS MARSDEN'S RESIDENCE ON WEDNESDAY. WHEN SHE RECEIVED THE MEMBERS OF THE BEXHILL COMMERCIAL ASSOCIATION AND OTHER LOCAL GENTLEMEN.

'Kate invited them all to go and view her personal collection the following Wednesday'

She was full of ideas. She wanted to make sure that the Pavilion was filled with interesting things and that they wanted them to help educated the children. The well-off schools were willing to pay for lectures at the museum and they could give the same lecture to the poorer children for nothing. They applauded her when she said they should help the younger generation and to help grow and develop the little town of Bexhill. When she was asked what the finality of her scheme would be she responded that a huge Commercial College would be built in Bexhill.

"Why should they not have a Technical College here?" She told them that her whole heart was in the work and she would use all her energy into making the Museum as comprehensive as possible.

Everyone was on her side, they laughed at all her jokes, agreed with all her ideas and she invited them all to go and view her personal collection the following Wednesday.

The Chairman, Mr H. L. Neale moved a vote of thanks to her and said, 'her speech had been quite an education in itself. Such a Museum as she proposed would be a magnificent asset to the town.'

And then, in what we see now as words of extraordinary irony, Mr Robbins, who represented the Commercial Association on the committee of the proposed Museum seconded the vote of thanks and said: "If ever the College came about, he said, Miss Marsden's name ought to be written in gold in the annals of Bexhill-on-Sea." There was more applause as the vote was carried with acclamation.

That speech was reported, those words were uttered, that applause thundered, laughter rang out – on the 25th January 1913. Barely six weeks later, on 14th March 1913, Kate's removed from a project she loved and believed in was humiliating and deeply upsetting for her. Once more the scandal had caught up with her, when someone

---

SOCIETY FOR ORGANISING CHARITABLE RELIEF AND REPRESSING MENDICITY.

OFFICES OF THE COUNCIL: 15 BUCKINGHAM STREET, ADELPHI, W.C.

N.B.—This Report is CONFIDENTIALLY communicated, and intended only for the information of

The Mayor & Town Clerk of Bexhill-on-Sea

Case No. 16,929. Date of Report, July 27, 1893. Despatched *14 March 1913* 189 .

Name—THE KATE MARSDEN LEPER FUND,
6 LOMBARD COURT.

anonymously sent the Mayor of Bexhill details of the scandal that erupted in 1893. The Mayor then disassociated Kate from the museum and any other community involvement with the small town.

Notes by the Yakut Costume Designer Augustina Filippova

I had been wondering how and what our ancestors had worn and why the costumes were decorated so beautifully. If people had worn the clothes just to protect their bodies from the winter frost and the summer heat, then the clothes would have been more primitive.

We talk about our traditions, but someone had to create them first and make them come true. In early times there were designers who designed the clothes and gave the special meaning to the decorations and these became the tradition. Someone designed dresses for the traditional festival for the Sakha people, Yhyakh, the beautiful girl wearing a smart dress and silver decorations was sung in songs called the Olonkho or fairytales in which she was the pride of the family. Our people are perceptive to beauty and comfort, and traditions were not a heavy burden.

Each epoch brought its novelties, in the seventeenth century clothes were made of well-dressed leather using the skins of horses, cattle, deer and wild animals. Some details of Steppe Turkic tribes, Tungusses, and Yukaghirs' clothes could be noticed in the dresses. In the eighteenth and nineteenth centuries, Russian culture influenced the design and materials used, these are the coats with the puffed sleeves and crinoline and skull caps. Every novelty became a strong Yakut tradition with symbols in the detail and decorations that represented protection.

Girls in costume from Chineke

The colour of the clothes are particularly important, generally four colours were used, black, green, red and silver-white. These colours are connected to the four seasons, black symbolises spring when the snow melts and the ground looks black. The Sakha people say, 'the spring has come, the ground turns black. Green symbolises summer, and red is the colour of autumn when bush leaves and field flowers turn red. Winter is a white fairytale when the snow sparkles with silver sparks in the sun, and at night silver stars twinkle in the sky'.

So, the perception of colour is distinguished by the Sakha people through natural features. When I create the Yakut traditional clothes, first I consider the whole ensemble: the silhouette of a woman wearing a coat with crinoline and a jab aka cap is reminiscent of a well-shaped uraha; the ornament made of woollen cloth on the back is reminiscent of a smart serge; the cut in hem as if sets a door ajar of yurta. Let's take a coat-tangalai – the bride's coat – where does the word tangalai originate from? The Sakha people have a phrase tangalai bylyt which is close to the phrase ribbed clouds.

In Yakut legends they say, 'The daughter of high skies, a beautiful Siberian crane girl, went down from the clouds-tangalai on foot to the Middle World. According to the legend, when a girl is given in marriage, she is blessed by the god Aiyyhyt. The god Aiyyhyt lets the bird kytalyk go from the clouds-tang-alai having cut its wings not to let it fly away, but become a custodian of a young lady's hearth. That is why coat-tangalai has short sleeves which symbolise the cut wings of a Siberian crane bride. Something is stored in our genetic memory, subconscious; something is dictated by surroundings, nature, close and like-minded persons. My designs are the view of a modern person feeling spirit of the past and the present'.

Diana at Dinner

From Punch, Volume 98, June 28th 1890
The first women-only restaurant in London

On the first page of the prospectus of the recently-established "Dorothy" Restaurant it is stated that it is for "Ladies only". On the last page will be found the following modification:—

> "At the request of many of the Lady customers, it has been decided to open the Restaurant from 6·30 P.M. to 10 P.M. to both Ladies and Gentlemen."

There was started in London, I mustn't say where,
And, beyond saying lately, I mustn't say when,
A sweet Restaurant, where the sex that is fair
Might attend undisturbed by the presence of men.
"We are forced to endure you in Park and in Row,
We must bear you unwilling in hansom or 'bus;
But if any stray *here*, they shall meet with a No,—
So attempt not the haunt that is sacred to Us.
"Be warned, O intruder, nor venture to lag
When the nymphs of Diana the huntress draw nigh.
Fly, fly from their presence as fleet as a stag.
Lest you meet with the fate of Actæon, and die."
Thus the Ladies addressed us; the tables were set,
The silver was polished, the viands displayed.
And, like doves in a dove-cote, the customers met,
In a plumage of silks and of muslins arrayed.
"This is sweet!" said Amanda. "Delightful!" said Jane.

While the rest in a chorus of "Charming!" combined.
And, declaring they cared not if dishes were plain,
So the men remained absent, they solemnly dined.
And they toyed with their *entrées*, and sipped their Clicquot,
And their smiles were as sweet as the wine that they drank.
But at last came a whisper—"Oh dear, this is slow!"
"Hush, hush!" said the others. "How dreadfully frank!
"Not slow; but there's something—I scarcely know what,
An absence, a dulness I cannot define.
It may be the soup, which was not very hot,
Or the roast, or the waiting, the ice, or the wine.
"But I'm sure there's a something." And so they agreed,
And they formed a Committee to talk of the case.
And a programme was issued for all men to read,
Bidding men (on page one) to abstain from the place.
But, since it is harder to ban than to bless,
"For their own sakes," they said, "we will humour the men."
If you turn to the last page, you'll find this P.S.:—
"Men allowed, by desire, from 6·30 to 10."

The Red Cross Sister

Poem written by Benjamin Wells A.R.A.M 1879 for his daughter
Janet, known as Sister Janet who worked alongside Kate Marsden:

The Red Cross sister sails over the Main
On a mission of mercy, no greed of gain
Leaves Father and mother and dearest friends
To Succour the wounded they dying to tend.

Strong in her faith this sister so brave
Fears no danger wherever there's life to save
And when that's past hope she cheers their last breath
With the glorious promise of life after death.
This Red Cross sister has powerful friends
Who vie with each other to further her ends
So when war and pestilence ravage the land
True Charity comes from the Stafford House Band

Benjamin Wells A.R.A.M 1879

Her Story is False:

The damning book review written by Isabela Hapgood

This is the transcript of Isabela Hapgood's review of Kate Marsden's book, 'On Sledge and Horseback to Outcast Siberian Lepers'. The exact date in 1893 and publication are unknown. This is less a book review than an attack on Kate herself with no editorial culling of the fierce hatred that is implied throughout. Sadly, Queen Victoria was sent a copy as the review is amongst the archives at Windsor castle.

HER STORY IS FALSE

Kate Marsden's Book Describing Life
Among Russian Lepers.

★

HAS NO FOUNDATION IN FACT.

★

She Saw but One Sick Person and Drew
on Her Imagination Throughout.

A few months ago – perhaps only weeks – a book which attracted wide notice and deep attention was presented to the public. The subject of the book was its recommendation to notice, for it treated of outcast Siberian lepers, (sic) and gave a thrilling account of adventures among them, the heroine of which was the author, Miss Kate Marsden, now proved most indubitably, by cumulative evidence piled high, to be an imposter.

New Zealand first exposed Miss Marsden. Her pretended experience among Maori lepers gave her her first prestige in England; but she is either a daring and reckless liar or else had no realization of the present transportation facilities, for it took the Wellington (New Zealand) *Post* a very short time to give the lady the lie direct. There are no Maori lepers it seems!

But the Siberian yarns have received much more widespread notoriety than the New Zealand tentative efforts – little feelers as they were. Her tales of her adventures at Yakutsk and Vilyuisk, her frightful hardships, nauseating experiences while visiting in the same huts with decaying lepers some days dead, would, and did fill a volume. And the volume was read and created deep sympathy and admiration for so courageous a heroine.

But an honest Russian named Petroff, who accompanied the strange embroiderer on her wanderings, contradicts all her assertions, and in such a way as to leave no doubt as to his own veracity and Miss Marsden's mendacity. Everything she says in her book is false, apparently! One might 'caviare' it a la Russe, sentence by sentence, and there would be nothing left but black gridirons on every page. What was the woman thinking of! Is she mad? Or only wicked?

Makes Many Misstatements

The very information concerning the leper colony which Miss Marsden published as the result of her own investigations had been collected, forwarded to St. Petersburg, and even published a year and a half before Miss Marsden issued her bogus book! This is rank ignorance, leading to suicide! She traveled with a folding bed, had a tent to herself all the way, excellent service, basins, combs, sponges, brushes, clean linen and other comforts of life denied to many and many a better traveler. She relates in her book that she was obliged to sleep in the open air, when not occupying the fetid atmosphere which dead lepers polluted and that she never could change her linen or even her dress.

She also tells harrowing tales of her struggles with 'nothing but tea and a sort of hard toast of sour black bread' for two months. M. Petroff declares that 'Miss Marsden brought from Irkutsk bouillon, potted roast beef, reindeer tongues, dried vegetables for soup, prepared coffee, condensed milk', and also that she had had barley, cognac (teetotal lady that Miss Marsden depicts herself to be!) fruit, game until she could eat it no longer, fresh meat – everything in the world that the heart of man or the palate of a Marsden could desire!

There are sixty-six lepers. It seems, in Russia; the very hairs of their head are numbered. Money sufficient to take care of them was collected long ago; nuns went from Moscow to attend them. The lepers told M. Petroff – who did all Miss Marsden's investigations for her, as she could not bear the disagreeable sights and smells – that they lacked nothing. And then Miss Marsden deliberately, and with no other source of information, goes and publishes a book in which she falsifies every statement he gave her, and makes up others equally false as well!

Drew on Her Imagination

As for the 'herb' which Miss Marsden uses as a pretext for her business trip, she must have known it be worthless as a cure for leprosy before she started on the journey, because in Yakutsk she was definitely told of its inefficiency. As for Miss Marsden's 'discovery' of the lepers, that is a yarn, too, since their existence and state are annually reported to the government. The 'untraveled' roads over which this bogus heroine rode were as well known as any country roads, since her coming was heralded from place to place and arrangements were made for her reception everywhere. She had pacing horses provided for her, and everything was done to make her journey not only comfortable but luxurious and absolutely regal when we think of the country.

Miss Marsen never saw a dead nor a dying leper, and only one living one, for care was taken that she should not be exposed to anything so disagreeable. Leper nurses are hired to look after the helpless ones. And in spite of what Miss Marsden states to the contrary, the grassland in the Yakutsk region is marvellous fine, and the Yakuts are great cattle breeders.

The lot of a leper is not a happy one. Many things might be done to alleviate it, no doubt; and judging from all accounts these things are done in the country of which Miss Marsden writes so harrowingly. They have the same food which the communities about them eat, and in the right quantity. Of course that cannot be boarded at grand hotels in cities, but in the name of all that is merciful, let us give the Russians their due.

As for the authority upon which Miss mars den's statements are denied, it is so genuine and so numerous that it cannot be disputed. Among many the New York *Evening Post* names the *New Zealand Mail* (two issues), the *Wellington Evening Post* (three issues), the Wanganui *Chronicle, the* Christchurch *Weekly Press* and the Oamaru *Mail* for refutations of the new Zealand slanders.

With these as references the Russian refutations have a right to be heard, and they are the faithful and ready to produce witnesses in support that one can see no reason for denying them.

Kate Marsden's time-line,
set against what others thought of her.

13th May 1859:	Kate born in Edmonton, youngest of eight children.
5th August 1859:	Baptised at St James Church, Edmonton
1861:	The last year that the Marsden family is complete and living at 10 The Parade, Edmonton Joseph Daniel Marsden, 47, Sophia Matilda Marsden, 39, Joseph, 12, James E. 11, Eleanor M, 10, William H, 7, Annie J, 6, Alice, 5, Frank, 3, Kate, 2.
1861:	James dies of consumption age 11
1870:	Alice dies of consumption age 13
4th August 1873:	Mr Marsden dies
1875:	Kate is accepted for nurse's training at Tottenham Hospital in Snell's Park November 1877: Kate goes to Bulgaria to tend Russian soldiers wounded in the Russo-Turkish War.
1878:	Kate is working at Westminster Hospital
1879:	Kate becomes Sister-in-Charge of Woolton Convalescent Home in Liverpool
1882:	First breakdown in Kate's health
1883:	Eleanor dies of consumption in Hastings age 32
1883:	Kate leaves Woolton
1884:	Kate sails to New Zealand with her mother to see Annie who has consumption who dies within six days of arrival
1885:	Kate appointed as Lady Superintendent at Wellington Hospital
9th July 1885:	Elected secretary of the Wellington St John's Ambulance Association
28th Sept 1885:	Kate has an accident and falls out of a linen cupboard at the hospital, she becomes 'dangerously' ill, possibly a nervous breakdown. In recovery she resolves to devote herself to the cause of leprosy.
6th March 1889:	Lecture given at Wakapuaka
1889:	Sails back to England with her mother

5th March 1890:	Presented at court
8th March 1890:	Meets the Princess of Wales
April 1890:	Arrives in St Petersburg. Presented to Empress of Russia
May 1890:	Decorated for her services in Bulgaria by the Russian Red Cross, hears about Russian lepers. Returns to England.
17th July 1890:	Article in Evening Post New Zealand published titled 'An Imaginative Lady' questions her work in New Zealand.
18th Sept 1890:	Living at 20 Kensington Crescent, she left for Russia from here (Street now gone.)
Sept 1890:	Sets off for Russia via Alexandria, Jerusalem, Constantinople and Tiflis.
Nov 1890:	Arrives in St Petersburg
Dec 1890:	First article in Girl's Own Paper
1890:	Trouble begins to brew for her in New Zealand
1st Feb 1891:	Leaves Moscow with Ada Field
26th February 1891:	Topics of the Day Paper: New Zealand, biased article about Kate Marsden in Constantinople and meeting the lepers there.
28th Feb 1891:	In Tobolsk: Ada returns to Moscow
28th April 1891:	Kate arrives in Irkutsk
1st May 1891:	Kate's birthday. First meeting with Irkutsk committee.
22nd June 1891:	Kate leaves Yakutsk on horseback
31 July 1891:	Kate returns to Yakutsk
5th Sept 1891:	Interview with Ada Field in Women's Herald
17th September 1891:	Article in The Nursing Times paraphrasing Ada Field's article in Women's Herald
Dec 1891:	After 10 months Kate returns to Moscow and stays for 5 months
Sept 1892:	Kate is in Hastings writing her book, 'On Sledge and horseback to Outcast Siberian Lepers', which is published in 1893.
27th October 1892:	Silver Badge meeting
19th October 1892:	Kate writes to Sir Henry Ponsonby asking what to wear to Balmoral and how to get there
27th October 1892:	Letter from Henry Ponsonby on behalf of the Queen endorsing Kate's work
October 1892:	Summoned to Balmoral where the Queen gives her a brooch.

October 1892:	Princess Christian presents her with a silver medal. An anonymous account of her journey is published in Russian. Royalty and Charity article published with details of the Balmoral visit.
3rd November 1892:	Interview with 'The Nursing Record' Speaks at Lady Jeure's house in Harley Street
23rd November 1892:	Elected as one of the first female fellows of the RGS
19th December 1892:	The Wanganui Chronicle, New Zealand. Extremely damning article about Kate.
23rd February 1893:	The Nursing Record. Meeting of Princess Louise and many other well-known ladies and gentlemen held at the Vicarage, St Mary Abbott's in Kensington held by the Marquis of Lorne in support of Kate Marsden.
February 1893:	German Embassy request more details about her book for the German Emperor
2nd March 1893:	Favourable book review in The Nursing Record Hospital World Supplement. 'Fresh Pages' by E. M. Harrington.
6th April 1893:	Unfavourable book review printed in The Nation, titled 'Philanthrpoy on Horseback'
May – October 1893:	Exhibits at Chicago World Fair, Chicago, United States Publishes her book.
24th May 1893:	Letter from Albert Barker to Sir Henry Ponsonby from the Press Club of Chicago, enclosing an American review of her book.
14th June 1893:	J. Goldsmith Procter, the Hon. Treasurer of The Kate Marsden Leper Fund, writes to Sir Henry Ponsonby asking whether Her Majesty will accept a copy of photographs of the model of Miss Kate Marsden's Leper Colony in Siberia.
1st July 1893:	The palace answered yes.
21st June 1893:	Queen Victoria's daughter Vicky writes to her mother asking whether Miss Marsden would send a copy of her book to Olga who is very anxious to have one and from the author herself.
July 1893:	Charities Organisation Society critical report
1893:	Travelled to St Petersburg to defend herself before the Russian Committee
8th December 1893:	The Grand Duchess Elizabeth Feodorovna writes to her grandmother Queen Victoria that she has seen Miss Marsden and 'What a remarkable woman she is'.
17th August 1894:	'Exposure of Kate Marsden' Evening Post

18th August 1894:	Exposure printed in The Times
20th August 1894:	Written notes from the Privy Office suggest that the Queen was being consulted about what to do about the issue of Kate Marsden
1894:	Committee withdraws support
27th August 1894:	Taranaki Herald, "nemesis has at last fairly overtaken that astute adventuress"
29th August 1894:	Letter sent by Eastleigh to Sir Henry Ponsonby, the Queen's Private Secretary, discussing Kate Marsden
9th October 1894:	Shocking Revelations article printed in NZ Star – runs to many pages
October 1894:	In Germany to escape accusers
December 1894:	Sent by Eastleigh to Sir Henry Ponsonby, the Queen's Private Secretary, 'Only one word more to say that I hope we shall never hear more of Miss Marsden for she proves to be an infectious disease.'
2nd November 1895:	Kate writes to Queen Victoria telling her that she hasn't enough money to continue the libel action against The Times but pleading that she is innocent of all charges
2nd November 1895:	Kate writes to The Times saying that while all the fuss is going on that 'the work for the poor outcast lepers, numbering over two million scattered over the world, as they and their needs seem to have been entirely forgotten'.
23rd October 1895:	The first meeting of the St Francis Leper Guild at the house of Baroness Gudin at 27 Redcliffe Square, London, who consented to take the chair. It was proposed and carried unanimously that Miss Ada Field be asked to become a corresponding member for Russia. It was also proposed that Kate Marsden be reimbursed for the expenses incurred in organising the guild to the present point.
11th November 1895:	Sir Fleetwood Edwards (Keeper of the Privy Purse to Queen Victoria) writes to Colonel Biffe telling him that Kate has written to Princess Beatrice and that Colonel Gordon said the same about Princess Christian 'So I expect all the ladies of the Royal Family are being similarly pestered'.
3rd December 1895:	Second meeting of the St Francis leper Guild at Baroness Gudin's house. It was proposed that Miss Kate Marsden be appointed lecturer and organising director to the guild at a stated stipend.

340

9th January 1896:	Truth magazine publish an article in which she is charged with 'immoralty, dishonesty and lying'
1896:	Withdraws due to scandal Travels
1897:	Leper hospital opens in Vilyuisk
1898:	Resident in Philadelphia Travels in Paris, USA and Hawaii
30th September 1898:	Article in The Hawaiian Gazette saying that Kate was a passenger on the Warrimoo but did not disembark at Honolulu as a letter had gone ahead warning the Board of Health that she was on her way.
1899:	Withdraws from leprosy work
1900:	Tried to exhibit at Exposition Universalle.
1902:	Hospital in Vilyuisk has 76 patients
1904:	D F Rishitillo paid her a tribute
1906:	Attended court
1912:	Becomes a founder of Bexhill Museum
14th March 1913:	Letter from The Society for organising Charitable Relief and Repressing Mendacity to the Mayor of Bexhill informing them of the scandal. It appears to be a copy of an earlier letter.
17th March 1913:	Letter from Daniel Mayer, the Mayor of Bexhill asking Kate whether she is the Kate Marsden written about in The Times article of August 1894. If so he will have to disassociate himself from her.
19th March 1913:	Letter to Mr Mayer putting her side of the scandal.
6th April 1913:	Letter from Kate written from Chine Side, Shanklin, Isle of Wight to the Committee of the Central Office of the Charity Organisation Society. In this furious letter she demands to know what she is accused of which necessitated their writing to the Mayor of Bexhill. She asks why they 'browbeat and drive to desperation, those whose only wish is to try and do good and live in peace'. Withdraws due to scandal
1916:	Nominated a Free Life fellow of the RGS
1917:	Hospital has 19 patients
23rd October 1919:	Letter from Harry de Windt eulogising over her and her work in Vilyuisk. 'I heard nothing but good spoken of you while I was in Yakutsk.'
28th October 1919:	Letter from Kate to the RGS from Silver Willows in Bexhill-on-Sea saying she has seen de Windt and he has actually seen her leper colony. Would they like to talk to her?

1921:	Vindication published
1926:	Starts a world wide collection for leprosy
26th March 1931:	Dies at Springfield House, Beechcraft Road, Wandsworth.
30th October 1932:	Emily Norris writes to Bexhill Museum offering a photograph of Kate Marsden; it is refused.
26th March 2014:	On the anniversary of her death Kate Renouf, Elena Kychkina, Kupriyan Mikhailov, Oyars Semenov, Paul Manning, Robert Adling ton, Morgan Hill-Murphy and Jacki Hill-Murphy clear Kate Marsden's grave in Hillingdon Cemetery untouched for 83 years.

Select Bibliography

Best, Brian and Katie Slossel. Janet: Nurse and Heroine of the Anglo-Zulu War 1879, Pen and Sword Military 2006

Betts, John. Bexhill Museum – The Story Unfolds 1912 – 1914, Bexhill Museum Ltd 2014

Boyle, Franny., Constance The Tragic and Scandalous Life of Mrs Oscar Wilde, John Murray 2011

Dixie, Lady Florence. Across Patagonia, Richard Bentley and Son 1880

Edmond, Rod. Leprosy and Empire: A Medical and Cultural History, Cambridge University Press 2007

Frazier, Ian. Travels in Siberia, Picador 2011

Hewitt, Ellen., Looking Back, or, Personal Reminiscences by the Widow of a New Zealand Settler, Leopard Classic Library 1914

Lonely Planet – Russia by Simon Richmond, Published by Lonely Planet 2015

Marsden, Kate. On Sledge and Horseback to Outcast Siberian Lepers, First published by the The Record Press 1892

Middleton, Dorothy. Victorian Lady Travellers, Routledge and Kegan Paul 1965, London

Ryan, S. Charles, M.B., C.M. Edin., in association with John Sandes, B.A. Oxon.

Under the Red Crescent: Adventures of an English Surgeon with the Turkish Army at Plevna and Erzeroum, 1877-1878

Skinner, Michael. What we did for the Russians and what the Russians (some of) did for us., Lulu Press Incorporated 2008

Sutherland, Christine. The Princess of Siberia, Quartet Books, 1984

Tayler, Jeffrey. River of No Reprieve, Descending Siberia's Waterway of Exile, Death and Destiny, Mariner Books, 2007

Watts, Sheldon J. Epidemics and History: Disease, Power and Imperialism, Yale University Press 1997

Tebb, William. The Recrudescence of Leprosy and its Causation, Swan Sonnenschein & Co London 1893

Thomas, Sue, editor. Victorian Traffic: Identity, Exchange, Performance, Cambridge Scholars Publishing 2008

Tweedie, Ethel. A Girl's Ride in Iceland, Horace Cox, Windsor House. 1889

A Remarkable Career Barrier Miner (Broken Hill, NSW : 1888 – 1954), Tuesday 28 August 1894

New Zealand Papers Past

The Telegraph, Rupert Christiansen, 22 Sep 2007

The Native Flowers and Ferns of the United States in their Botanical, Horticultural and Popular Aspects, Boston: L. Prang and Company, 1878-80

Beautiful Ferns from Original Water-colour Drawings after NatureBoston:D. Lothrop and Co.,1882

Yakutia Modern Guidebook, PressPass, LLC, 2015

Jacki Hill-Murphy has travelled to some of the most inhospitable places on earth to re-create the journeys of daring women adventurers from the past. In tracking valiant women who left inhibition at home and journeyed into the unknown, she pays tribute to their invincible spirits and achievements. She has followed in the footsteps of Victorian explorers Isabella Bird who travelled by yak across the Digar-La in Ladakh, India; Mary Kingsley, who pioneered the route to the 13,255 ft summit of Mount Cameroon; and Kate Marsden who trudged from Moscow to Siberia in search of a cure for leprosy. Jacki also braved piranha-infested waters in a dugout canoe to replicate the 1769 expedition of Isabel Godin, the only survivor of a 42-person, 4,200-mile expedition along the Amazon River. Jacki says: "We are all adventuresses who need to travel to be who we are and we are better people for it."

KATE MARSDEN.